Remembrance
Loss, Hope, Recovery after the Earthquake in Haiti

Re-mémoire
Chagrin, souvenir, espoir après le séisme en Haïti

Edited by
Nadège T. Clitandre, Claudine Michel, Marlène Racine-Toussaint,
and Florence Bellande Robertson

Published by
UCSB Center for Black Studies Research
as part of the *Onward!* series
in conjunction with
Multicultural Women's Presence
2016

Remembrance: Loss, Hope, Recovery after the Earthquake in Haiti
Re-mémoire : Chagrin, souvenir, espoir après le séisme en Haïti

Published 2016

ISBN: 978-0-9983235-0-3

Cover artwork: "Earthquake," by Bertelus Myrbel

Published by:

Center for Black Studies Research
University of California, Santa Barbara
4603 South Hall
Santa Barbara, CA 93106-3140

Phone: (805) 893-3914

Fax: (805) 893-7243

Email: ctr4blst@cbs.ucsb.edu

http://www.research.ucsb.edu/cbs/index.html

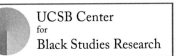

UCSB Center
for
Black Studies Research

in collaboration with:

Multicultural Women's Presence
9441 NW 15th St.
Pembroke Pines, FL 33024

Phone: (954) 447-7277

Email: multiculturpress@aol.com

Women's Presence

TABLE OF CONTENTS

Publisher's Note   7

Preface   9

Introduction: Archiving Voices   11
  Nadège T. Clitandre

PART I
MAINSHOCKS: EYEWITNESS TESTIMONIES

Notes of a Haitian Daughter   30
  N. Frédéric Pierre

Chacun son destin   35
  Odette Roy-Fombrun

My Dearest Ana   39
  Nadève Ménard

La Colère de la terre   44
  Edith Lataillade

Les Heures qui suivirent   46
  Johanne Elima Chachoute

Séisme . . . 12 janvier 2010, 16h53   49
  Françoise Beaulieu-Thybulle

Vivre   51
  Évelyne Trouillot

Survie miraculeuse   53
  Marie Andrée Manuel Etienne

Kinam : Le 12 janvier 2010   57
  Joëlle Vitiello

One Is Never Alone in Haiti   60
  Lynn Selby

Being Together   67
  Laura Wagner

Foreshocks   71
  M. J. Fièvre

Haiti Earthquake Aftermath, Journal Entries   74
  Kathuska Jose

Les Grandes douleurs sont muettes   76
  Gysèle Th. Apollon

Pour eux et pour nous   80
  Kettly Mars

PART II
AFTERSHOCKS: DIASPORIC REFLECTIONS

False Starts and Hopeful Beginnings   82
  Nadège T. Clitandre

Lòt Bò Dlo, the Other Side of the Water   88
  Edwidge Danticat

God Gives, God Takes Away!   98
  Myriam Nader-Salomon

Séisme, enfer, misère   100
  Geneviève Gaillard-Vanté

Les Femmes, après le séisme : « Tout le monde nous
a oubliées »   104
  Lucie Carmel Paul-Austin

Changing Perspectives   109
  Christalie Parisot

The Thing   111
  Michèle Voltaire Marcelin

Les Oranges de l'espoir   115
  Jan J. Dominique

Reclamation   118
  Anne-christine d'Adesky

Saved by Service: *Mwen Sèvi, Mwen Sove*   125
  Charlene Désir

Nou Se Fanm Tout Bon   128
  Grace L. Sanders Johnson

Haïti chérie   133
  Mathilde Baïsez

Le Sort a encore frappé Haïti   136
  Raymonde Maureen Eyi

Thriving amid Chaos   138
    Carolle Jean-Murat

Wishing I Could Have Done More   142
    Evelyn Ducheine Cartright

In Memoriam   145
    Florence Bellande Robertson

PART III
ACTIVE FAULTS: RESPONSIBILITY AND BLAME

Mon pays paradoxal   150
    Michèle Duvivier Pierre-Louis

The Faces of Poverty   152
    Jacinthe Armand

Le Séisme du 12 janvier 2010 : Mes réflexions deux ans après   155
    Alexandra Philoctète

"After They Beat Us They Are like Dogs at Our Feet":
An Oral History of Vulnerability and Violence in
Post-earthquake Haiti   158
    Claire Antone Payton

We Fall Down, but We Get Up: Calling for Mental Health
Intervention for Haitian Women   165
    Olga Idriss Davis & Lyvie François-Racine

Quel est mon mêle ? Le Manfoutisme haïtien   170
    Florence Etienne Sergile

Insoutenable seconds   173
    Viviane Nicolas

Je suis fatiguée   175
    Dolores Dominique-Neptune

In Haiti, Two Years after the Earthquake   178
    Josiane Hudicourt-Barnes

Cri du cœur pour Haïti : Changement et reconstruction
sont-ils des utopies ?   181
    Marlène Racine-Toussaint

Unforgotten   185
    Claudine Michel

PART IV
FORESHOCKS: REPRESENTATION AND IMAGE

Haiti ou la santé du malheur   198
    Yanick Lahens

When I Wail for Haiti: Debriefing (Performing) a
Black Atlantic Nightmare   201
    Gina Athena Ulysse

Vessels for Haiti   208
    Anna Wexler & Catherine Tutter

Haiti: The Price of Freedom   211
    Carolyn Cooper

The Uses of Vodou   214
    Kate Ramsey

An Unnaming: The Haitian Earthquake Metaphor   219
    Danielle Legros Georges

Under the Photographer's Gaze   223
    Toni Pressley-Sanon

In a Room without Windows   229
    Manoucheka Celeste

Dead Citizen   237
    Jerry Philogene

Art, Artists, and the Shaking of the Foundations   244
    LeGrace Benson

L'Espoir après le séisme   255
    Danièle Mangonès

Divine Descent of Christ   257
    Gessy Aubry

Before and After   259
    Philippe Dodard

Her Saving Grace La Sirène   260
    Edouard Duval Carrié

CONCLUSION

Yo Prale Lakay: A Homecoming   264
    Claudine Michel

Author biographies   275

Mission Statement: Multicultural Women's Presence   290

PUBLISHER'S NOTE

UCSB Center
for
Black Studies Research

ONWARD! A HAITI BOOK SERIES

Remembrance/Re-mémoire is a volume of reflections on the earthquake that occurred on January 12, 2010, which led to over 300,000 deaths and devastated the country's already challenged infrastructure. The book, prepared in collaboration with the publishing house Multicultural Women's Presence, records the horrific experiences of survivors of the earthquake as well as the involvement of those deeply affected in the Diaspora. It endeavors to document aspects of the recovery process and the attempts of the Haitian people to heal as they slowly rebuild their lives and put structures back into place. It also chronicles major government failures, the shortcomings of a heavy foreign presence, and, most importantly, the local solidarity efforts that have allowed the Haitian citizenry to regain some level of hope, fostering a collective response to the monumental challenge of rebuilding Haiti.

The *Onward!* series published by the UCSB Center for Black Studies Research includes studies, texts, and narratives that destabilize long-standing views and misrepresentations about Haiti and its people as well as Haiti's rapport with the international community. These volumes combine the extremely quotidian with the visionary and challenge normative notions of objectivity, reason, and voice. They offer rich testimonies and analyses that dislocate, reassemble, and aim to (re)empower. Additionally, these texts create opportunities for growth and responsible engagement: they serve as platforms to critique and educate, as new spaces to heal and restore self and community. All in all, the *Onward!* series is about scholarship that transforms. These books look at the relationship between power and history, engage issues of representation, and urge us to work toward new and sustainable possibilities for personal, cultural, and political regeneration in Haiti and beyond.

ABOUT THE UCSB CENTER FOR BLACK STUDIES RESEARCH

In 1968, insurgent students at the University of California, Santa Barbara, demanded the inclusion of Black Studies in the university's curriculum, leading to the creation of the Department of Black Studies and the Center for Black Studies Research—actions linked to historical freedom movements that challenged legally sanctioned injustices and the absence of certain groups in institutions of higher learning. Today these units continue to lead in recording past achievements, charting new research, and empowering marginalized communities in the United States and throughout the African Diaspora. Since 1996, the Center for Black Studies Research has embraced Haiti as one of its primary areas of research and involvement on the ground. The Center also serves as publisher for the *Journal of Haitian Studies* (JOHS), the scholarly journal of the Haitian Studies Association (HSA).

We take this opportunity to express our appreciation to Haiti's friends Dr. Judy Hamilton and Dr. Charles Nicholson, whose generous donations are making this series of publications possible. The Center for Black Studies Research team also deserves our kudos—director Diane Fujino, business officers Mahsheed Ayoub and Rosa Pinter, and especially, Rose Elfman, our brilliant and dedicated JOHS/*Kalfou*/ *Onward!* managing editor, for her immense contributions to the field of Haitian Studies. Thank you also to Nancy Doan from Student Affairs and the JOHS/*Onward!* associate editors Patrick Bellegarde-Smith and LeGrace Benson for their steadfast support, and to the leadership of the Haitian Studies Association as well as Haitianists everywhere for believing in our vision and projects.

Onward! *Annavan!* We have work to do.

Claudine Michel

Series Editor

PREFACE

Like many other books that originate in a Haitian academic *lakou*—a core communal space—this project is a *kombit*, a product of the collective work of a group of Haitian women joined by other friends and colleagues from the United States, Canada, Jamaica, and as far away as Gabon. Together we wanted to honor and celebrate the lives of those we mourned after the quake, bring about healing still needed six years after the disaster, and offer a space of reflection to help us continue to grow and remember. It is also a call for solidarity to alter narratives and platforms and rebuild the country differently on the basis of a new social contract.

In the process of collecting these stories and testimonies, we were moved by the protective stances of Haitian women everywhere *vis-à-vis* the people and the country that they are so viscerally attached to. We learned about the ties that bind women to women in Haiti and across the Diaspora. We expected the eyewitness accounts to be heartrending, but we were perhaps less prepared to discover how women born in Haiti but living in the Diaspora also dealt with a certain kind of deeply rooted trauma. In all instances, women relayed their experiences in ways that are profoundly unforgettable. And always, creating communities of solidarity was a way of coping with trauma and moving on—together.

The editors of this volume are four Haitian women, each feminist in her own right, from three different generations. Over many years we have worked both in the academy and on the ground to make a difference in the lives of those who continue to face challenging conditions at home. We were committed to the advancement of the country and the defense of the marginalized, especially women and

children, before the quake; our efforts doubled after the disaster. We
worked alongside Foundation Hope/Fondation Espoir, we supported
the important work of Direct Relief International, and we stood by a
community library, the Bibliothèque du Soleil; we joined forces with
grassroots efforts that delivered first aid to the wounded, offered
shelter, rebuilt schools, and assisted survivors with finding a sense of
normalcy. Here we credit Multicultural Women's Presence (MWP)
for creating a space where all women's voices could be heard and
establishing a forum for their stories to be told. This book is a product
of that feminist vision and honors the commitment to the collective
that animates our engagement to support Haiti, Haitians everywhere,
and all others in search of dignity and hope.

Lastly we thank the authors—fifty-six women and two men—
who believed in the project and were brave enough to commit their
stories on paper or offer their art as testimony. The stories collected
in this volume are powerful no matter the means used to narrate
the experience. Some authors trace connections across multiple
vignettes while others distill their thoughts in a single poignant page
or paragraph; some of the essays were written the day after the quake
while others were long in gestating—two of them were written only
a month before publication. All the accounts came deep from the
heart, and each story is a special treasure recounting an experience
lived, a moment shared, a life honored. The authors we present to
you in *Remembrance/Re-mémoire* reveal their fears and lamentations,
their shortcomings and moments of hope, but also the abiding love
that makes us human.

In solidarity,
The Editors

INTRODUCTION: ARCHIVING VOICES

Nadège T. Clitandre

When the earthquake ravaged the city of Port-au-Prince, Haiti, at 4:53 p.m. on Tuesday, January 12, 2010, it threw the entire country into unprecedented limelight. Over the following six years, however, less journalistic and social media attention has been paid to the aftermath of the quake: its lingering political, economic, social, and psychological impact on this small nation inhabited by ten million citizens. This is not surprising as, in the era of technological advancement that contributes to fleeting attention spans, retaining the world's awareness of the country is most challenging. Nevertheless, scholars, researchers, writers, artists, and activists who have been attentive to Haiti's difficulties long before the earthquake, or who have since gained renewed interest in the country that shares an island with the Dominican Republic, persist in sustaining an important dialogue on Haiti's future development and its role in today's global arena.

These scholars, artists, and activists also insist that the envisioning of a new Haiti in the national and global imaginary simultaneously involves both reflexive and reflective harking back to a past often misconstrued by the international community. Thanks to a number of important essays that have been published since 2010 in works such as Martin Munro's edited volume *Haiti Rising*,[1] Paul Farmer's *Haiti after the Quake*,[2] and Gina Ulysse's collection of short essays *Why Haiti Needs New Narratives*,[3] links between the earthquake, Haiti's past, and its future are well articulated. So are the narratives of some individuals who offer testimonies to what happened on that dreadful day as well as in the days, weeks, and months following the earthquake; and of others who, at a distance, raise awareness about the country's people and culture or find other means of offering their support. So too is the creativity of writers who, as evident in the 2012 anthology *So Spoke the Earth*,[4] unearth unknown stories, rehash foundational ones, and invent new ones for generations to come; and of artists who visualize both the imaginable and the unimaginable, like the earthquake that Haitians have come to refer as "bagay la" (that thing), or the successes and failures of a revolutionary struggle in 1791 that clutches to the nation's pride as well as its insecurities.

But with an estimated 300,000 deaths and the displacement of over one million people, the loss is immense and the stories endless. A handful of volumes can never completely account for the damage that has been done. Yet there is comfort in recognizing that this new post-earthquake reality fosters unceasing living archives that point to lives, narratives, and a sense of place; offer reverence to the dead; and provide dynamic spaces, physical and virtual, for survivors to tell their own stories in their own voices. These archives counter the misrepresentation of Haiti and the sweeping generalizations that many individuals with little to no knowledge of the country often make. Our modest collection of short essays by fifty-eight authors has been conceived and produced in the spirit of sustaining the conversation; exposing the complexity and diversity of the Haitian nation and its people, wherever they reside; debunking assumptions and misconceptions that too easily get recycled; and documenting the experiences of individuals who have been directly or indirectly impacted by the earthquake. This too is in honor of the dead and the living.

The idea behind *Remembrance* is a genuine attempt to capture the voices of women who carry this immeasurable loss while maintaining, although sometimes challenging, a keen sense of hope for Haiti. Marlène Racine-Toussaint, one of the editors and the original architect behind this collection, is among the first to have envisioned a project of this type. This volume adds to Gina Ulysse's project of publishing in *Meridians* journal, just a year after the earthquake, eleven reflections composed in various genres by Haitian women in Haiti and in the diaspora. In her introduction to these pieces, Ulysse astutely states, "As with any other natural disaster, it is women who are disproportionately affected."[5] The contributions in this volume offer a more expansive look at the various ways in which Haitian women have been affected by the earthquake. *Remembrance* also makes room for the narratives of non-Haitian women who are in solidarity with women on the ground through research, feminist organizations, social activism, and personal relationships. Collectively, these narratives—written from various geographical spaces and diverse viewpoints—point to a circle of sisterhood that transgresses national borders, engenders transnational alliances, and produces global reverberations. Their words remind us that despite the lack of consistent attention to Haiti, the struggle continues.

Remembrance is structured thematically, with four main parts we are calling **Mainshocks, Aftershocks, Active Faults,** and **Foreshocks.** These terms are key in the study of earthquakes. *Mainshock*, in the lexicon of earthquake science, refers to the largest shock. In the case of Haiti, it is the 7.0-magnitude quake (with its epicenter, Léogâne, approximately sixteen miles west of the capital) that caused the most damage, especially in the densely populated region around Port-au-Prince. The largest recorded mainshock in Haiti's history is the 8.1-magnitude earthquake on May 7, 1842, which destroyed most of Cap-Haitien in northern Haiti and significantly damaged King Henri Christophe's royal palace, Sans-Souci, in Milot. We use the term *mainshock* in this collection to describe the eyewitness testimonies that offer readers an eerie sense of what happened on the ground right before, during, and immediately after the earth shook for about thirty-five seconds. Each piece in Part I provides an individual and unique angle of vision, to borrow the phrase by Black feminist Patricia Hill Collins.[6] Indeed the standpoints, undoubtedly impacted by class, race, color, and educational background, are varied. But what the essays in Part I have in common are the descriptions of scenes and places that no longer exist; the naming of family members and friends who have perished; the haunting images of dead bodies, white dust, and chaos; and the shared sensation of fear, shock, and bewilderment coupled with an overwhelming sense of solidarity.

Part I begins aptly with the reflection of N. Frédéric Pierre, a young Haitian American woman who insists that the "first responders" of the earthquake were the survivors who, as she powerfully asserts, "used their fingers as bulldozers." Feeling like an insider-outsider when she arrived in Haiti one day before the earthquake to conduct research for her dissertation, Pierre is forever transformed by the experience. She writes, "The earthquake shattered my hyphenated identity and reconstructed an authentic Haitian self that emerged from the rubble." As a child of Haitian migrants, Pierre thoughtfully considers the sacrifices poor Haitian mothers make for their children through an intimate look at her relationship with her own mother. Interestingly, children emerge as a recurring image in Part I. Odette Roy-Fombrun begins and ends her story of survival by summoning the image of a young girl and her blue shoes. Such an apparent image of innocence is transformed into a haunting, cruel image of tragedy as Roy-Fombrun finally reveals the fate of the young girl. Through her narrative, we are reminded of the collapse of well-known buildings in Haiti, such as the Caribbean Market in Delmas, one of the biggest supermarkets in the country, and Hotel Montana, the illustrious four-star hotel and landmark built in 1946 that caters to the elite, tourists, MINUSTAH, and aid groups.[7] We are also subtly prompted to recall a lesser-known, but now infamous building: College La Promesse Evangélique, a Protestant primary school in Nerette, which collapsed in 2008 and caused the deaths of over one hundred schoolchildren.

Writing a letter to her daughter just a few months after the earthquake, Nadève Ménard cannot imagine what it must feel like to lose a child. She wonders how her own daughter will process the earthquake in the future and if she will ever question her mother's decision to continue to live in Haiti. She asks her daughter: "Will you understand by then what it means to love a country like a person?" And then there are those who do imagine what such a loss must feel like. Edith Lataillade describes the experience of a mother who helplessly hears the call and cries of her son buried and dying beneath the rubble. Expressing shock, despair and bewilderment, Johanne Elima Chachoute, one of the younger voices in this collection, is, like Roy-Fombrun and others, haunted by an image of a young girl trapped under the rubble of her home, a young girl who called out Chachoute's name while she herself was fleeing the scene and screaming "like a hysteric." Disclosing the girl's identity, Chachoute honors the memory of this young child she had watched grow up in her neighborhood right in front of her eyes.

Françoise Beaulieu-Thybulle, in the essay that follows, remarks, as do the other contributors in this section, on the sense of solidarity, fraternity, and generosity she witnessed the night of the earthquake and the days to follow in the face of such gut-wrenching misfortunes. Alluding to the many lives lost, Beaulieu-Thybulle describes the event as a "seismic holocaust." But she maintains optimism in hoping that this national tragedy can, as she claims, "paradoxically stimulate urban and economic development" so that Haiti can be reborn from its ashes. The notion of renewal evoked in Beaulieu-Thybulle's narrative is juxtaposed with a sense of normalcy in Évelyne Trouillot's "Vivre." While Trouillot recognizes that she and other survivors are completely changed by the experience of the earthquake and must confront, painfully, a new reality and new responsibilities, she also knows all too well that life, in all its banality, goes on. "Life settles and refuses to remain underground," Trouillot concludes. This is perhaps the weapon that survivors in Haiti claim as the ultimate act of defiance. Is this how Haitians overcome what Marie Andrée Manuel Etienne calls "the apocalypse" in her essay? Like Trouillot, who sees this disaster as an event that reinforces her commitment to her homeland, Etienne, who felt the quake in her home along with her husband, Haitian writer and artist Frankétienne, and a journalist who arrived from Puerto Rico just ten minutes before the quake, finds that this "profound injury" fortifies her investment in developing and supporting psychosocial programs.

There are those who, like Pierre, set foot in Haiti right before the earthquake to forever be transformed as a witness and a survivor. Joëlle Vitiello, one of many individuals who arrived on the day of the earthquake for the Etonnants Voyageurs Festival that would commence on January 13 in celebration of the recent successes of Haitian writers, became a witness to what was happening in Pétion-Ville at Kinam hotel and Place Saint Pierre, one of the public spaces that would later turn into a tent city. She offers thoughtful descriptions pervaded by sounds: rhythmic drumbeats and chants at times interrupted by painful cries. The witnesses who are living in spaces outside this local community of survivors confront the trauma caused by the quake with an overwhelming sense of guilt. They too mourn the death of loved ones, but at a distance; in what some describe as privileged spaces, they feel the loss of home and community. Lynn Selby, at the time a graduate student from Texas who had been in Haiti for two years and had only three months left in the country, found herself crouched under a desk with the laptop that contained her dissertation. She was rescued by the mentors, friends, and neighbors who had become her family in Haiti. Staying true to her profession, she documented the extent of the destruction by handwriting a list of destroyed buildings and names of survivors. She admits that it took time and courage to find her way back to the community she built in Haiti. Laura Wagner is a survivor who, instead of writing about her own story from that day, concentrates on relationships with others: her involvement six months later with a group of young writers called Konbit des Jeunes Penseurs, who wrote about this feeling of loss, and her friendship with a Haitian woman going through treatment for advanced lung cancer in the United States, a friend with whom she went to church on the second anniversary of the earthquake. Unlike some foreigners, or "blan," as Haitians like to call them, who centralize their own stories by unjustifiably marginalizing and exploiting the stories of Haitians who become nameless or faceless, Wagner, like Selby, takes a different path. She astutely explains: "We write people down, the people we love and lose, to bring them back to life, and to say goodbye." The title of our collection, *Remembrance*, evokes this sentiment.

Another theme that is echoed in Part I is faith in God. For some, spiritual faith, like the Haitian people, remains resilient. M. J. Fièvre, now a member of the Haitian diaspora, returns to her homeland shortly after the earthquake only to find remnants of Église du Sacré-Coeur, a landmark church, in ruins, its pews covered with dust. Acknowledging the presence of God in this space that evokes childhood memories, she writes: "I can't stop believing in His love and am angry for this faith that I carry around like excess baggage." There are others in this collection who, like Kathuska Jose, admit to the fear of losing faith in the face of other disasters to come. Jose writes in her journal: "I have been unable to talk to God for weeks."

Other disasters did indeed follow the earthquake, testing the faith of many. As if by an act of mercy, the anticipated hurricane, Emily, largely spared Haiti, though hundreds of homes were flooded in the department of Artibonite. But in 2012, Hurricanes Sandy and Isaac caused substantial damage in the south—and six years later, Hurricane Matthew. For a small country, Haiti has endured repeated disasters, natural and unnatural. However, some disasters were unprecedented. For example, thousands of bodies were unceremoniously buried in Titanyen, a burial site made infamous during the Duvalier dictatorship that began in 1957. Ten months after the earthquake, Haiti faced the worst cholera outbreak in recent history, with a reported 500,000 infections and nearly 7,000 deaths. Moreover, a year after the quake, over one million people in Haiti still lived in tent cities with makeshift camps. For a country that often appears to be on the verge of collapse, it is faith, along with the sheer and very human will to survive, that keeps it from reaching the breaking point. Still, much has been broken. Gysèle Apollon's essay offers a detailed breakdown of physical losses—governmental buildings, schools, churches, businesses, and homes marked "to demolish." Maintaining a sense of optimism, she evokes the still-standing statues of heroes in Champ de Mars to remind the reader of the nation's sustained struggle against all odds. We end Part I with Kettly Mars, whose powerful words read like Aimé Césaire's *Notebook of a Return to the Native Land*.[8] In one long sentence, Mars articulates the resiliency of the Haitian people. It is in many ways a beautiful counternarrative to the idea that Haiti is dead.

The second part of the book, "Aftershocks: Diasporic Reflections," includes pieces from scholars, activists, and writers in the diaspora who articulate experiences that conjure childhood memories, individual familial stories, and ancestral ties. Their reflections are consumed by the challenge and guilt that come with living away from the beloved homeland. *Aftershocks* are defined as tremors that follow the largest shock of an earthquake sequence and continue over weeks, months, years. At least fifty-two aftershocks were recorded in Haiti. While the unrelenting emotional shocks the Haitian diaspora experienced cannot compare to the physical and psychological shocks felt on the ground, we would be remiss to discount the tremors felt abroad. We also play on the word *reflection* in the subtitle of Part II. A reflection is the energy or wave from an earthquake that returns after encountering a boundary between two different materials. Certainly, the question of return, physical or metaphorical, is fundamental to the diasporic reflections presented in Part II. The myriad forms of return by the diaspora blur the fixed boundaries that separate Haiti and its people abroad.

Members of the Haitian diaspora, nearing one million in the United States alone as a result of mass external migration since the 1970s, know all too well that leaving the homeland comes with a price; the return, if one has the privilege of doing so, is made in different ways. This too is the result of the disaster that is the twenty-nine-year reign of the Duvalier regime—which, although it ended in 1986, caused irreparable damage for generation after generation. Despite this traumatic history that follows Haitians wherever they find themselves, the diaspora never ceases to express love for, commitment to, and responsibility toward their homeland through various forms of what Michel Laguerre describes as Diaspora citizenship.[9] They contribute to tourism, form or engage in hometown association projects, and send remittances to family and friends. In 2012, the year the diaspora sent a reported $2 billion in remittances—20 percent of Haiti's GDP—then-president Michel Joseph Martelly published an amended version of the constitution that legalized dual citizenship.[10] Despite this change, ongoing questions about the role of the Haitian diaspora in Haiti's future remain unanswered. But as the pieces in this section show, Haitians in the diaspora are not waiting for the government to sustain and systematize the link with the homeland; they remain actively engaged.

Part II begins with my own contribution to this collection. In my essay, I reflect on my experiences in Port-au-Prince in December 2009, the month before the earthquake. I, along with my father, journalist and novelist Pierre A. Clitandre, were focused on completing a computer lab at Bibliothèque du Soleil, the community library project we have been developing since 2006, which had necessitated multiple returns annually for a daughter who learned to love Haiti through her father. The essay is a reflection of what I initially perceived as a debilitating silence, only to realize that it too is a significant part of the process toward healing after the earthquake. I write, "Some of us are silent because we are still digging." Accepting my own pace, I finally come to recognize the beauty behind everyday, banal narratives that get lost in the rubble. The notion of progress, which I witnessed during the days before the earthquake, is disrupted by the following four essays, which bring the reader back to the "apocalyptic" depictions presented in the eyewitness testimonies. This time, it is the gaze of the diaspora affixed to television news channels, computers, and telephones in desperate need of information on the ground. In writing her story of loss from "the other side of the water," renowned Haitian American writer Edwidge Danticat finds an opportunity to share stories of other individuals in the diaspora who lost family members. Danticat asserts, "It would be disrespectful to equate my pain and bereavement with that of those who nearly lost their lives and sanity to the devastation." Experiencing shock from her living-room sofa while glued to CNN, Myriam Nader-Salomon resorts to Facebook to receive news of family and damage to property in Haiti. Geneviève Gaillard-Vanté, mourning the death of her cousin, thinks of fond childhood memories and old neighborhoods in Haiti. Lucie Carmel Paul-Austin, who returned to Haiti two months after the quake, witnesses the differences in a city forever transformed. Despite the changes, such as the heightened focus on hygiene as a result of cholera, there is still a sense of simplicity and pleasantness that, as Paul-Austin writes, makes her feel like the country is "still reserved for me and my children." If the country remains a birthright, it is one that now houses, as Christalie Parisot asserts in her piece, only memories of the past and "unrecognizable" homes. Parisot's return to her hometown deepens her empathy for communities who experience disaster, but also brings a keen understanding of how disasters are capitalized. This too is another catastrophe.

Michèle Voltaire Marcelin's return to Haiti a month after the quake resulted in the preservation of extraordinary stories of survival, full of descriptions of "bagay la." She states, "One should not witness certain things, even secondhand, even a month later with impunity." Living in Montreal during the time of the quake, Haitian writer Jan J. Dominique admits that her family did not mark the tenth anniversary of the death of her father, agronomist and journalist Jean Dominique, who had died on April 3, 2000. They felt it would be too indecent. Dominique's father believed deeply in the land and its people and was an eloquent, colorful speaker. Were he alive at time of the earthquake, he would have found the right words to comfort his listeners. Anne-christine d'Adesky sees her multiple returns to Haiti after the quake as a process of reclamation, but she remains haunted by an image that both encapsulates the vulnerability of girls in Haiti and serves as a moral compass. In Charlene Désir's essay, reclamation is an act that involves a special relationship with not only the homeland but also its ancestors. For Désir, homage to the ancestors—to the spirit of grandmothers, sisters, and aunts—is an important part of her service to Haiti. The circle of sisterhood, as evident in this book, extends beyond ancestral membership.

In North America, the members of the Haitian diaspora were not the only individuals who suffered from loss. Many non-Haitian citizens, particularly in the United States and Canada, grieve friends and even family members who were in Haiti at the time of the earthquake. Grace Sanders Johnson, who was in the process of booking a flight to Haiti when the earthquake struck, reconnects with a circle of women in Montreal and later Haiti to ceremonially acknowledge the deaths of feminist leaders who have now joined the ancestors—Myriam Merlet, Magalie Marcelin, and Anne Marie Coriolan, among others. Mathilde Baïsez, in imagining an "unknown sister" who represents the challenges women her age face in Haiti, realizes how privileged her life is in Montreal, Canada. At a distance, she feels a keen sense of solidarity and contributes in her own way by sending money, clothes, and other needed products. All the way from Gabon, Central Africa, Maureen Raymonde Eyi feels this connection to a country that suffers so much, a country she has learned to love through a dear friend. She writes about others in her community who admire Haiti and come together to assist in fundraisers and relief efforts.

Part II ends with three essays that home in specifically on relief efforts after the earthquake. Carolle Jean-Murat, a gynecologist who coordinated medical teams in the United States as a liaison to help communities in La Vallée de Jacmel and Bizoton in Carrefour, shares important lessons learned from the experience. One is that you cannot take care of everyone; each person can best contribute within their own professional realm and particular location. The following two essays offer a glimpse of the tireless work that members of the diaspora did toward relief efforts on university campuses to support

Haitian students and honor the students and faculty members who died during the quake. Summing up the sentiment of all members of the diaspora in the title of her essay—"Wishing I Could Have Done More"—Evelyn Ducheine Cartright details her work with students and faculty, involvement in campus activities that raise awareness and funds for relief efforts, and successful attempts to secure scholarships for students who suddenly became orphans on her campus. What more could she have done? Florence Bellande Robertson, one of the editors of this collection, also reflects on the efforts of a local campus in Boca Raton, Florida, to archive memories and celebrate lives. She marvels at the memorial plaza built in homage to the faculty and students of Lynn University who perished during the tragedy while on a mission trip, and at the orphanage located at the epicenter of the quake in Carrefour—a gift from the family of one of the Lynn students lost in the earthquake.

"Active Fault: Responsibility and Blame" is the title of the third part of this collection. An active fault is one likely to have another earthquake in the future, one that has moved once or more in the past ten thousand years. We use this term to encompass the ongoing factors and vulnerabilities, both internal and external, that have impeded Haiti's development since its inception as an independent nation in 1791. We also play on the word *fault* to bring into focus the "blame game" that quickly followed the earthquake. Whether the blame is on the Haitian government and its lack of infrastructure; a corrupted political system with an individualistic mindset; international strategies such as the trade liberalization policies of the '90s and interventions by outside organizations, such as the International Monetary Fund, that stunt sustainable development; or natural and unnatural disasters that continue to wreak havoc on the country's ecology and natural resources, the essays in this section reveal that any conversation about Haiti's future development must contend with longstanding structural issues that have yet to be resolved or acknowledged.

We begin with Michèle Pierre-Louis, former prime minister of Haiti and the second woman to serve the country in that capacity. Pierre-Louis writes of the paradox of despair and hope Haitians experienced immediately after the earthquake and her

disappointment in the face of another missed opportunity to turn
Port-au-Prince into a real city that proudly expresses its renewed
humanity. The earthquake sheds light not only on the challenges of
development and urban planning plaguing Port-au-Prince, but also
on the importance of further developing cities outside the capital and
rural areas more generally. Indeed, decentralization is one of the main
enduring issues in any discussion of development in Haiti. Jacinthe
Armand's essay on Salagnac farmers and market women offers a stark
example of the status of the peasantry after the earthquake and the
way in which humanitarian aid efforts negatively affected farmers
in the countryside. Armand views the earthquake as a wake-up call
for decentralized Haiti and a new wave of development. Alexandra
Philoctècte expresses frustration with the empty promises of the
international community, NGOs in particular, that contribute to
Haitian dependency. Her essay explicates some of the dangers of
camp life after the earthquake, especially for women and children,
who are most vulnerable to sexual violence.

The two essays that follow rely on individual oral stories of
women to expose more broadly the physical and emotional hardships
women face in Haiti both before and after the quake. Claire Antone
Payton offers the story of Maryse to explore the relationship between
the commodification of sexuality and an increase in violence after
the earthquake. In an interview, Maryse gives an account of being
assaulted by her husband while at the same time exposing the
danger women face when they do not live up to gender ideals and
expectations. Through her story, Payton concludes that the Haitian
legal system is not equipped to effectively handle gender-based
violence. Olga Idriss Davis and Lyvie François-Racine write about
women's resilience by focusing on the narrative of a mother who
saves her son by cutting off his arm. The story is used to advocate
for mental health programs in Haiti and call for global action in this
area. The authors insist that strategies for development in Haiti must
also focus on mental health.

Education is another key factor in the conversation. Florence
Etienne Sergile, a trailblazer in the fight for ecological sustainability,
asks: What are we, the educated, doing to contribute to development?
For her it is important to integrate the study of science in Haitian

schools and to change our ways of thinking in order to be able to contribute to the preservation of the nation's rich resources. Viviane Nicolas reminds us that the land itself, a gift from the Taino ancestors, is a natural resource that has been spoiled by the colonial experience and that we must honor and preserve it. Indeed, there is plenty of blame to go around. Dolores Dominique-Neptune's essay is not only a testimony to the horrific experience of having to bury her son but also a steadfast critique of the political system and a Haitian government that would spend $44 million on elections and not its citizens. She asks: How many must die for the government to prioritize its people?

Josiane Hudicourt-Barnes expresses a similar critique by calling out the government machinery, which, she says, rarely cares for its citizens and is unable to respond to their basic needs. But she also calls out opportunist Haitians in the country who, like international aid organizations, capitalize on the disaster. Her response shows that "disaster capitalism" is not immune to local interests.[11] Marlène Racine-Toussaint, an editor in this collection, places the blame internally on the elite and an unwavering hierarchical class system. Attentive to the treatment of domestic workers, she defines the solidarity in Haiti as circumstantial. She also places blame externally on the international community of donors and aid organizations whose plans are not appropriate or in line with Haiti's reality. We end the section with "Unforgotten" by Claudine Michel, another editor of this collection. Michel tells the story of a five-year-old earthquake survivor who comes to represent the forgotten children of Haiti, of the world. She examines the plight of children with little to no access to education as well as the tool of language, and dreams of a Haiti with a bright future for young girls.

"Foreshocks," the final part of this collection, consists of essays that wrestle with what Gina Athena Ulysse describes as the trendy "dehumanization narrative" that "took off on a subhumanity strand" after the earthquake.[12] Foreshocks are smaller earthquakes that precede larger ones. Here we use the term to refer to the lingering ways, both subtle and overt, in which Haiti's dignity and humanity are put into question through the overproduction of images that misrepresent the nation and reduce and simplify the country to a disparaging moniker, "the poorest country in the western hemisphere." The essays take on the challenge of producing counternarratives that put into question the visual and narrativized image of Haiti in popular media coverage of the country and rightly historicize the problematic gaze of Hollywood, celebrity activists, aid workers, and journalists within a colonial context and a global racial imaginary. They expose the difficulty of truly achieving a peaceful global community and foreground the contributions Haiti makes to modernity and to the very understanding of what it means to be human.

Here, we commence with Yanick Lahens, who asserts emphatically that Haiti is not peripheral: it is a nation with a history equal to the rest of the world, and as such should be on equal footing in terms of dialogue with other nations. For Lahens, Haiti offers to the world "luminous creativity" through its artists and writers, whose work combats negative or simplistic images of the first Black republic. Gina Athena Ulysse's "When I Wail for Haiti" explores the role of performance more broadly, and the "wail" more specifically, as a mode of intervention in processing trauma. Ulysse explains how she transforms her one-woman show "Because When God Is Too Busy" into a "hybrid living newspaper" that includes and honors the voices of people in Haiti. Anna Wexler and Catherine Tutter write about the process of creating a memory vessel, a community-engaged object of spiritual remembrance and compassionate response. Performative in its own right, the project is also a mode of healing intervention that honors the Vodou tradition.

Carolyn Cooper reflects on an encounter with a Haitian painter to connect the process of framing an artwork with the way in which we frame reality. She takes on Pat Robertson's notion that the successful revolution of 1791–1804 was a direct result of a "pact with the devil." In her reflection, she reminds us that such ludicrous remarks coming from the United States are also echoed by other nations, including Haiti's close neighbors. Kate Ramsey explains that such longstanding assumptions about Haitians as devil worshippers and Haitian culture as "progress-resistant," as circulated by Robertson, David Brooks, and others in the United States, necessitate a historical analysis of the enduring denigration of Vodou, Haiti's ancestral religion. Depriving Haiti of its humanity and creativity, these notions feed on the reality of poverty in the country.

Those who know and study the country cannot ignore the significant level of creativity that is produced in Haiti under challenging circumstances. Danielle Legros Georges pays attention to the imageless metaphor Haitians created to describe the earthquake. She views the unnaming of the quake as a genius response and counter-image to the overproduction of images that are not adequate to express Haiti's complexities and realities. The next three essays in Part IV provide historical contexts for understanding the influence of the racialized Western gaze on the global visual representation of Haiti. Toni Pressley-Sanon looks at the circulation of photographs and examines what she views as a dysfunctional contemporary relationship between the First World photojournalist and the Third World subject. As she astutely asserts, "People in the throes of disaster are not afforded privacy or dignity." Thus she deliberately leaves photos out of her essay in order to consider alternative ways of analyzing images. Manoucheka Celeste then offers a close reading of texts where the politics of blame is obvious, concentrating on how the negative portrayal of Haiti by US media is used to justify assumptions about blackness and the plight of oppressed black Americans. In "Dead Citizen," Jerry Philogene scrutinizes what she calls the "voyeuristic fascination" of a world that views Haiti "as a permanent ward of the global community." Investigating the way images of Haiti render Haitians anonymous beings to be pitied and aided, Philogene calls for a "rearticulated visual historicity." For this to happen, one must also be familiar with the history of visual arts in Haiti as form of empowerment and resistance. LeGrace Benson also focuses on artists, art historians, and art lovers who risked their lives to save national art treasures. They grieved not only for loved ones but also for "the work of human hands [that] perished." An art historian herself, Benson provides a succinct historical overview of the impact of previous earthquakes in the eighteenth and nineteenth century on artists, writers, and musicians to further discuss the work of various artists who produced powerful work after the earthquake. She writes that these artists, musicians, poets, dancers, and filmmakers "have the ability to eject their own mute and invisible dread into a calculated and tolerable sound and fury and thus provide viewers and listeners with a vicarious release from the terror."

What follows Benson's essay are four paintings completed by Haitian artists after the earthquake. Danièle Mangonès, who started working on the painting that became "L'Espoir après le séisme" three days before the earthquake, views her work as a visual manifestation of the revelation of the disaster and an expression of hope and renewal. Gessy Aubry presents her artwork "Divine Descent of Christ" as a testament to the Christian crosses that stood erect in the midst of rubble throughout the capital and in service of what she calls the divine "feminine energy" in Haiti. Phillipe Dodard, one of two male voices in this volume, offers "Before and After" as an abstract representation of the thousands of lives lost during the earthquake. Edouard Duval Carrié then conjures the spirit of La Sirène, the beautiful Vodou goddess of the seas, to offer solace to the Haitian people.

As a conclusion, we present a thoughtful reflection on the importance of Vodou in sustaining Haiti and its people, and a call for more balanced relations among humans, for a re-embrace of values that elevate the soul and honor our passage on this planet. Claudine Michel takes the reader on a journey of how she wrote the preface to the third edition of Karen McCarthy Brown's influential book *Mama Lola*.[13] In the process, she provides a prescription for understanding the intricate working of the Haitian cultural imagination and collective consciousness, grounded in ancestral knowledge and reverence to the spirit world. The foreword she eventually writes turns into a eulogy for the earthquake victims. Feeling like a chosen mourner, Michel calls on the ancestors to guide the victims home. All the voices in this volume are mourners who graciously open windows into their intimate lives in memory of the hundreds of thousands who perished on January 12, 2010. Let this book be an offering of hope to sustain and strengthen our beloved Haiti.

Notes

[1]   *Haiti Rising: Haitian History, Culture and the Earthquake of 2010*, ed. Martin Munro (London: Liverpool University Press, 2010).

[2]   Paul Farmer, *Haiti after the Quake*, ed. Abby Gardner and Cassia Van Der Hoof Holstein (New York: Public Affairs, 2011).

3   Gina Ulysse, *Why Haiti Needs New Narratives: A Post-Quake Chronicle* (Middletown, CT: Wesleyan University Press, 2015).

4   *So Spoke the Earth*, ed. M. J. Fièvre (South Florida: Women Writers of Haitian Descent, 2012).

5   Gina Ulysse, Section Editor Introduction, "Pawol Fanm sou Douz Janvye (Women's Words on January 12th, 2010)," *Meridians: Feminism, Race, Transnationalism* 11, no. 1 (2011): 93.

6   Patricia Hill Collins, *Black Feminist Thought: Knowledge, Consciousness, and the Politics of Empowerment* (New York: Routledge, 2000).

7   MINUSTAH is the United Nations Stabilization Mission in Haiti, which was established on June 1, 2004.

8   Aimé Césaire, *Notebook of a Return to the Native Land* (Middletown, CT: Wesleyan University Press, 2001).

9   Michel S. Laguerre, *Diasporic Citizenship: Haitian Americans in Transnational America* (Basingstoke: MacMillan Press, 1998).

10 The announcement was made on June 19, 2012. See for example a report by Council of Hemispheric Affairs at http://www.coha.org/haiti-amends-constitution/.

11 See Naomi Klein, *The Shock Doctrine: The Rise of Disaster Capitalism* (New York: Metropolitan Books, 2007).

12 Gina Athena Ulysse, "Why Representations of Haiti Matter Now More Than Ever," *NACLA Report on the Americas* 43, no. 4 (2010): 38.

13 Karen M. C. Brown, *Mama Lola: A Vodou Priestess in Brooklyn* (Berkeley: University of California Press, 2001).

PART I

MAINSHOCKS
EYEWITNESS TESTIMONIES

NOTES OF A HAITIAN DAUGHTER

N. Frédéric Pierre

From beneath the earth's surface, a thunderbolt lashed up to crack Port-au-Prince's shell. The roar of crumbling mountain merged with the shrieks of children, men, and women. Here and there, the expression *san du Jezi* punctuated our collective death sentence. I sat on the balcony of the Hospice St. Joseph, a medical clinic doubling as a bed and breakfast, confused and silently wondering where this thunderous train would emerge. It took a wooden entertainment unit rushing across the linoleum floor for me to realize there were no trains in Haiti. Before the inevitable crash, I fell to my hands and knees into an embrace of chalky rubble. The dust invaded my lungs, blinded my eyes, and tinted my locs a greyish white. On my forearms, I crawled toward my yelping hostess and used her calves to pull myself upright. The building squirmed like jello and melted beneath my bare feet. Still mute, I followed her counsel and said, "God," when a fresh burst of smoky rubble tickled my throat. I chose to keep my mouth shut for survival and continued to do so for years.

This collection provides me an opportunity to speak, and I can speak again because bearing witness is itself a value. My experience of the 12 January 2010 Haitian earthquake clashes with popular narratives. For the record, the first people to respond to the earthquake were the survivors themselves, who used the equipment of their fingers as bulldozers, moving mountains of cement in search of the buried living. I repeatedly witnessed aftershocks and crumbling mountains claim the lives of these first "first responders." Narratives that suggest otherwise insult their memory and heroic effort. The next thirty-six hours are a collection of images: flying off a green three-story building, an elderly man with a bright red hole between two stunned eyes; a sunset sharing its pink and deep purple wavelengths; the possibility of a tsunami washing over our bedding made of broken branches; prayer warriors rapping verses of unknown spirituals; the muffled moan of children pleading, "*Tanpri manman.*"

I murmured to my own mother and hoped that, unlike the newly orphaned children around me, she would hear me. For me, to think about the earthquake is to think about my Mom and the aspirations mothers have for their children. In his poem "The Prophet," Kahlil Gibran tells a mother with a babe to her bosom: "You are the bows from which your children as living arrows are sent forth. The Archer sees the mark upon the path of the infinite, and He bends you with His might that His arrows may go swift and far."[1] This beautiful verse pops into mind with one of the most haunting memories seared into me. A group of men uncovered a mother and child who transitioned with the baby's lips latched on the mother's breast; in death as in life, she would provide for her babe. Although this baby arrow did not soar far, it is this image that came to mind when I finally spoke with my mother from an airport hangar in the Dominican Republic. I simply croaked, "*Manman mwen vivan*" and knew, then and now, that part of my survival was the consequence of her earnest prayer. For the breath of relief my mother exhaled, over two hundred thousand other mothers did not because their breath is trapped in the earthquake that claimed their children.

Haitian children have been especially vulnerable to plots beyond their mothers' imagining. For example, shortly after our nation's founding, a French general occupying the Dominican Republic demanded that Haitian children without the etch marks of slavery on their person be kidnapped and sold off to North Carolina in exchange for rice.[2] How did that generation of mothers cope with the loss of the first generation of freeborn Haitian children? The peripheral position of Haiti within the world economy certainly contributes to the decision-making process that leads impoverished mothers to choose to send their children to live with friends or family members with access to resources in Port-au-Prince. Others, like my Mom, chose to migrate to countries that speak unintelligible tongues and systematically train the child to reject the cultural mores of the parent.

The children of Haitian migrants develop hyphenated identities. On one end, bound to vivid memories of home shared by our parents; on the other end, bound to the incomprehensible structures of our host country. The prime example I have of this from lived experience was my complete lack of awareness of the Million Man March but my vivid memory of the first coup d'état against Haitian president Jean-Betrand Aristide. These two events happened within a few years of each other. But as a migrant Haitian child I mainly recall the hushed tones of my elders as they anxiously awaited word of a cousin, an uncle, or a brother who between a rock and a hard place chose to become "boat people." Migrant children are trained to translate, pursue education, and secure careers that yield incomes generous enough to send remittances home. Commingling this dutiful pursuit of the immigrant's mission with the exile's yen to elevate the place of origin and memory, I went to Haiti on 11 January 2010 to conduct dissertation research on early post-independence Haitian society. I had been in Haiti for less than twenty-four hours when the earth cracked and there was nothing I could do. I was a stranger to the wounded around me. I was a stranger in my homeland with nothing to offer but silence.

The earthquake shattered my hyphenated identity and reconstructed an authentic Haitian self that emerged from rubble. With this altered self-perception, I returned to New York and plunged into relief efforts coordinated by members of my community. We developed a course to teach native Haitian Creole speakers how to read and write in the language they dream. It took us eighteen months to translate Michel-Rolph Troullot's *Ti dife boule sou istwa Ayiti* into the standard orthography. During this time, my classmates, ranging from 9 to 76 years old, read, analyzed, and translated the only history of our revolution written in Haitian Creole. It was an intergenerational dialogue about our ancestors that nourished my broken spirit. My mother joined the class, too, and I learned so much about her because she was my student. For Haitian Mother's Day, I assigned a prompt that would help us write notes of appreciation for our mothers. I, being a fastidious reader of Toni Morrison, brought up the example from *Sula* wherein a mother manually moved her baby's bowels as an example of mother love.[3] The women around the room politely nodded. When it was my mother's turn to share, she said that Haitian mothers would use their lips to relieve their babies' nasal passages of mucus. I cringed, and she leaned over to whisper the wickedest joke in my ear. The earthquake created the space for these types of memories to be formed, and for that I am grateful.

My search for healing through service transformed me into an education advocate. Through our community course in Creole, I learned about the educational disparities faced by teenage Haitian migrants in New York City, particularly those who are English Language Learners (ELLs). Their education was interrupted due to Haitian schools being closed after the earthquake. Imagine surviving the epic catastrophe of the earthquake, migrating to a foreign country, and being told that because your child is too old, they could not enroll in high school and must opt for a General Educational Development (GED) certificate? This is not the dream Haitian mothers have for their children. Though I am not a mother, my upbringing makes me uniquely qualified to advocate for education programming that meets the needs of fellow earthquake survivors.

There is no conclusion to this story. But in lieu of closing, I will say that on that day the earth's shell felt as fragile a raw egg. When the ground cracked and the tremors were zinging our feet, I felt as if I were surfing on the slippery surface of an egg yolk. I witnessed what was lost as the ground opened up and skipped like a calf. But, for now, I focus on what was birthed in that moment. From this awful destruction, there is active creation. Haitians with hyphenated identities like myself are now, more than ever, eager to return home. They visit for reasons ranging from vacations at swanky hotels built with monies earmarked for reconstruction to building parks for children in need of safer spaces. The bonds I have developed with family members and colleagues working in Haitian studies cohere around the earthquake. What was once a gaping hole of loss is now a space for recovery.

Notes

[1] Kahlil Gibran, *The Prophet* (New York: Vintage Books, 2015), 20.

[2] Proclamation of Louis Ferrand, 6 Jan. 1805 in Thomas Madiou, *Histoire d' Haiti*, III (Port-au-Prince: Editions Henri Deschamps, 1985), 237–238.

[3] Toni Morrison, *Sula* (New York: Penguin, 1982), 33–34.

Chacun son destin

Odette Roy-Fombrun

Et pourquoi cette fillette aux chaussures bleues ?

—Que se passe-t-il donc Frère Joseph ? Vous qui partez toujours le dernier. Il n'est pas encore 4h.

—J'ai terminé mon livre et je viens remettre la dédicace à Vilaire pour contrôle.

Comme lui, un peu fatiguée, je quitte le bureau pour me rendre chez moi à Musseau où ma fille Marie-Claude m'attend pour le souper. Brusquement je change de parcours et décide de me rendre chez mon fils Daniel. Nous sommes encore debout quand un bruit insolite, comme une grande marée roulant vers nous, se fait entendre.

—C'est un tremblement de terre, crie Daniel, entrainant sa femme, Carine, et moi vers la sortie.

Agrippés l'un à l'autre, terriblement angoissés, nous regardons leur grand immeuble qui menace de s'écrouler. Les locataires effrayés se précipitent dans la cour.

Après un long, très long silence les langues se délient et c'est la tour de Babel où chacun exprime son émotion et partage son expérience. Mais aucun de nous ne comprend l'étendue des dégâts puisque le grand bidonville adjacent, 'Jalousie' est en place. Par prudence, tous ses habitants se précipitent vers la Place Saint-Pierre, en priant Dieu et chantant des cantiques.

Des appels téléphoniques annoncent que les dégâts sont énormes à Port-au-Prince, que le *Caribbean Market* s'est écroulé et que de nombreux éboulements paralysent totalement la circulation des véhicules. Cependant, pas une minute ne me vient à l'esprit que notre

maison, aux murs de béton tellement durs qu'on avait du mal à y
mettre un clou, pouvait s'être écroulée. Marie-Claude ne répond pas
aux appels téléphoniques, mais je la pense en sureté avec le personnel
de maison. C'est en apprenant que l'Hôtel Montana, proche de chez
nous, s'est écroulé que commence mon inquiétude.

—Marie-Claude ! Voici Marie-Claude !

A mon grand étonnement, ma fille nous arrive dans un piteux
état : échevelée, pieds nus, blessée, un tricot délavé par-dessus une
robe d'intérieur déchirée et poussiéreuse.

Après d'affectueux baisers, très entourée, elle raconte :

> Vers 4h30, mettant fin aux travaux de rangement des
> dossiers de la FORF (Fondation Odette Roy-Fombrun
> pour l'éducation) je m'apprête à prendre un bain bien
> mérité. Poussée par je ne sais quel destin, je quitte la salle
> de bain—où je serais certainement morte emmurée—
> pour aller ranger quelques objets dans l'armoire-dépôt.
> C'est alors que j'entends un bruit sourd, incroyable,
> indescriptible, que j'assimile à un engin extraordinaire
> passant dans la rue. Puis, tout s'est mis à secouer autour
> de moi. Comme dans un film d'horreur, les objets de
> l'armoire sont projetés sur moi comme des missiles. Ils
> me jettent par terre à coté d'un lit. Je sens le sol s'effondrer
> alors qu'un très épais nuage de poussière m'aveugle. Que
> se passe-t-il chez moi ? Est-ce une explosion ? C'est alors
> que, juste au dessus de ma tête, je vois la dalle de béton
> du plafond. Je l'aurais reçue sur le crâne si je n'avais pas
> été projetée par terre dans ce triangle de vie.

> Reprenant mes sens, je réalise qu'il me faut à tout prix
> sortir de là en me dirigeant vers le trou d'où vient une
> lumière. J'essaie de me lever, mais, impossible de bouger :
> j'ai un pied coincé ! Je crie à l'aide. Mes appels désespérés
> résonnent dans le vide. La panique me saisit. Je pense aux
> victimes du 11 Septembre 2001 à New York. J'en appelle
> alors à Dieu : « Toi seul peux m'aider. A nous deux donc !
> Un, deux, trois ! »

> Miraculeusement, une force indescriptible me traverse
> la jambe et j'arrive à arracher le pied de cette masse qui
> l'emprisonnait.

> Les secousses continuent. La peur dans l'âme je rampe. Il
> me faut atteindre la lumière avant que la toiture de béton
> ne s'écroule sur moi.

J'entends au loin les voix de nos fidèles servantes, Yvonne et Sefize, qui hurlent de désespoir : *Madan Bayard mouri! Nou p ap wèl ankò!*

Impossible de répondre.

J'arrive enfin au puits de lumière. Nouveau miracle : un grillage de fenêtre est posé là. Il me sert d'échelle pour atteindre la cour où les deux servantes, couvertes de poussière, échevelées, émues jusqu'aux larmes, m'embrassent à m'étouffer. En effet, une bonbonne de gaz, en se détachant, avait violemment heurté Yvonne qui cuisinait.

Les cris qui montent de la ville et l'immense nuage de poussière qui obscurcit l'horizon confirment que le désastre n'est pas circonscrit à notre seule maison.

Sans nouvelles, pieds nus, je me rends chez notre voisine dont la maison s'est aussi écroulée, heureusement, sans faire de victimes. C'est son beau-fils, arrivé plus tard, qui m'a généreusement conduite ici.

Le lendemain, des nouvelles surprenantes nous parviennent. Ma belle-sœur qui se trouvait sous les décombres du Caribbean a été sauvée par un inconnu tandis qu'une alliée était encore dans les décombres de l'hôtel Montana.

Quant au frère Joseph, il a été tout bonnement enseveli dans sa chambre. Le miracle a voulu que l'on retrouve dans les décombres son ordinateur et le texte du livre qu'il venait d'achever. Etrangement, le livre était dédicacé aux élèves ensevelis deux ans auparavant sous les décombres de l'Ecole de Nérette.

La solidarité est à la mesure du drame. Toutes les classes sociales sont unies dans un même élan de générosité. Ensemble, on fouille pour sauver des vies. Ensemble, on soigne les blessés. Rien que des *konbit* d'entraide.

Que de drames partagés ! Que de vies généreusement sauvées ! Que de sans abris spontanément hébergés !

Mais le tableau que je n'oublierai jamais c'est la grande pelle mécanique ramassant les cadavres empilés qu'on ira jeter dans des fosses communes. Une image cruelle restera gravée dans ma mémoire : deux petites jambes d'une fillette suspendues hors de la benne à cadavres avec chaussettes et chaussures bleues, mises sans doute ce matin-là avec amour par une mère attentionnée ! Où est-elle la mère de cette fillette ? Voit-elle ce que je vois ? Est-elle couchée près de sa fille dans une dernière étreinte ? Un dernier baiser.

My Dearest Ana

Nadève Ménard

August 2010

My dearest Ana,

I've never been good at keeping journals, although I have tried at several points in my life. To be honest, I'm not even that great at letter-writing, although I do it from time to time. But this letter is different. There are things I want to say to you and I worry I might forget them by the time you are old enough to understand. We are at such different moments in our lives. How strange that this one event has strengthened our bond, yet underscores our differences at the same time.

January 12, 2010, was a Tuesday, only your second day back at school after the holiday break. I picked you up in the afternoon and off we went to run errands. I was on the organizing committee for a literary festival that was to start on January 14, and there were so many details to finalize. We headed to Pétionville to buy a welcoming gift for my advisor, whom I hadn't seen in years but who would be in attendance at the festival. We then went to a shoe store where I purchased a pair of overpriced black sandals for the cocktail party to be held Wednesday evening. And then we arrived at Groupe Croissance in Delmas, which housed the festival headquarters. You were so excited to help me put together the welcoming satchels for the participating writers. One of the other organizers called to say she was picking up the T-shirts and would soon be back. Those of us in the office were scurrying back and forth—crossing names off of lists, packing bags . . . I felt a rumbling beneath my feet. And heard a strange sound, a very loud strange sound. I don't remember if you said anything, but I felt your fear as you began moving toward me. I'll never forget the fear in your eyes. I told you to stay put, walked over to you, gathered you beneath me and we waited. Just a few seconds and it was over, although I still had no idea what *it* was. All I knew was that you were okay, and therefore, so was I. Even today, I cannot comprehend the stories of parents losing children, children losing parents, families losing each other. My heart refuses to process those stories as truth, even when I know several victims personally.

That evening, when I finally felt brave enough to drive us home, I tried not to see the horrors on both sides of the street. The people covered in white concrete dust and blood, the collapsed buildings, the blank stares. I kept the radio firmly tuned to Visa FM so that upbeat konpa played in the car. You could sing along and not be frightened. Meanwhile, I focused on maneuvering around the people and abandoned cars in the streets. I tried to find my way home when most of the landmarks I drove by every day were gone. And I was not sure of what home would look like once we got there.

Will you always remember camping out in my uncle's yard? How happy you were to have the entire family in one place, how excited to be sleeping in a tent. There were fourteen of us in all, huddled together on makeshift mattresses under the stars. I don't know if you will ever fully realize just how vital you were to all of us in those early days. And to be honest, just as there was anxiety, frustration, and confusion during that time, there was also a lot of laughter and love. We were all happy to be together, to be safe and to be alive. We had bread and peanut butter for breakfast every morning, with a side of bananas. You were thrilled to be allowed coffee, which was usually a special treat.

Those first weeks, I was scared to take you out with me; I didn't want you to see the destruction. To be honest, I was scared to face the streets myself. Even now, my heart hurts each time I drive past the collapsed National Palace on my way to the university. So, in the early days, going to our own house to work on putting things in order was your only outing. And you enjoyed it so much, always happy to be able to bring another toy back to camp.

There were so many things I meant to tell you, but never did out of cowardice. How do you tell a five-year-old that the supermarket where she always gets free lollipops no longer exists? That her great-aunt's school where we attended Vendredi Littéraire had collapsed?

That the school where I had chosen to register her for the following year was crushed? I am sure that you gleaned many things from the conversations and silences around you. I know I am among the lucky just by virtue of being able to choose how much to expose you to. There is no gaping hole where your parents or grandparents should be. No gaping hole where your home once stood.

That first week, I heard on the radio that the École Normale Supérieure where I teach had collapsed. A colleague was rescued after two days. So many former and current workplaces of relatives and friends crushed, destroyed. So many possibilities for disaster averted.

When I resumed my office job in late January, I dreaded going in every day because I knew I would be doing nothing of consequence, and yet there was so much to be done. I felt guilty about that. When you finally returned to school several weeks later, you were so happy to see your friends and teachers, to have some semblance of normalcy in your life. And while I desperately craved that normalcy for you, it seemed absurd to me that anything could ever be normal again.

Once you returned to school, you'd tell me where this one or that one of your friends was during the earthquake, what he or she was doing at the time. Teddy was sleeping and his father carried him out of the house. Laurie and her cousin were playing on the stairs. I realized that no matter how much we tried to shelter the children, you and your friends went through the same process as everyone else, in terms of reliving the earthquake, recounting it, assessing how we each lived through it.

A few weeks after the earthquake, when we had returned to our house, you were playing with blocks on my bed. You created a complicated story about a family whose home was repeatedly destroyed by earthquakes. In June, I took you to visit my sister in Manhattan. As we waited to cross the street one day, a train rumbled underground and I could sense your small body stiffening beside me. We all have our aftershocks.

I wonder if you will ever question my decision to stay here after the earthquake. When you see the footage of hundreds of people fleeing by the planeload, will you wonder why we were not among them? Or will you understand by then what it means to love a country like a person? Will you understand how leaving could have been unthinkable at that moment even though I was unsure of how I'd be able to help or even what my own future would look like?

It is easy to despair when seven months after the earthquake so much remains to be done. Hundreds of thousands of people remain homeless and rubble still clutters the streets. But I cannot despair knowing that it is your future that hangs in the balance.

Just today I went shopping for your school supplies. Next month you will begin first grade. How lucky you are to be able to attend the school I had picked out for you last year, in spite of the fact that it was completely destroyed in the quake. That's something I plan to insist upon throughout your childhood—the fact that you are lucky. Not because it makes you entitled. On the contrary, so that you can always strive for a society where a child doesn't have to be lucky to be able to go to school or to receive a solid education.

I wonder if you'll be able to look back at January 2010 as a turning point, identify it as the moment when we all said enough is enough and decided to change things for the better. So far, I doubt it.

I moved here as a child in 1987. Those older than me lament that my generation never knew a stable, prosperous Haiti. All we know is political instability, ecological disasters, and societal chaos. Will your generation become accustomed to the rubble everywhere, the scarred landscape and tent cities?

When you ask me what I did to help others after the earthquake, once you are old enough to appreciate the magnitude of what occurred, what will I be able to say? How can I explain that strange blend of paralysis and frustration that held us in its grip? Will you understand the limits we faced, or will they just sound like excuses?

One day in late May, I was stuck in traffic after teaching at the university. Glancing out of the window, I saw two little girls looking at me hopefully. They wore bright blue uniforms and had ribbons in their hair. They were only a little older than you. They were waiting for a tap-tap to Delmas, so I gave them a ride. I asked them why they were in school so far away. One family had lost their house in the earthquake. The other family's house was intact, but the neighborhood was mostly abandoned and no longer deemed safe. One little girl was confused by the roads in Delmas and not sure exactly where she was staying. Her friend explained where she needed to be. She lives just down the street from us and was so grateful for the ride. It was so little to do.

Living here now means inhabiting two parallel universes. The biggest, most pressing problem remains how to improve the lives of those seriously affected by the earthquake. And yet, we still have to deal with minor everyday occurrences like cars breaking down and the lack of electricity, rising prices, and enforcing bedtime.

I think of our constant conversations throughout the day, the ways in which you ground me. The way my life has structured itself around your existence, around your very being, and I realize how few seconds it would have taken for me to be annihilated. Your constant chatter and endless questions. Your smile as you inform me that you're going to be a singer and dancer when you grow up, and your absolute belief that it can happen. The sweet baby smell of your scalp. Your hand in mine. Watching you sleep. Those precious gifts I had begun to take for granted. How much you've grown since January, half a shoe size, almost a full dress size. When I think of this year, 2010, will I remember these details of your life or will the earthquake overshadow everything else?

I cannot imagine what the future holds for you, what your future here will look like. Will that terrible day and its aftermath fade into distant memory for you? Will you always notice the missing landmarks as you walk down the road? Will you remember going downtown to look at the National Palace decorated with lights at Christmastime? Will you help find ways to make life here more beautiful?

Sometimes I wonder how I can have so much hope in this situation, but I do. And I hope that if I pass nothing else on to you, I give you that much, the love and hope for a country that has been through so much, has given so much, and has so much more to give. I hope we'll both remember the abundance of fruit everywhere in the streets in January 2010. Sweet and juicy tangerines.

Love always,
Manman

Note

"My Dearest Ana," by Nadève Ménard, was originally published in *Meridians: Feminism, Race, Transnationalism* 11, no. 1 (2011): 108–113. Copyright © 2011 by Smith College. Reprinted with permission of Indiana University Press.

La Colére de la terre

Edith Lataillade

Nouvelle secousse, nouvelle colère de la terre !

Charlène est face à ce qui fut sa demeure. Elle supplie, elle crie et, dans un sanglot, appelle quelques jeunes sauveteurs improvisés : « c'est lui, c'est mon fils ! C'est Tilic ! se pitit mwen ! sove li tanpri ! »

Tilic appelle, crie, hurle.

L'enfant a le dos et les membres coincés sous la masse de béton et les gravats. Trois jeunes garçons se précipitent ; ils essayent de libérer Tilic. Ils sont poussés par la force de désespérance de la mère, et par le souci de servir la vie. Ils n'ont que leurs mains et des barres de fer, trop flexibles pour l'emploi. Une nouvelle secousse les fait fuir.

La mère reste seule, face à la souffrance et aux appels de son fils. Elle se tord, elle crie et supplie, mais ces appels puissants se perdent dans les échos de la foule en prière dédaignant les insuffisances de son langage.

Les sauveteurs improvisés s'emploient déjà à d'autres sauvetages, d'autres tentatives de délivrances.

Charlène entre dans l'effroi, avec l'angoisse et la peur dans ses entrailles. Elle appelle ses dieux. Autour d'elle, les actes de solidarité et d'entraide se multiplient. Ils expriment des mots de vie, des gestes de respect et d'encouragement : « Ou pa bezwen pè nou la, kouraj. » Entre deux secousses, les sauveteurs se mettent à l'œuvre, se replient, et reviennent. Charlène supplie : « Tanpri, sove Tilic ! » la voix de Tilic s'affaiblit.

Une rumeur de tsunami court et casse la force de l'entraide et de cette humanité spontanée les mains nues. Charlène n'entend plus la voix de Tilic. Elle court vers les sauveteurs, supplie; mais ils sont déjà à d'autres sauvetages, d'autres délivrances et libérations. Ils ont dans l'âme la force de la solidarité et le sens de l'entraide.

Mais Tilic est silencieux !

Tilic ne crie plus ; il ira trouver ceux de la fosse commune. Charlène ne pourra pas lui offrir une sépulture à la hauteur de son amour. Charlène quitte le corps de Tilic. Elle court en hurlant vers son chagrin qu'elle portera le reste de sa vie.

Note

Tiré du recueil inédit, *La Colère de la terre*.

LES HEURES QUI SUIVIRENT

Johanne Elima Chachoute

Le plus angoissant fut l'obscurité qui tomba brutalement, comme pour cacher à nos yeux l'étendue de la tragédie. Mais ça se voyait, tout le monde en avait peur de cette obscurité qui se mêlait de ce qui ne la regardait pas. Si la terre se remettait à trembler, comment pourrions-nous voir d'où viendrait le danger et fuir le plus loin possible ?

Choqués, crevant de peur, nous nous serrions les uns contre les autres, énervés par des mots des badauds qui essayaient déjà de vaincre ce trop-plein de peur par le rire. Comment pouvait-on avoir le courage de rire alors que la seule chose qu'on croyait stable dans notre pays, se mouvait sous nos pieds ?

Je ressentais des sentiments contradictoires, j'avais envie de revenir au stade de fœtus, de regagner le doux ventre de ma mère pour y trouver une sécurité bienfaisante. Mais en la regardant délirer sans même avoir conscience que son mari, mon père, pouvait être en ce moment même en train d'agoniser sous les décombres de notre maison, j'avais encore plus envie de cacher à sa vue les cadavres que déjà on alignait sur le trottoir d'en face, de la mettre quelque part où ses pieds ne toucheraient pas le sol.

J'avais peur, j'avais soif, j'avais froid. Je ressentais une vacuité incompréhensible. Je ne comprenais pas que trente-cinq secondes aient suffi pour que je me découvre aussi poltronne, pour que d'un coup il fût impossible de trouver à boire !

Les radios, qui d'habitude polluaient le silence étaient muettes ! Ce soudain mutisme donnait une impression de fin du monde. Haïti venait-elle de disparaître de la surface du globe ? Le président était-il mort ? Où était la MINUSTAH ?

J'imaginais qu'en des moments aussi terribles un président devait expliquer à la nation ce qui venait de se passer. D'habitude, je n'aimais pas l'entendre, le président; mais en ce moment ce besoin se faisait terriblement sentir, comme si le fait de savoir qu'il était vivant signifiait que les gens qui allaient et venaient devant moi, et moi-même n'étions pas les seuls rescapés. Oui, entendre sa voix voudrait dire que dans quelques minutes des équipes de secours allaient arriver et que la MINUSTAH allait prodiguer les premiers soins aux gens que j'avais entendus crier, prisonniers des tonnes de bétons.

Mon Dieu, j'avais peur !

Je cherchais de temps en temps une espèce de sécurité que je souhaitais contagieuse dans le regard d'Anne Fedorah que sa mère serrait trop fort contre elle, car elle criait en se débattant. En ce moment, elle était calme, comme si elle sentait le drame qui se jouait autour d'elle du haut de ses deux ans. Chaque fois que nos regards se croisaient, elle me montrait sa menotte, où elle venait, il y a juste quelques minutes, d'être égratignée dans l'effondrement de la maison familiale. Elle balbutiait : « Nainainne, Fedo blessée . . . » Mon Dieu petite filleule chérie, une égratignure ce n'était vraiment rien à côté de ce qui se passait vraiment, si tu savais !

Ma tante gémissait sous le choc des images dont nos yeux en faisaient le plein stockage pour les réserver pour les cauchemars; Nathalie sursautait à chaque réplique; Judly se serrait contre sa mère en réclamant de l'eau tandis que cette dernière comptait les cadavres qu'on alignait les uns à côté des autres. Tout cela me désespérait !

Qu'est-ce qui se passait ? Une obscurité dévorant un après-midi aussi vite, des radios silencieuses, l'impression que quelque chose d'insaisissable vous empêche d'appréhender ce qui se passe sous vos yeux, cela n'arrive que dans les rêves !

Je venais, il y a quelques minutes, de voir Gary Victor passer derrière une moto, vêtu seulement d'un jeans et d'une chemisette, dans la réalité il ne ferait pas ça Gary Victor, hein ? J'avais donc là une preuve solide que je rêvais. Seulement si ce que je voyais là était bien réél, il aurait toutes les raisons du monde de passer en trombe derrière une moto avec ce regard un peu fou.

Maintenant, c'était l'obscurité totale. J'entendis une voix grésiller, un son familier qui tombait dans la stupeur tel un bon signe. Je me levai pour le chercher ce son, ma mère s'accrocha à moi en criant : « Kote w prale pitit ? » Je la repoussai doucement en lui promettant de revenir vite, mais j'avais peur de m'éloigner d'eux et de trouver la place vide en revenant, et peur aussi que le sol puisse les engloutir sans moi, alors je me rassis.

Tout était si beau ce matin, il faisait un temps magnifique ! Je me souviens de mon clin d'œil au miroir tandis que je terminais mon maquillage pour aller travailler. En attendant un taxi sur la route du Canapé-Vert, j'avais souri de voir un jeune homme m'observer à la dérobée. J'étais sûre qu'il me trouvait séduisante dans mon uniforme de travail : un pantalon bleu marine qui m'allait à ravir, un corsage d'une blancheur immaculée et des hauts talons qui me donnaient une assurance sans bornes. En ce moment, j'étais pieds nus, les ongles de mes pouces arrachés, je ne portais que mon pantalon et ma chemisette, le reste je l'avais abandonné sur la route en hurlant telle une hystérique.

Le visage de cette petite fille pris au piège sous les décombres de sa maison et ses cris lorsque je m'étais enfuie en ressentant les premières répliques, vinrent danser dans ma tête. C'était surtout de l'entendre crier mon nom qui m'avait frappée. Cette enfant, je l'avais vu naître, grandir dans le quartier et j'avais fui en l'abandonnant à son sort de peur de mourir avec elle.

Fedorah s'est endormie !

Elle fermait les yeux sur tout et demain lorsqu'elle se réveillerait, tout ce que ses yeux de bébé avaient l'habitude de voir ferait partie du passé, rien ne serait comme avant. Mais ça, Anne Fedorah l'ignorait…

Je me serrai contre ma mère et en parfaite égoïste enfouie mon visage dans son cou et me mis à sangloter avec rage. Moi, je comprenais et c'était … insoutenable !

Séisme… 12 janvier 2010, 16h53

Françoise Beaulieu-Thybulle

J'entends au loin des cavaliers, des fantassins qui galopent, sabots sonnants ; la route se fragmente en éclats. Ça pulvérise partout. L'effet est fulgurant, une scène primordiale où les bottes des Dieux défoncent, fendent et crevassent le sol, anéantissant tout sur leur trajet. C'est un tremblement de terre. Une croûte qui s'ouvre, une déchirure terrestre qui fissure l'âme et le corps.

La terre fendue, traversée de secousses, de vibrations, de convulsions, d'explosions. Une terre-cimetière qui décapite, broie les os, ouvre les ventres. Une terre qui grossit de la graisse de nos corps. La ville est soumise au scalpel d'un éventreur arrivant du tréfond de la terre. L'horreur d'un drame comme seule une nation pauvre peut engendrer.

Personne ne devine ma frayeur. C'est l'obscurité totale. Je suis tétanisée de la tête aux pieds.

Incapable de rester impassible devant la fulgurance des images qui suivent, je saute, cours, bouscule. Ma demeure est lointaine et inaccessible. Je trouve refuge dans un cul-de-sac, où m'y accueillent, en me faisant une petite place parmi eux, des concitoyens, des Haïtiens qui ne sont ni amis, ni parents. Dans le frisson de cette nuit solidaire, je redécouvre la fraternité. Thé et larmes sont échangés. Accrochés l'un à l'autre nous égrenons avec le seul bouclier de la chaleur humaine, les secondes fatidiques où nous espérons pieusement survivre la quarantaine de répliques qui annonce l'arrivée de l'aube.

Le rideau solaire se lève enfin sur la noirceur du drame. Réveil brutal qui ôte les épines de mon cœur pour les enfoncer dans ma chair. La situation est grave, le récit impossible, les voix inaudibles, le tableau indescriptible. Nos frères sont mis en croix. Une femme se serre les entrailles pour hurler son désespoir. C'est un holocauste sismique.

Nos morts, éparpillés sur les trottoirs sont portés dans les chars, les grues et les camions. Nos morts sans noms attendent en coulisse, après cette chute dans le néant, d'être dévorés par la peste et la vermine. Sans monuments, sans sarcophages, ils sont embarqués, cap vers le nord, guidé par Saint Christophe, patrons des voyageurs.

Ceux qui ont eu la chance de survivre la catastrophe, attendent dans la faim, la soif, le dénuement, à ciel ouvert, le matin clément, la fenêtre qui devrait s'ouvrir sur une étoile lumineuse qui guidera vers une difficile mais courageuse ascension vers la reconstruction.

Sur des béquilles, la ville se redresse et avance. On charrie l'eau, on sort les casseroles, on fait chauffer les marmites. Au rythme du soleil, les papillons folâtrent et les abeilles butinent. Ce sont des signes que la vie reprend. Les marchandes reins serrés, têtes chargées de victuailles font descendre des vivres des cimes fraîches et inébranlables. Elles tournent la page et laissent les morts reposer en paix.

Quels pansements suffiront à rapiécer mes mille morceaux ? Quelles secousses vont encore nous faire vibrer ? Sous quels abris reposerons-nous ? Combien de temps encore sentirons-nous les vertiges de ce crépuscule morbide ?

Et les sinistrés nomades croient sur la place publique. Telle la mauvaise herbe, elle dérange. On l'arrache. Transplantée dans le désert, elle meurt à petit feu. Quel sarclage !

Puisque rien n'est fait pour commémorer ceux que l'on ne peut oublier, nous entonnons, quand même, un cantique d'espérance en hommage aux disparus, le destin nous ayant permis de rester en vie. Espérons que cette tragédie nationale va paradoxalement stimuler l'essor urbain et économique. Les villes vont se relever. Haïti renaîtra de ses cendres.

VIVRE

Évelyne Trouillot

Nous sommes le vendredi 15 janvier. « Il est 5 heures du matin, dit soudain une voix. Vous n'allez pas prier aujourd'hui ? » J'entrouvre les yeux et la réalité me happe sans aucune transition bienheureuse. Au-dessus de moi, les étoiles insolentes de beauté ; autour de moi, les bruits familiers de toute la famille couchée sur des matelas de fortune, tous blottis les uns contre les autres, tous vivants. Ce n'est pas un cauchemar et nous sommes chanceux d'être en vie. Nous nous sommes réunis dans le jardin de mon frère. Juste à côté, un camp s'est établi sur un terrain vague. « Vous n'allez pas prier aujourd'hui ? » répète la voix. Hommes, femmes et enfants mêlent leurs voix dans la fraîcheur du petit matin, une fraîcheur si douce que je clignote les yeux, conjurant le cauchemar de prendre fin. En vain.

La douleur revient. Comme je l'ai écrit hier à mes parents et amis, cela fait si mal de voir les maisons détruites de la ville de mon enfance, les rues encombrées de carcasses, de regarder les cadavres allongés sur les trottoirs, de suivre l'errance de centaines gens sans abri, sans recours. D'entendre à chaque fois la liste des morts s'allonger de noms de gens qu'on a connus, professeurs d'université, écrivains, féministes, étudiants, enfants, jeunes femmes et hommes anonymes mais qui, comme moi, étaient de cette terre, portant en eux sa cadence et ses déboires, sa rage de vivre et sa soif de beauté. Cela fait mal et cela change pour toujours ma conception de la vie et des choses. Le tremblement de terre a secoué plus que les maisons, les immeubles et la terre. Une minute et quelques secondes pour nous rappeler brutalement que nous sommes tous unis par l'imminence de la mort. Pour moi, chaque minute devient un cadeau fragile et tremblant du destin, une responsabilité nouvelle d'être forte et d'en profiter au maximum dans le respect de mes convictions. La vie a pris un goût d'absence.

Nous sommes le samedi 16 janvier. Vers les 3 heures du matin, une nouvelle secousse assez forte pour réveiller ceux d'entre nous qui dormaient vient détruire toute illusion de retourner bientôt à la normalité. Des coups de feu sporadiques nous rappellent que, comme dans toute catastrophe, des instincts rapaces et meurtriers se réveillent au mépris du collectif. Assez pour nuire avant d'être placés sous contrôle, mais pas plus qu'ailleurs. N'en déplaise à certains médias étrangers qui profitent de la tragique occasion d'une catastrophe naturelle pour présenter et ressasser des images stéréotypées d'un pays qui souffre et qui se bat. Des images qui ne servent qu'à augmenter inutilement l'angoisse des compatriotes à l'étranger sans nouvelles de leurs proches, des nouvelles qui contribuent à éveiller l'indignation de tous ceux qui compatissent avec les victimes de cette tragédie.

Nous sommes le dimanche 17 janvier. Le quartier s'est organisé en comités pour gérer un quotidien qui trébuche encore. Le soleil joue à la marelle avec des nuages polissons et semble gagner la partie. Dans le camp d'à côté, des mouvements annoncent le réveil. Un voisin se réjouit qu'une adolescente blessée qu'il avait conduite à l'hôpital soit sauvée, elle ne perdra pas son œil.

Un bébé pleure.

Des rires d'enfants éclatent avec un bruit de galopades heureuses.

La vie s'installe, refusant de rester sous terre.

Survie miraculeuse

Marie Andrée Manuel Etienne

Trente-cinq secondes de battements telluriques pour une éternité
d'angoisse et de malheurs innommables.
Ma maison a bougé à une onglette de l'effondrement.
Mon corps et mon âme ont vibré à quelques millimètres de la mort.
Et ma ville s'est affaissée dans un fracas de poussière
nuageuse crépusculaire.

Personne n'ignore combien notre planète a été affectée par de nombreux désastres naturels souvent provoqués et aggravés par l'irresponsabilité des dirigeants politiques et le comportement insouciant des humains en général. C'est le cas de la terre Haïtienne qui a été violemment secouée par le séisme du 12 janvier 2010. Ce fut une épouvantable catastrophe qui emporta plus de 250,000 vies et provoqua l'effondrement de milliers d'immeubles. A Port-au-Prince et dans ses régions avoisinantes, des églises, des écoles, des centres commerciaux, des hôtels, des édifices publics et des maisons privées s'effondrèrent en un terrible crescendo d'horreurs.

Ce jour-là nous avions reçu la visite d'un journaliste portoricain Angel Dario qui participait à un Congrès religieux en tant que Président de la Conférence Episcopale de son pays (ce que j'ai appris un an plus tard quand il est revenu nous voir et surtout revoir la maison où il a failli mourir). Il m'a avoué que dans cette maison il est né une deuxième fois. Angel est arrivé le 12 janvier 2010 à 4h40. Il m'a vue dans la bibliothèque en train de travailler et s'exclama : « Quel beau studio ! je vais en prendre quelques photos ».

Ensuite il est monté voir mon mari, l'artiste écrivain Frankétienne, au second étage pour photographier quelques tableaux. Dix minutes plus tard nous avons perçu les premières secousses. On eût dit un opéra insupportable. Une effroyable série dévastatrice qui paraissait interminable suivit. Le beau studio s'est effondré au milieu d'un amas de décombres hétéroclites. L'interview n'aura lieu qu'en janvier 2011.

Goudougoudou . . . je déteste ce vocable qui fait référence au séisme du 12 janvier 2010 qui allait ravager notre pays et bouleverser nos vies. Je n'arrive toujours pas à effacer de ma mémoire cette blessure profonde qui m'a marquée physiquement et moralement. Au moment où un soleil abricot nous inondait de ses derniers rayons magiques, la terre a commencé à trembler. J'étais seule au 1er étage où je subissais la rage déconcertante de ce monstre chaotique qui me balançait d'avant en arrière et me projetait contre le comptoir de la cuisine et la table de la salle à manger. Toute la vaisselle s'est brisée sur ma tête. J'ai vu tous les murs s'écrouler autour de moi. Je ne cessais de répéter calmement : « Jésus j'ai confiance en toi ». Après le séisme j'ai dû subir des tractions de la colonne cervicale et de la colonne vertébrale.

En 35 secondes tout a basculé. Ce n'était plus qu'épouvante. Terreur. Chaos. Meurtrissures. Cris affreux d'outre-tombe. L'apocalypse . . . Et des intervalles de silence et puis les questionnements : Comment et pourquoi suis-je vivante ? Cette blessure profonde que je porte en moi a laissé des cicatrices indélébiles.

Ce fut une hécatombe génératrice de panique, de traumatismes et de chaos généralisé. La vie quotidienne devint un véritable enfer : privation d'eau potable, absence d'énergie électrique, dysfonctionnement systématique des communications téléphoniques. Toutes ces anomalies durèrent plusieurs jours. Et les survivants, désemparés tout au début, apprirent à vivre dans une précarité que l'on croyait éphémère et qui pourtant a continué encore pour devenir un vrai cauchemar malgré la solidarité et l'aide généreuse de la diaspora haïtienne et de la communauté internationale. Les cicatrices et les traumatismes sont restés visibles. Insupportables. Et presqu' insurmontables.

Etant présidente du Club des Femmes de Carrières Libérales et Commerciales de Port-au-Prince (BWP), de concert avec nos membres, nous avions pris la décision de nous aider mutuellement et d'aider nos sœurs traumatisées. Nous nous demandions comment survivre aux innombrables désastres causés par ce monstre apocalyptique.

Avec le support financier de la Fédération Internationale (IBPW) et en partenariat avec le Centre de psychotrauma URAMEL, nous avons essayé de nous reconstruire en participant à des séances d'accompagnement psycho-social à travers le programme : « *Grandir à travers l'épreuve* ». Ce programme comprenait 3 volets :

- Projet d'appui psychosocial
- Assistance financière à une vingtaine d'étudiantes
- Support financier à une vingtaine de commerçantes du secteur informel.

Ce programme a eu un impact positif sur les deux groupes cibles, soit 82 femmes vivant dans deux camps : l'un à Delmas 31 sur la cour des Sœurs de Saint Paul de Chartres et l'autre sur la cour de l'église de Saint-Gérard.

Je participais régulièrement à ces séances avec les psychologues d'URAMEL. Cet accompagnement a appris à ces jeunes femmes comment elles pouvaient relever deux défis : celui de se reconstruire et celui de construire une nouvelle Haïti. Nous n'oublierons jamais ceux qui sont partis. Nous les survivants avons chacun un devoir de mémoire. Nous devons témoigner pour dire. Pour guérir et pour prévenir.

Je crois que je suis investie d'une mission : celle de poursuivre au sein du BPW le travail que j'ai commencé il y a une vingtaine d'années. En effet dans le cadre des activités engagées depuis sa création, en faveur de l'amélioration du statut de la femme haïtienne dans le domaine du travail et son intégration progressive dans l'activité nationale, le BPW Club de Port-au-Prince a donc décidé de relancer ses activités en dispensant aux jeunes femmes des cours que nous appelons « Les Classes du Weekend », qui auront lieu tous les dimanches : savoir vivre, hôtellerie, restauration et culture générale.

Il est urgent de susciter le réveil des consciences endormies à travers un immense mouvement de rapprochement culturel et spirituel qui nous permettra non seulement de limiter les dégâts irréparables mais surtout de créer un climat d'harmonie, d'amour et de paix. Apprenons à vivre ensemble et surtout à garder vivaces nos utopies !

Trente cinq secondes de battements telluriques pour une éternité d'angoisse et de malheurs innommables.

Trente cinq secondes qui ont transformé nos vies et ont redoublé mon propre désir d'aider et d'épauler mes compatriotes et en particulier, les femmes de mon pays.

Kinam : Le 12 janvier 2010

Joëlle Vitiello

Deux ans après le tremblement de terre qui a mis Haïti à genoux le 12 janvier, les traces de la minute-charnière qui a divisé le temps en un « avant » et un « après » demeurent vives et profondes. Quand j'évoque le 12 janvier, c'est toujours l'« avant » qui se présente d'abord. L'atterrissage en fin de matinée, dans le bonheur de retrouver Port-au-Prince, d'apercevoir le Palais National, trônant, superbe, dans le bas de la ville. C'est à partir de lui que je me repère dans la ville à chaque retour. J'éprouve aussi l'anticipation de revoir les visages familiers. Je suis venue cette fois-ci pour un hommage à la poète et artiste Yanick Jean, prévu la veille de l'ouverture du festival littéraire des Etonnants Voyageurs. J'espère aussi entendre les voix émergentes de la poésie haïtienne, et continuer un travail sur les droits de la personne humaine, en particulier auprès des femmes. C'est la première fois depuis que je viens en Haïti, que je vais loger à Pétion-Ville, au Kinam, plutôt qu'à l'Hospice Saint-Joseph ou à l'Oloffson. En route, je remarque que les rues sont dégagées de tout fatras et que le commerce semble actif. Haïti est debout.

A peine dans ma chambre, je teste mon nouveau téléphone Digicel et texte les mots « Arrived safel . . . » à mon compagnon, lorsque le téléphone me tombe des mains. Je n'aurai pas le temps de taper la dernière lettre, le « y », et le téléphone ne fonctionnera plus. A partir de là, ce sont les sons qui me reviennent le plus nettement. D'abord un vrombissement de marteau-piqueur qui fait trembler les murs, puis qui ressemble à des tirs d'armes automatiques. C'est le bruit d'Haïti en train de se défaire. Lorsque le grondement s'amplifie et que je peux à peine me tenir debout, j'imagine soudain que c'est la montagne derrière le Kinam qui va s'effondrer et tout ensevelir. La

Joëlle Vitiello

pensée fulgurante que je vais mourir en Haïti me traverse la tête et en réponse à la seconde de terreur qui envahit mon corps tendu, je me réconcilie avec cette idée, l'accepte. Enfin, je reconnais le tremblement de terre et me tiens aux murs dans l'embrasure de la porte.

Une fois dans la rue, c'est un silence inouï qui me frappe alors que la ville se fracasse. Puis, petit à petit, des cris, des pleurs, des enfants qui courent en pleurant, d'autres pieds nus. Les adultes aussi ont peur, mais restent calmes. Une petite fille qui a perdu ses chaussures se réfugie dans l'hôtel. Les adultes dans la rue consolent un petit garçon qui pleure, son cartable sur le dos.

Très vite, le Kinam devient un lieu de refuge et la vie va s'y organiser, plus précisément, entre les cours intérieures et la place Saint-Pierre. Des chirurgiens y séjournant en fin de mission vont de suite se mettre au travail et rejoindre une clinique située de l'autre côté de la place, travaillant jour et nuit jusqu'à l'épuisement. Une Américaine dont le Blackberry fonctionne encore donne à son fils les noms des personnes autour d'elle et les numéros de téléphone à appeler pour rassurer leurs familles.

La nuit s'organise dehors. Parmi les réfugiés de l'hôtel, il y a des Canadiens spécialisés dans la construction antisismique, des docteurs, des familles françaises venues adopter des enfants, des voisins qui ont tout perdu, un jeune homme de l'Union Européenne qui a vu son bâtiment de plusieurs étages s'effondrer après la deuxième secousse. Grâce à son talkie-walkie, nous avons pu, au fil des nuits, écouter tous les plans d'évacuation des ressortissants européens élaborés par leurs représentants.

La propriétaire de l'hôtel, malgré ses pertes familiales, est restée au poste et a démarré immédiatement la génératrice de sorte à éclairer la rue à l'extérieur pour aider toutes les personnes qui se sont regroupées spontanément sur la place Saint-Pierre pour la nuit et tous ceux qui tentent de rejoindre leurs maisons.

Des chants liturgiques s'élèvent partout dans la ville. Sur la place Saint-Pierre, j'entends aussi les tambours. Tous les dieux sont convoqués. En cette période de Carnaval, j'entrevois dans la nuit les bandes de quartier circuler avec leurs offrandes et leurs bougies, s'arrêtant devant chaque maison. Au cœur du désastre, la communauté trouve le moyen de se soutenir, de commencer à panser les plaies. Les rythmes sont parfois interrompus par de longs cris de douleur lancinants. Le ciel étoilé est limpide, et si la terre n'avait pas tremblé, la nuit aurait été magnifique. J'essaie en pensée de recoller les morceaux d'Haïti, pour ne pas me réveiller face à l'inimaginable.

C'est seulement au petit matin que je suis sortie dans la ville avec Sophie, une jeune Française travaillant pour une organisation de microcrédit et qui restera presque deux ans après le séisme, travaillant sans relâche auprès de la population haïtienne. C'est grâce à elle, qu'une fois rentrée aux États-Unis, je trouverai du travail pour des Haïtiens, à une période où aucune NGO n'en emploie. Partout où nous avons pu circuler, les gens s'aidaient les uns les autres. Au Karibe, qui a été sérieusement endommagé, les écrivains du festival des Etonnants Voyageurs attendaient leurs transports. C'est là que j'ai appris le décès de Georges Anglade et de sa femme Mireille.

La vie sur la place Saint-Pierre s'est aussi tout de suite organisée. Les bâches apparues dès la deuxième nuit anticipent les tentes. Cette nuit sera aussi longue que la précédente, plus tragique aussi au fur et à mesure que la réalité du *tremble terre* pénètre les esprits.

Entre le moment où j'ai quitté le Kinam et celui où j'ai quitté l'Ambassade pour l'aéroport, le pays a changé. Partout sillonnent des convois militaires avec des soldats armés jusqu'aux dents. A l'aéroport, j'assiste à des pugilats entre soldats et humanitaires de tous horizons. Les seuls avions qui se posent dégorgent des journalistes-photographes et repartent vides.

Le travail de solidarité continue : informer, enseigner, inlassablement témoigner d'une Haïti se relevant d'elle-même, forte de sa culture et de son histoire. Défendre aussi et surtout les plus vulnérables, les petites filles et les femmes, contre les nouvelles violences post-séisme. En juin 2012, ce sont les jeunes Haïtiens et Haïtiennes qui travaillent dans les camps, inlassablement, pour faire du soutien psychologique et éducatif, qui m'impressionneront le plus.

ONE IS NEVER ALONE IN HAITI

Lynn Selby

I spent most of Tuesday, January 12, 2010, in my Port-au-Prince apartment with my mentor and friend, Tibebe, the driving force of my "book," which is what she called my dissertation. Over the two years I had lived in Haiti, Tibebe shared with me stories of her life and the different communities where she worked and organized. She introduced me to different people who helped me with my dissertation questions. She encouraged me to overcome my timidity, and advised me on how to sustain relationships in the neighborhood that hosted my research. That particular Tuesday, I was in the final phase of my research and confident about the three months that remained of my stay in Haiti.

Tibebe was in the back room of my ground-floor apartment when the earthquake struck. I was working in my socks at my desk in the front room. I recognized the tremors, grabbed my laptop, and crouched under the desk. When the shaking stopped, I was unable to dislodge myself from the rubble but could hear her voice. She had somehow leaped through an opening created during the duplex's collapse. Able to see light in sight but pinned down by debris, I cried out to her in fear that I would lose the use of my legs. She talked with me continuously as she darted around the fallen structure, looking for openings, and made short forays into the street to look for help. Down the block she found my landlord, Bony, who had been like a father figure to me.

When Bony arrived with only a couple of people to dislodge the debris that held me down, it dawned on me that the situation was very bad. How many times had I seen people gather spontaneously in large numbers to respond to accidents? Most of my neighbors were occupied with their own families' survival. Tibebe stayed until I was pulled out with the laptop, which I had protected with my body. She then left to walk the four miles home to find her own three daughters.

As I was lying on the ground with neighbors massaging circulation back into my legs, I began to take stock of the larger situation around me. The second floor where Bony and his family lived had shifted forward and sandwiched the ground floor. When the tremors stopped, the only other person in the duplex at the time had been able to step from the living room of the apartment on the second floor onto the sidewalk. The other tenants of the duplex had returned while I was being dug out. A sense of shame started to take hold as I realized that my rescue had delayed Tibebe's own return home to her family.

Bony and his family took my American housemate Chelsey and me under their wing, and we spent the first night in the middle of the street in order to avoid the debris that might be set loose by the aftershocks. Bony would leave sporadically to scope out the surrounding areas and assess resources at hand. He would never tell us when he would return. I felt frustrated that we were not making plans together but indebted to him for rescuing me. All in all, I was unable to assert myself with him. While he was gone, I ventured out to visit my friend Michel's elderly mother nearby. Vesta was homebound with high blood pressure and diabetes, so I wanted to check on her first. Together, Chelsey, another student, and I slowly made our way to her home a block away. Once there, we found Vesta hosting people who had taken refuge in her courtyard, entertaining them with stories and providing them with food and bedding. We reluctantly left her and her family, so our absence would not cause Bony any alarm.

Neighbors continued to dig through the night to rescue and recover their loved ones. During past periods of national crisis, my neighbors could not and did not expect outside help from the Haitian state or the UN. Buffered by middle-class amenities like municipal water services to their homes and a friendly relationship with the street vendors who worked in the area, they had their own practices of disaster-preparedness. These practices were critical to their survival after the earthquake, especially when they had to extend any stockpiles of rations, water, and batteries retrievable from the rubble.

We sat with our neighbors and passers-by who had not been able to return to their own homes. After procuring a pen and paper from Chelsey, I wrote down any useful mobile phone numbers I had in my contact list on my laptop before its battery died. I tried to use Chelsey's and a stranger's cell phone to no avail.

I watched the ways my neighbors consoled a young mother grieving the loss of her four-year-old. They procured white clothes to put over her dress, holding her up as she stretched out her body in the shape of the cross. In stark contrast, a Baptist member of Bony's family proclaimed loudly that the earthquake was punishment against the Catholics for worshipping entities other than God. I felt like it was an accusation leveled at the mourning mother and a way to blame the rest of us in general. Yet in her own terror during the aftershocks, she would reach out to me, squeezing the injuries on my side at each new tremor, "*Jezi* [Jesus]!" A teenager I knew from a neighboring area joined our group. Jean Vince had only been able to find his father and noticed that I was injured. I tried to convince him that the smaller tremors were going to abate and that we had been through the worst part of the earthquake; I held his hand throughout the night.

When daylight arrived, some friends came through to find out how we were doing and to inform us about their own families. Jean Vince went back to his home and then circled back to let me know that a couple of his friends and neighbors had survived. I asked after his family. "Everyone is fine, my mother is fine, everyone is fine," he answered. Then, under his breath, in a soft voice, "My brother is dead." Jean Vince left to rejoin his surviving family.

We moved into Bony's office three-quarters of a mile away. With Chelsey's help, I documented the extent of the destruction and the names of survivors. Bony's family, friends, and strangers who lived nearby clothed and fed me and provided me with enough adequately clean water to wash my wounds. I felt encouraged to persevere each time I encountered someone I knew in person and heard news of another person's survival, but I was still anxious to reach other friends about whose whereabouts and condition I knew nothing.

Our world shrank to an area that could be covered in a fifteen-minute walk. I can only recall out-of-sequence snippets from those first few days when I was still in the streets in Port-au-Prince. I remember the volunteers who distributed drinking water, the young man at the back of a tap-tap who imitated a siren sound as the driver made the rounds to pick up more bodies, and the middle-aged grandmother who tapped into her food reserves to feed people who passed through. This grandmother was generous *and* strategic; she reached out to Chelsey and me since we were Americans and her grandchild was a U.S. citizen. She wanted to find out how she could get him to safety. I overheard morbid speculations concerning which neighborhoods had been obliterated; they seemed to be a grim form of diversion used to fill the hours of uncertainty and give some sense of control over the situation. "Such and such neighborhood? *Kraze* [destroyed]! Such and such landmark? *Kraze!*" On Wednesday night a rumor of an impending tsunami triggered a running procession from the city center up the main street of Lalue. This rumor was later attributed to thieves who wanted to take other people's belongings.

While I found comfort from many of the people I encountered, the eerily cool weather, the scarcity of food and drinking water, and the proliferation of flies added to the sensation that our situation could rapidly become worse. Bony became strained under the weight of the loss of his home and the responsibility of taking care of so many people. I had enjoyed a jocular mentoring relationship with him before the earthquake; now I was as dependent on him as his much younger common-law wife along with the rest of the people in his household, which he managed in benevolent paternalism. I was torn between a sense of obligation to him and the desire to connect with my own networks, where I felt like I could be decisive and take action. By Wednesday evening, January 13, I thought I could shift the burden of my care to Michel's family. His mother Vesta had reassured me about my injuries when I visited her with him that afternoon. She spoke to me about working together to get some *lwil maskriti* (castor oil) and *zoranj si* (sour oranges) in order to massage the bruised areas of my body and clean the lacerations.

Thursday, January 14, Bony was able to procure some gasoline on the black market so he could drive his car. He drove Chelsey and me on roads that were clear of debris to the American Embassy so that my injuries could be evaluated. The Embassy doctor informed me that I had a nerve compression injury on my leg that would likely heal on its own over several weeks and urged me to consider evacuation. While I was touched by his concern, I was motivated to return to Vesta's home, to the warmth of the family, the *lwil maskriti*, the *zoranj si*, and her and Michel's counsel, and to strategize my next move. Chelsey and I exited the Embassy only to realize that our ride was nowhere in sight. I realized that Bony had needed to get us off his hands and had made the unilateral decision for this to happen at the Embassy. We were confronted with the dilemma of how to get back to the city eight miles away with a small amount of Chelsey's cash and uncertainty about public transport. While I could now walk, there were still times when my weakened and desensitized right leg would suddenly buckle under me. Plus, it was starting to get dark. We circled back to the Consulate's entrance and were let inside the grounds to stay the night.

Inside the Consulate, there were hundreds of U.S. citizens, permanent residents, and adult Haitian nationals accompanying U.S. national minors. There was also a gravely understaffed group of American Foreign Service Officers and Haitian security. My piece of paper to contact my mother was placed into a rapidly growing pile. A young woman from Queens, New York, who had been visiting her family let us use her phone so that Chelsey and I were able to call our families in the United States. Official channels moved much more slowly. After a night and half a day there, I decided to be evacuated with Chelsey. I was gambling on the possibility that we would be evacuated to Santo Domingo, where I planned to regroup and then return to Haiti within a few weeks.

A complex system emerged to address the medical urgency of the injured and infirm and the growing number of parentless minors. It was difficult to discern how the evacuations were prioritized, and some U.S. nationals asserted that they were more of a priority than other evacuees. A white male U.S. national loudly complained about his place in line and questioned if U.S. citizens were being prioritized— he was in line with the U.S. national group, but apparently he did not recognize the U.S. citizen status of Black people of Haitian descent.

Grateful for Chelsey's company but far from the community which had sheltered us and unable to contact them, I felt alienated by these petty disputes. I crouched down and put my head between my legs, feeling the greatest wave of despair yet.

I considered myself lucky that we were evacuated to Santo Domingo and were hosted by friends there. I conceded to take a flight to the United States two days later since I did not know how I would return to Port-au-Prince without a passport, a means to access money, or a place to stay. I felt like a burden to my Dominican hosts and could not justify my return to my Haitian friends who had more challenges ahead and the responsibility of taking care of their own children and grandchildren.

The earthquake of 2010 ripped open my world in a way that I had never before experienced. With the guidance of mentors and friends in Haiti, I was able to establish balance in my life and community relationships. Ever cognizant of my awkward foreigner mannerisms, I had tried to learn the improvisational agility and patience required to live in Haiti. I modeled my behavior after Haitians' attentive and relational ways with one another. I started to provide daily encouragement, to be consistent and present with others, and to be discreet about my own losses and aspirations. One is never alone in Haiti. While I had joked that I had undertaken an apprenticeship with friends and colleagues in order to learn how to live and labor in Haiti, I never underestimated the work of making a life there. My Haitian friends, colleagues, and neighbors had impressed me with their tenacity and resilience; when I lost my hard-earned equilibrium, I felt this loss deeply.

The initial numbness wore off, and my hope that my survival could mean something more than just an arbitrary occurrence faded after my first two weeks back in the United States. I wanted to be grateful for my survival, but darkness set in. Thoughts of Haiti hurt, and all my thoughts were of Haiti. I was rendered mute, and I could not look much further into the future than the next day. I replayed the event of the earthquake and my departure as if I could go backward in time and change it. I clung to items like the list I handwrote of destroyed buildings and living survivors in the few days after the earthquake and the first shirt given to me by Michel's father to replace my own bloodied clothes. I hoarded memories of moments and other people's stories in the aftermath in a suspended state, fearful that I would distort these experiences if I opened my mouth. The loss of the home and sense of community that I had built over two years instilled a deep apprehension, a lack of trust within me, and a sense of having failed the people who had given me so much.

It took me a long time to reconnect with the people who had been so fundamental to my life in Haiti. I started by sending messages through friends who traveled between the United States and Haiti, gradually answering emails and making phone calls on my own, and visiting once a year. My recovery from trauma started slowly, was uneven, and is still incomplete. Each phone call and each trip back, I learn of more friends' and acquaintances' losses that they kept from me partly out of consideration for my own grief. I tentatively take steps to become familiar with the conditions on the ground there instead of fearing the worst, to recognize my own and others' renewed abilities and prolonged limitations as we build new plans together, as we generate hope.

BEING TOGETHER

Laura Wagner

As I half-lay, half-sat under the rubble I thought: *If I die now, I lose everybody.*

That wasn't the only thing I thought. When your body is crushed under the weight of a cement roof, your mind darts all over the place, frantically alighting and taking off again. I also thought: *I don't want to die. I don't want to lose everybody.*

When I reflect on the earthquake now, the saddest thing is everyone who died alone, either quickly or slowly. I worry about the people who died without knowing if their children or husbands or wives or lovers or sisters or brothers or mothers or fathers had survived. I worry that they died with their hearts full of fear. I worry that they thought it was the end and that they never got to say goodbye to the world and the people they loved in it.

In July 2010 and thereafter, I worked with a group of young writers from Port-au-Prince's *quartiers populaires* called the Konbit des Jeunes Penseurs. We met weekly in a temporary school building made of plywood and painted blue and white. Some of the poems and essays we wrote are racy (a lot of rhymes for *fant janm*); others were about love (*an verite, an verite fanm / se sik nan ji kachiman m*).[1] Some others about politics, poverty, NGOs, and life in Cité Soleil.

> *Boujwa yo menm tankou yon resò*
> *Depi yo [an]nik mate*
> *Yo rive lòt bò dlo.*[2]—ASSEPHIE

Sometimes the writers chose to write about the earthquake:

Mwen santi m bouke
Bouke dòmi anba kay plastik
Depi lapli tonbe m pran panik
Mwen vle pou sa chanje.[3]—ÉLIE

They wrote about what they've lost; sometimes they broke down as they read. As we all became comfortable with one another, the complicated details of people's lives slowly emerged. Their losses were crushing. Losses, from the earthquake but also from childbirth, diseases, *lougawou*, gang warfare, relatives who disappeared *lòt bò dlo* and never called again. Lost people.

I suspect that the writers have long known what the earthquake taught me: there is no *demen*, there is only *demen si dye vle*. I can't save Haiti, or the world. The world can do away with us at any moment it pleases. I am not exceptional; none of us is exceptional.

But we are present, and together, in the world right now.

Years have passed since the quake, and time rushes forward. I meant to write only about *douz janvye*, but my mind keeps wandering. Other losses loom. As I write this, a friend from Haiti is in the United States, going through treatment for advanced lung cancer.

When people ask how we're related, she says, "She is my spiritual granddaughter." They nod, perplexed and polite.

The long, anticipated goodbye wrings you out. Everyday activities are weighted with the creeping admission that, despite declarations of *kenbe fò pa lage*, no one can hold on forever. People say it's courageous to spend time with her while she is sick. But I'm not afraid of sickness or hospitals; I'm afraid of loss. Being together, however long you can be, is the opposite of loss.

The stale adage "A single death is a tragedy, but a million deaths is a statistic" taunts me. I think about politics. I think about privilege—the privilege of health care, of closure, of grieving without having to think about feeding yourself and your children, or securing your *prela* so the wind and rain don't blow your make-shift house away.

She misses Haiti—all of it, despite the dust, rain, and risks. She says, with her eyes wide, "It is my *home*," in a way that lets you know she's frightened she won't ever see it again.

On January 12, 2012, we went to church together in California and lit candles in front of *Notre-Dame de Perpétuel Secours.*

> *Bondye, beni Ayiti. Beni tout sa k mouri yo, sa k blese yo,*
> *sa k andikape yo. Moun ki frape, moun ki deplase, timoun*
> *kap viv nan lari, moun ki nan mizè.*[4]

She prayed, far from home, in the dim church on a Thursday afternoon in *peyi fredi sa a*, this cold land. She was so thin, under her heavy coat. I started to cry. I didn't know if I was crying for Haiti (or what it even meant, or if it means anything, to "cry for Haiti") or if I was crying for her. She rubbed my back and hugged me. I didn't want her to know that maybe I was crying for her, that I was crying because I'm afraid she's dying. So I said, "I can't do anything, I can't save anyone, I can't fix things in Haiti," because that's true, too.

She said, "*Se pa fòt ou, ti kokòt.* It's not your fault. *Se kominote entènasyonal la*, they are making money off Haiti."

I looked at her and started laughing. "I *am* part of the international community."

"No you aren't, *Ti Lolo, cheri.* You're just a *ti tèt kale.* You're just a pawn." She paused. "But you write to try to help Haiti, not to break it."

These days, everything feels like an act of existence, in defiance of the inevitable loss. When the Konbit writers declaim death and fear, or Haiti's social problems—and when they write about love—I think *men kouraj.*

We write to engrave people in our memories. We write to draw ourselves out of our own loneliness, into the light of day. We write because we are here. We write people down, the people we love and lose, to bring them back to life, and to say goodbye.

Notes

[1]   In truth, in truth women / are the sugar in my custard-apple juice.

[2]   The bourgeoisie are like a mattress spring
      With the slightest touch
      They fly off to the other side of the sea [the United States]

3   I feel tired

     Tired of living under a plastic roof

     When the rain falls, I panic

     I wish for this to change.

4   God, bless Haiti. Bless all those who died, those who were injured,
     those who are handicapped. People who were struck, people who were
     displaced, children living on the street, all the people in misery.

FORESHOCKS

M. J. Fièvre

Some things have not changed—the crunchy gravel of the dirt roads, the rooster's crow, the buzz of bees, the bright yellow sun of the Haitian dawn. The rest is spooky in its familiarity, yet wrong in detail. A chill settles onto the top of my stomach. Even my skin has gone cold. I drive holding the steering wheel close, among the crowds of unwashed faces and men asleep against their stomachs, the makeshift tent villages. Sometimes, a humanitarian truck comes barreling up behind me and rides my tailpipe.

In Turgeau, where rubble still blocks many streets, I slow down to look for the crumbs of recognizable memory. That's probably the time when I should blame God, wonder if He got angry for being mocked, if His patience simply ran out—the moment when I should decide that He probably sees us all, unblinking. But I can't stop believing in His love and am angry for this faith that I carry around like excess baggage.

As I park the car on Jean Paul II Avenue, I remember *la Fête Dieu*. In my childhood, many streets in Turgeau would be closed to traffic so that devoted Christians could assemble magnificent carpets, meticulously made of flower petals, pine needles, and palm fronds. At six o'clock in the morning, a procession of Roman soldiers mouthing sorrowful songs and purple-robed penitents carrying a statue of Jesus on the cross paraded in front of the houses, destroying the carpets, a great honor for those who worked all night creating them.

Now my city is lost, the ground covered in dusty dry blood. I've been driving around Port-au-Prince, looking for a face to hold on to. I want to look an unknown person in the eye, past my own incoherent grief, my own futility.

I walk to the end of the street, hugging the curb, walking along the lip where the asphalt falls away into a narrow ditch. I reach Sacré Coeur, where so many Sunday mornings my mother and I kneeled and recited our Credo. Father André said mass there. I tried Father André's cell phone after the earthquake. I wanted to speak about religion and God, discuss the meaning of life. He didn't pick up. As the phone burned in my hand, I tried to remember the instant before I learned about the earthquake, the ordinary moment when I leaned against my pillows.

A large cross remains standing outside the church, and all of a sudden, I fear the Jesus on the cross, as I had as a child. He looks so peaceful, yet threatening. I study the smooth shape of his hands, his face with its beatific expression. I hope to stop believing then, and start cursing God. But the fear goes away.

The roof is still intact, but most of the walls have fallen in. I walk inside the ruins and take in the smell of rotten flesh. The pews are covered with dust. A cell phone and a New Testament have been left behind. Hot afternoon sunlight streams through a crack, and dust particles whirl and jig across the beam, thousands floating up with each new footprint on the powdery carpet of dust. A silver spider dines on a green fly.

The church is destroyed, but this is still the house of God. Eyes closed, palms pressed together beneath my chin, I mouth a Hail Mary.

When we lived in Christ Roi, not far from Turgeau, my mother and I often visited Sacré Coeur, and every Sunday I hoped to emerge translucent and Catholic, clean as philosophy. One of the priests often paced the aisles during the sermon, and I tried to be as still as a statue, unnoticed as a candle before it burns. For many years after that, I positioned myself at a safe distance between God and Satan, tempting both. Until I grew closer and closer to God because of that room in the human heart that's older than the body. Sometimes, though, I wish I'd gone the other way so that I could freely cry, "Treason!"

I ache for the peace that faith doesn't bring.

"There's still a body stuck in that small hallway," a voice says. The voice is that of a young man in cut-offs. His hands are thick-veined.

He openly watches me, as he smokes a cigarette. He's got some kind of growth on his neck, shiny and red—a smooth round lump. He points at a cave in passage. "The body is right there."

"Any word about Father André?" I ask.

He shrugs. "Father André is fine. *Just fine.*"

Maybe it's true. Or maybe he doesn't even know who Father André is.

Some people begin to sing outside, huddled in the church garden beneath the hot glare of the sun. In another realm of reality, the hymns surrounding me would lift me up. Heat overwhelms me as I stand, still stunned, in the fierce, dry, completely still air. I go back to the street, walk around a little. Out here, the huge blue sky looms above us, bigger than ever, like it might swallow the rest of us up.

The naked crazy guy who walks by me does not see me. In fact, no one pays attention to me—not even the three-legged dog and the old beggar. I watch the slow breath of the dog on its side, stretched out, its legs raised a bit so that all three touch the wall, each paw making little shivers. The place where its leg once was is healed and covered with fur, weirdly beautiful. I wonder if the dog hates the missing leg for leaving.

I hear the flick of a lighter behind me and smell the stream of smoke as the man in cut-offs exhales. He tells me that dogs can feel earthquakes coming, and his voice is heavy with cigarettes. Before the ground shook, the dogs in Port-au-Prince barked and whined, nervous, restless.

"Not everything is lost," the man says.

He's not looking at me. But maybe he's talking to me. Maybe I will heal, even without understanding.

Note

Thank you to The Nervous Breakdown (http://www.thenervousbreakdown.com), where this piece previously appeared.

HAITI EARTHQUAKE AFTERMATH, JOURNAL ENTRIES

Kathuska Jose

Titanyen, Thursday, Feb. 11, 2010[1]

This is where they bury the dead, where white crosses stand on unmarked graves. Backhoe trucks drive back to the city to collect more bones to fill the dusty pits.

More bodies will surely follow.

I fear that Loulou will be one of them.[2]

Port-au-Prince, Saturday, Feb. 13, 2010[3]

Rainy season is approaching now. Politicians have been unable to come to an agreement about what to do with the homeless.

"Pèp la grangou," dit ma tante, "e solèy la ap touye nou !"[4]

There's no need for money . . . there's nothing left to buy.

Somerville, Sunday, Feb. 14, 2010

Church feels like a funeral service. I have been unable to talk to God for three weeks.

"All will turn out for the better!" says the pastor. He tells us all to wait and hope.

I'm not so sure I believe in that. The future looks too grim.

Port-au-Prince, Thursday, July 28, 2011

Tent cities have become the new capital and the cholera outbreak has decimated the population.

Hurricane Emily is now lurking.

Our sorrow grows.

Notes

[1] Titanyen is a burial ground for the earthquake victims, located on the Route 1 in Haiti near the capital city.

[2] Loulou, relative of the writer.

[3] Port-au-Prince was one of the areas hit the hardest by the earthquake.

[4] "The people are hungry," says my aunt, "and the sun is killing us!"

LES GRANDES DOULEURS
SONT MUETTES

Gysèle Th. Apollon

En cet après-midi paisible du 12 janvier, personne ne s'attendait à recevoir une gifle, où plutôt un coup de poing en pleine figure, un *uppercut*, pour emprunter le langage de la boxe. Le choc encaissé nous a tous laissés hébétés, refusant l'évidence. Il a fallu malgré tout se frayer un passage dans l'obscurité qui descend vite à cette époque de l'année, au milieu des cris et du brouhaha d'une foule gesticulante, en spectateur inconscient de tout ce qui se passait autour comme devant l'horreur d'un film d'épouvante à la télévision,

Le lendemain, après une nuit passée à la belle étoile, il a fallu récupérer la voiture abandonnée et affronter le contraste impressionnant d'une foule hagarde—dans un pays comme Haïti où le silence n'existe pas—, aussi dense que la veille, devant les cadavres étendus sur la chaussée, tant, il est vrai, que les grandes douleurs sont muettes. On a pu se rendre compte de l'ampleur du désastre et réaliser que RIEN ne sera plus comme avant.

Dieu merci, notre maison a tenu le coup. Le mur mitoyen en tombant a assommé l'un des chiens et la citerne a craqué mais aucune autre fissure sérieuse n'a été enregistrée. Cependant, de nouvelles secousses pourraient encore se faire sentir. Le respect de la consigne de ne pas s'aventurer à l'intérieur des maisons nous a forcés à dormir encore trois semaines en plein air sur la terrasse. Heureusement, nous étions en période de sécheresse.

Trois jours de deuil et de prières ont été décrétés. Il ne fallait pas s'enfermer dans sa citadelle. Pourquoi ne pas payer de notre présence à la grande cour de la Primature et serrer les mains des gens du quartier et de la foule sous les tentes qui récitaient des litanies accompagnées de cantiques et, ensuite, faire un tour au centre-ville, le cœur battant, traverser le Champ-de-Mars en distribuant des bonjours aux réfugiés sous les tentes ?

Tout a disparu : les édifices gouvernementaux, les écoles, les églises, les entreprises commerciales. Le Palais national a reçu un coup de Jarnac. Sa tête s'est enfoncée dans ses épaules. Le drapeau national a glissé de son mât et s'est mis en berne tout seul.

On a peine à imaginer l'effondrement du ministère de la Justice et qu'il ne reste que la balance sur le fronton de ce qui avait été l'imposant Palais de Justice. Le certificat de bonne vie et mœurs qui témoignait de la respectabilité a disparu. Il est vrai qu'il est difficile de faire justice; le vol, le crime et la corruption étant à tous les niveaux, tout le monde agit en toute impunité. Le Palais législatif s'est effondré. Les casernes qui représentent le prestige, la rectitude de notre défunte armée, et aussi la fierté haïtienne ont perdu un étage. Il ne reste plus que le rez-de-chaussée chapeauté par le régiment de fenêtres des combles semblables à des képis qui se seraient enfoncés jusqu'aux épaules.

Les églises ont l'air d'avoir subi un bombardement tout en épargnant les crucifix (on avait commencé par brûler l'ancienne cathédrale et celle de St-Jean Bosco) et les cloches se sont tues. Elles ne sonnaient d'ailleurs plus depuis belle lurette, les paroisses ont cédé le pas aux petites chapelles individuelles. On s'est mis à tutoyer Dieu et à changer les rites. A l'exception du « AMEN » mis à toutes les sauces (créole/français)—

« Ainsi-soit-il » étant perçu comme un gros mot—, le latin a fait place au faux lyrisme pleurnichard des cantiques infantiles. Peu ou pas de presbytères et le clergé qui, autrefois, visitait les familles, n'a plus aucun contact avec les paroissiens qu'à travers les homélies aux messes du dimanche. Il faut chercher—et trouver—un officiant pour célébrer un mariage ou un enterrement.

La quasi-totalité des écoles méritait d'être restructurée pour une uniformisation des programmes et la restauration du civisme. Leur affaissement en même temps que le ministère entraînera-t-il (enfin !) cette réforme tant souhaitée d'un système éducatif inefficace et médiocre. Il est plus que temps que soit sérieusement inventorié ce commerce scandaleux de livres (n'importe quel bétisier fait l'affaire) et des frais scolaires onéreux de douze années d'écolage que les

parents s'esquintent à payer pour qu'en fin de parcours les élèves ne détiennent qu'un papier sans grande valeur ?

Le commerce informel a pris le pas sur l'autre. On ne pouvait déjà plus faire de lèche-vitrines nulle part, les dernières vitrines de ce qui restait du centre-ville ont subi les excès des récentes émeutes de la faim.

Les Postes se sont effondrées et la TELECO est fissurée de part en part. Si indispensables autrefois, elles brillent à l'heure actuelle par leur absence depuis l'installation de l'internet, des cybercafés et des compagnies privées de téléphones.

On citerait à n'en plus finir la liste des édifices publics détruits : Direction générale des impôts (DGI), Palais des ministères (particulièrement celui de la salubrité publique), grands hôtels dont l'hôtel Christopher (siège de la MINUSTAH).

Des murs, des clôtures portant la marque en rouge À DEMOLIR sont restés ironiquement debout pendant longtemps. Port-au-Prince était déjà laide avec les graffitis et les inscriptions style MUCI, OCODE prétendant instruire un peuple toujours en quête d'alphabétisme, Depuis qu'il a été décidé que le vieux Port-au-Prince ne faisait plus partie du patrimoine, à l'instar du vieux San Juan à Porto-Rico, et qu'il fallait élargir les rues des anciens quartiers résidentiels en coinçant les devantures d'honnêtes petites maisons, les affiches publicitaires de DIGICEL, de NINO CELL et autres avaient pris la ville d'assaut. Nombres d'autres bâtiments sont aussi tombés. Serait-ce pour nous inciter à renverser les barrières de l'égoïsme et de l'individualité dans la nostalgie des temps révolus où il faisait bon vivre séparé du voisin seulement par des haies d'hibiscus ou de buis retenus par des fils de fer qui facilitaient les communications en raccourcissant les parcours, parfois d'une rue à une autre, et faisaient passer cette belle sentence en proverbe : « vwazinay se fanmi » ?

Comment vivre dans cette désolation ? Ceux qui sont morts sont-ils, peut-être les plus chanceux ? Ensevelis dans la poussière des décombres ou partis vers les fosses communes, ne nous forcent-ils pas à nous rappeler, en cette période de Carême, que nous sommes poussière et que nous redeviendrons poussière ? Et les nantis qui ont vu s'écrouler en quelques secondes, dans un fracas épouvantable, tout ce qu'ils se sont enorgueillis d'avoir amassé durant des générations, ne doivent-ils pas réfléchir sur les biens de la terre auxquels on ne doit pas s'attacher ?

Au Champ de Mars, nos héros, sont restés debouts, imperturbables et sereins, en seigneurs que rien ne peut troubler ni émouvoir. Leur image doit nous servir à reproduire au plus haut point leurs grandes qualités, tout en ayant la sagesse de renoncer, de prévenir, et d'attendre car tout n'est pas perdu.

POUR EUX ET POUR NOUS

Kettly Mars

Sous peine de perdre notre restant d'âme, qu'un hommage tellurien soit rendu à nous tous qui ne sommes pas morts, qui avons échappé à la mort part volonté divine ou par hasard, héroïnes et héros sans lendemains qui avons arraché des vies du chaos avec nos ongles et nos dents, nous les miraculés, les estropiés, les déplacés, les orphelins, nous qui avons erré dans les rues poudreuses de la ville les yeux remplis du même effroi, le sang encore frais sur nos bras, nous qui n'avons pas fini de compter nos morts, qui ne comprenons toujours pas cette houle qui a broyé la vie, à nous qui avons vu ensemble les visages innombrables de la mort, qui n'aurons jamais de réponse aux questions de notre impuissance, qui avons pleuré les larmes de nos ventres, qui avons pleuré les mêmes larmes amères, qui avons survécu et survivons à la peur, qui survivons à l'angoisse, à nous tous qui avons encore une identité, qui ne nous sommes pas suicidés, ne sommes pas devenus fous, qui continuons à scruter d'autres soleils, à lutter, à nous indigner, à nous révolter contre ceux qui veulent nous voler ces jours que nous avons arrachés au hasard de la mort, contre ceux qui nous veulent morts ou morts-vivants, à nous qui laissons monter la sainte colère en nous, qui appelons de tous nos vœux le feu sacré, nous qui croyons qu'un jour nous aurons eu raison d'avoir survécu, même un jour d'une autre vie, nous qui avons le courage de rire, de retrouver dans nos rêves les jours heureux qui nous sont ravis, de nous créer dans le chaos des raisons de vivre, à nous qui obéissons quand le souffle de la vie ordonne à nos mains et à nos yeux, à nous qui disons non au désespoir qui guette le rire des enfants . . .

PART II

AFTERSHOCKS
DIASPORIC REFLECTIONS

FALSE STARTS AND
HOPEFUL BEGINNINGS

Nadège T. Clitandre

*I believe that I needed to make that false start in order to get to
my destination.*

—Edward Belfar, "On False Starts and Detours"

*If you do not breathe through writing, if you do not cry out in
writing, or sing in writing, then don't write, because our culture
has no use for it.*

—Anaïs Nin, diary, winter 1953–1954

For the past two years, silence has been my survival mechanism, the façade that masked the guilt I could not face for not doing more, for not doing enough. Along with my guilt came anxiety, uncertainty, and self-doubt. Not all of these gut reactions had to do with the January 12 earthquake in Haiti that ravaged the capital city of Port-au-Prince, and damaged, beyond repair, the family home that had been transformed into a community library. Some of these sentiments came from ending a six-year relationship after finally realizing that it had no future; some from transitioning from being a graduate student to a tenure-track Assistant Professor; some from buying a home all by myself; and some from just gaining the thirty pounds I swore I would never gain back. But nothing weighed more heavily than the devastating impact of the 7.0-magnitude earthquake that hit my native homeland.

When I began writing this essay as a serious attempt to break my writer's block, I realized that it wasn't just guilt that silenced me. It was also the false start, or, rather, a series of false starts. Since that fateful Tuesday afternoon in January, I have made a number of attempts to put into words the many emotions that came over me as I processed what some describe as an unimaginable event. There were times when I jotted down a few words on a notepad or a napkin. But I would find myself starting over a number of times, only to end in failure. I was struggling to find the words to express myself, to work through the images of chaos and destruction. How do I speak the unspeakable? To be honest, I didn't want to be still in silence long enough to unearth my pain. I didn't want to bleed on the blank page.

Then one day I actually wrote down the first few lines of what I thought would become a poem: "The soft blow of a smiling kiss / from her face / reminds me of Christmas / on a hot afternoon." I stopped. This beginning felt strange, but authentic. There wasn't any blood. No earthquake. No exceptional story to tell. Just a glimpse from a lived moment turned memory. But this too I feared, and so I stopped. Somewhere deep down, I felt the guilt of expressing so much joy in a time consumed by so much pain. It finally dawned on me that the previous false starts had everything to do with me suppressing this moment of happiness. I couldn't write because I assumed a false beginning. Every time I sat down to write, it wasn't the destruction that occupied my thoughts, it was the days prior to the earthquake, when I was in Haiti and felt so much hope for its future.

In December 2009, I spent nearly the entire month in Port-au-Prince. Haiti Soleil, the nonprofit organization I started in 2006 when I was a Ph.D. student at the University of California, Berkeley, had received a grant from the Irene S. Scully Family Foundation. This generous grant was earmarked for a modest computer lab at Bibliothèque du Soleil, the community library my father founded in 2005. It was an exciting time for the library and for Haiti Soleil. After nearly five years, we were beginning to finally see the fruits of our labor. We were pleased with the library's slow but steady growth. The library by then had 400 members with library cards. It received 30–50 patrons on a daily basis. It had developed a positive reputation in the community of Carrefour-Feuilles as an oasis for reading, writing, and both creative and intellectual exchange. We held presentations that included prominent Haitian literary figures such as Frank Etienne, Dany Laferrièrre, and Gary Victor as well as non-Haitian authors such as the Cuban exiled writer Zoe Valdez. Other well-known Haitian artists like the filmmaker Arnold Antonin graced the library with their presence. We hosted conferences on topics ranging from Vodou and Christianity to the influence of jazz on contemporary Haitian music and the environmental challenges in Haiti. We also organized film screenings and cultural events. At times we were amazed to find out that our modest library could receive an audience of 300 people. The youth in particular were quite fond of the space; the services we offered allowed them not only to study and engage with friends, but also to be creative. We made it a priority to foster and support their creativity. In our mind, the new computer lab with PCs equipped with internet access was just the beginning. We were preparing to offer even more services.

Installing a computer lab is quite challenging in a country where there is little access to electricity and the cost of computer equipment is high. Fortunately, I had a small but skilled team. Edouard Leneus, who was working for Haiti Soleil at the time, laid the groundwork for the computer lab before I came, while Timothy Suttle, the board member of Haiti Soleil responsible for the organization's technology concerns, and Roberde Madhere, at the time the Hainet technical engineer, handled the installation for the lab's internet networking system. Tim made the trip to Haiti from Oakland, California, the week before the quake, to install the Ncomputing system that would allow all the computers to be linked to a main system.

I was running around with staff, electricians, and IT technicians, workin to get the computer lab up and running by the end of the month. I was also helping the staff prepare for the library's annual Christmas party for the youth in the community. The major aim of this joyous event is to showcase the talents of the participants of Camp d'Éte du Soleil, the library's annual summer camp, and Soley Pou Tout Timoun, the library's afterschool program. Both programs cater to youth ages 5–15. The Christmas party ended up being a success. I watched and applauded proudly as participants danced, recited poetry, acted in skits, and offered comic relief. The sound of youthful laughter filled the library courtyard with such positive energy. And there was light, not only figuratively. The community had EDH (electricity offered by the state) for an unusually extended period of time and Christmas lights were everywhere. I recall going for a walk with my father in the Champ de Mars area one night. I was in awe of the decorated National Palace showered in Christmas lights. As I pulled out my camera to take a photo, a young man, walking by with a group of friends, said something like, "What's the big deal, it's just the palace, it's not going anywhere." We ignored this remark and continued to enjoy the view of the palace from where we stood. Dad and I felt a strong feeling of progress, not just for us, but for the country at large. I have been making trips to Haiti consistently since my first initial return in 2000. I don't think I had ever felt so happy in Haiti.

On New Year's Eve, I wore a yellow dress, the one my mother bought me in April of that year to attend a friend's wedding. I went out dancing with my father in a resto-bar on Rue Capois, not too far from the Champ de Mars. Edouard joined us for a drink. When my father and I returned home, there was someone waiting for me. Much later, when our different worlds converged in surprising and wonderful ways, he told me that there was only one thing he was sure of that night before confessing to a crush: He didn't want to start the New Year without me by his side. Although I did not reciprocate the feelings until nearly two years later, I remembered that fateful night. It was black and marvelous. Like the National Palace waiting to salute Independence Day, I too was shining . . . and waiting . . . for the dawn to break a new day.

Bibliothèque du Soleil's computer lab was finally completed exactly a week before the quake. Tim had arrived the day after New Year's. When he left on Tuesday, January 5, the heavy lifting for the computer lab was all done. I returned to California two days later, the Thursday before the quake, tired but feeling as though I had accomplished something wonderful.

A few minutes after 2 p.m. California time on Tuesday, January 12, I received a call from Edouard in Haiti. I had not answered the call, as I was getting on a bus to head to work at the University of California, Santa Barbara. A few minutes later, when I was able, I listened to the message Edouard left. Something about an earthquake and something about my father being ok. I didn't grasp the gravity of the message, but I felt that something was wrong. When I arrived on campus, I found myself heading to the office of Raphaëlla Nau, a fellow Haitian friend who was working in the English Department at the time. There are only three of us on campus. Claudine Michel, a dear colleague, mentor, and sister-friend who is a professor in the Department of Black Studies, is the other Haitian on campus. We are all women, all strong and independent, all natives of Haiti, and all connected to the country in our own meaningful way. When I hugged these two women for the first time after the quake, I felt the pain our bodies carried in each sisterly embrace. Like mine, their bodies shook, as if the aftershocks traveled on this side of the water to remind us that we are forever tied to this beloved island we call home. Those sisterly embraces were moments of comforting silence; words were not necessary.

Three weeks after the quake, my father finally mustered the courage to tell me that three of the kids who had participated in our youth program had died during the quake: Berline Senacharles, Lucvenia Zamor, and Yolande Sherly Felix. There was that uncomfortable silence again. I knew their faces, I heard them laugh, and observed, with curiosity, their quiet demeanor. Of the three, I remembered Sherly the most. In the summer of 2009, she participated in the library's third annual summer camp program. I was in Haiti to observe their activities. I have a photo of her on the day the kids wore their "I love being black" t-shirts, which were donated by California entrepreneur Kumi Rauf. In the photo, Sherly is blowing a kiss at me. I remember smiling back in gratitude! She's the subject of that poem I have yet to complete. It's her face that came to mind every time I attempted to write about the quake.

When I finally made the trip to Haiti in mid-March, my sister, Arabelle Clitandre, a photographer and graphic designer who is also on the board of Haiti Soleil, came with me. Along with my father and Jeansoir, the library's security guard, we visited numerous sites heavily impacted by the quake. One day, while we were walking around a nearby neighborhood, Jeansoir pointed to an open area covered in rubble. The space was vast and full of sunlight. He pulled me aside and with a soft voice he told me that this was the place where Sherly died with her mother, probably holding her tightly. And for the first time, since the quake, I let out a loud uncontrollable cry that surprised even me. It lasted for a few minutes.

Haitian feminist anthropologist Gina Ulysse states in a small collection of Haitian women's reflections on the earthquake she compiled for the feminist journal *Meridians*: "There are times when we are called upon to speak for others. Our responsibility when we are the transnational bearers of the pens, the ones with the language and access, takes on particular significance especially when the stories we have to tell are counter-narratives."[1] Certainly, new words need to be found to articulate the unimaginable disaster. New counter-narratives need to be created to dismantle the problematic ones that continue to linger. But there are still old counter-narratives of Haitian voices, both male and female, that lie deep beneath rubbles left behind from previous disasters, both natural and manmade, like the fragmented narratives my father tells me, or the ones my mother is perhaps too ashamed to tell, even though they too find their way in the haunting silences I often confront in my writing.

And there are everyday banal narratives of human activity like the one of a young girl blowing a kiss that brightens someone's day, or of a community library's Christmas party, or a photo being taken of the National Palace. In the aftermath of the earthquake, these narratives get lost in the rubble. They need to be excavated now more than ever. Some of us are silent because we are still digging. Some of us are digging because we don't want the silence. And some of us embrace the silence to reflect, knowing that if not now, sometime in the future words will spill out on the blank page. In any case, what matters most is that someone eventually tells the story, some way, somehow. I am beginning to tell mine, starting with the story of Sherly, the little girl who blew me a kiss that reminds me of Christmas on a hot afternoon. It's the story that allows me to breathe, cry, and sing all at once. I suppose I needed the false starts to get to this destination, which, after all, is just another beginning.

Santa Barbara, CA
September 10, 2012

Note

1 Gina Ulysse, Section Editor Introduction, "Pawol Fanm sou Douz Janvye (Women's Words on January 12th, 2010)," *Meridians: Feminism, Race, Transnationalism* 11, no. 1 (2011): 97.

Lòt Bò Dlo,
The Other Side of the Water

Edwidge Danticat

I was in a supermarket in Miami's Little Haiti neighborhood with my two young daughters when my cell phone rang.

"Edwidge, are you home?" asked my former sister-in-law, Carole, whose birthplace—Kingston, Jamaica—has a history with earthquakes.

"No," I told her. "I'm in the supermarket with the girls."

"You haven't heard then?" she asked.

"Heard what?"

"There's been an earthquake in Haiti."

"An earthquake in Haiti?" I said this so loud that a few people stopped to look at me. Being in Little Haiti meant that many of the people working and shopping at the supermarket were Haitian. One or two nodded as if to confirm what I was hearing. They already knew, I realized. Others immediately began dialing their own cell phones as if to get further clarification for themselves.

Although I had been hearing and reading about a possible massive earthquake in Port-au-Prince for years, it always seemed beyond the realm of possibility. It simply seemed inconceivable that an earthquake could rattle the country—my country, even though I had not lived there consistently for thirty years, since I was twelve years old.

"I'm watching CNN now," Carole said. "They're saying the earthquake is 7.0."

The significance of that number did not immediately register. A 7.0 earthquake might cause little damage in one place, while it could devastate another. It all depended on the population density and the capability of structures to withstand the shaking.

"They're saying it's catastrophic," Carole explained.

Catastrophic, I could understand.

"Just get home," she said. "I'll call you later."

Soon after she hung up, my cell phone started ringing nonstop.

My husband, ever so cautious, asked when I picked up, "Where are you?"

"In the car," I said, not sure how I had gotten myself and the girls and the groceries in there.

He wasn't sure I knew and he didn't want to worry me. I brought it up myself while keeping my ears tuned to National Public Radio.

"I'm calling everyone in Haiti," he finally said, "but I'm not getting through."

During the drive home, I looked out the window but could barely see the brightly colored homes and storefronts of Little Haiti. Dusk comes quickly on January nights, and this night was no different. Still, it felt as if dark clouds had swallowed the day a lot faster than usual.

My heart was racing as I started running down, in my mind, a list of the people that I would need to call, e-mail, text, or fax to check on in Haiti. At that moment, the list of aunts and cousins and friends in different parts of the country seemed endless. Most of them lived in Léogâne (the epicenter of the earthquake), Carrefour, and the eye of the storm—because of its population density and its ever-precarious buildings—Port-au-Prince.

I tried to think of the most efficient way to learn about the greatest number of people. It would be best, I told myself, to call several people who would have news of everyone else, the family leaders, if you will. My cousin Maxo was one of those people.

Maxo had lived in the United States for nearly twenty-five years before returning to Haiti in the 1990s. At sixty-two, he had been married several times and had eleven children ranging in age from forty-two to fifteen months. He was a generous, lively, and overindulgent soul who had taken over the family homestead after his dad had died in 2004. Maxo and five of his youngest children and his wife were living in Bel Air, the poor hillside neighborhood where I grew up. Maxo's was the first number I dialed at a red light on the way home. I heard a strange sound on the other end of the line, not quite silence, but not quite a busy signal either, something like air flowing through a metal tube or thick cloth.

When I got home, my husband was in front of the television watching CNN as he dialed and redialed his mother's cell phone number in Les Cayes, a southern town more than a hundred miles from Port-au-Prince. The television screen showed a map of Haiti with a bull's eye on Carrefour, where my husband's two uncles live. There were no images yet of the devastation, just phone and studio interviews with earthquake experts, journalists, and the occasional survivor (often via Skype) by the ever-changing news anchors. The Haiti-based eyewitnesses were describing a catastrophic scene, in which the presidential palace and several other government buildings had collapsed. Churches, schools, and hospitals had also crumbled, they said, killing and burying a countless number of people. Aftershocks were continuing, prompting a tsunami warning. The earthquake, we learned, had probably been caused by a strike-slip fault, where one side of a vertical fault slides past the other. It was barely six miles deep, leaving little cushion between the fault and the houses precariously perched upon the earth. (Later, we would find out that the earthquake was caused by a previously undetected fault, leaving the potentially cataclysmic danger of the other faults intact.)

"It was as if the earth itself had become liquid," one survivor said, "like the ocean."

On Twitter, the Port-au-Prince-based hotelier and musician Richard Morse announced that the Hotel Montana was gone. My husband and I had stayed at the Montana several times, often with our oldest daughter in tow. Entire neighborhoods had slid downhill, others reported, each row of houses pressing down on the next in a deadly domino effect. Daniel Morel, a veteran Haitian photojournalist, sent out some of the first pictures online: pancaked buildings and dust-covered silhouettes stumbling out of the rubble, many bloodied and nearly dead.

My husband and I kept dialing the phone numbers of friends and relatives in Haiti and getting no response. While keeping an eye on the television and an ear to a local Haitian radio program, we managed to get some dinner together for the girls, who at first did not seem to understand what all the fuss was about.

Before falling asleep, however, my oldest daughter, Mira, asked if her grandmother was okay. We tried to reassure her as best we could, but we did not know ourselves whether my mother-in-law—who often traveled from Les Cayes to Carrefour—was alive, or whether anyone we knew was alive.

The routine became (1) dial phone numbers of friends and relatives in Haiti; (2) go online—including social networking sites—for a bit more information; (3) dial friends and relatives all over the United States and Canada, who were also dialing and checking networking sites, and ask, "Have you heard from anyone?" They had not.

No new information was coming through the radio or television. The news was breaking all evening, but the same information was being repeated. U.S. State Department spokesman P. J. Crowley told CNN that we should expect "serious loss of life."

Occasionally, my cousin Maxo's phone would ring when I dialed it.

I tried texting.

No reply either.

I then got a call from the producers of *AC360*, CNN anchor Anderson Cooper's signature show. They had found me through my publisher and wanted to know whether I would come on the show.

"What will I say?" I asked my husband.

"What you feel," he said.

What I was feeling was nearly indescribable even for a writer. I was extremely worried about my loved ones, but I was also feeling a deep sense of dread, a paralyzing fear that everything was gone, that Haiti no longer existed, that the entire country had been destroyed.

We had been watching Haiti's ambassador to the United States, Raymond Joseph, on CNN and other media outlets. He had explained not only the gravity of the current situation but also a bit of Haiti's history and how Haitian fighters, after they had gained their independence from France in 1804, had traveled throughout the world, including to Greece, Latin America, and the United States, and had helped others gain their independence.

"This is the worst day in Haiti's history," he said. Haiti has helped the world before. Now it was the world's turn to help Haiti.

"Ask for help too," my husband said. "The country's going to need lots of help."

Ask for help, I kept telling myself, as I sat in the satellite studio in Miami Beach waiting to go on Anderson Cooper's show. I had no word from anyone in Haiti. The phone calls were still not going through. We had only heard rumors of some famous Haitians having died in the earthquake. Many of those rumors would later prove untrue.

Also on *AC360* was Wyclef Jean, the internationally known musician, who had also moved from Haiti to the United States as a child. I felt like sobbing when Anderson Cooper turned to me on the monitor and said, "Edwidge, I know you have been trying to get in touch with your family as well. Have you had any luck?"

I explained that I had not.

In some circles, many of us who were asked and went on television that night, the next morning, and in the days that followed were accused of trying to make heroes of ourselves. However, I will never regret this particular media outing because one of my maternal cousins would later tell me that he had somehow managed to see that program on his cell phone while lying on a blanket on the street in front of his flattened house in Léogâne. Before that, he said, he'd thought that the earthquake had happened all over the world and had feared that even if we'd managed to survive it in Miami, we might still be in mortal danger from the announced-then-called-off tsunami. He had been as worried about me as I'd been about him. We laugh about this now, but it makes perfect sense because one of the first videos broadcast after the earthquake was of a young girl watching a cloud of dust rise up to the hills from a broken Port-au-Prince and screaming, "The world is coming to an end!"

"This is probably one of the darkest nights in our history," I managed to tell Anderson and his viewers that night. "We're going to need an extraordinary amount of help in the days and months and years to come. I think the whole country basically is going to need rebuilding. And people who are the poorest of the poor, least able to withstand something like this, are suffering. And we absolutely need help. We desperately, desperately need help."

After the program ended and other programs began, the dark night dragged on. My brother-in-law came over with some friends and we put together a kind of command center, trying to make our efforts at reaching loved ones more efficient. We were still watching the television news programs, but some of us were now delegated to the phones and others to the computer and the radio stations.

Around midnight, we managed to reach my mother-in-law on her cell phone in Les Cayes. There had been no damage where she was in Les Cayes, but she was still feeling tremors.

"The ground is shaking," she kept saying. "The ground is shaking."

Her radio transmission had gone off that afternoon and she knew very little about what was happening in Port-au-Prince and the surrounding areas. We told her the little we knew and she was shocked. Before she could ask about her brothers in Carrefour, we were cut off. We would not be able to reach her again for five days.

***

With daylight the next morning came the first vivid images of the devastation. Piles of rubble were everywhere, many with both frozen corpses and moving limbs peeking out of them. Watching a video of one trapped little boy reaching for his mother from a pancaked house, I saw the little hand and cried. Little did I know then that my cousin Maxo and his ten-year-old son Nozial had already died and that three of Maxo's other children—including the fifteen-month-old—would be trapped in the rubble for two days before being rescued.

Perhaps because the images of the helplessly trapped were so hard to take, a lot of the television news coverage quickly shifted to successful foreign-led professional rescues. Many months later, I was surprised to learn that fewer than two hundred people had been rescued by professional rescuers. The rest, like Maxo's wife and children, had been saved by their Haitian friends and neighbors.

As for the foreign-led rescues, even if the rescued person died an hour or a day later, that person's predicament needed a dramatic arc, not unlike the short stories and novels that someone like me might write. The viewer needed an ending, and it had to be uplifting so that he or she could continue to watch the heart-crumpling rest. Of the many stories that might have been too devastating to watch are some that my family members told me: of hundreds of people who individually or in small groups kept vigil near a pile of rubble and spoke to their buried loved ones as they slipped away, dying an agonizing death so close, yet beyond reach. Of the trapped loved ones who exhorted their family members to go and leave them behind, to go on with their lives. Among the many things that is most haunting about this disaster is how many people could have been, might have been saved, if only love and good will could have rescued them all, if only there had been the right equipment . . . if only . . . if only . . .

Since January 12, 2010, I have often been asked what it was like to experience the earthquake from a distance. Was it traumatic?

Frankly, I have seen too many people who've been irreparably scarred by both physical and psychological wounds to say that I have suffered many. It would be disrespectful to equate my pain and bereavement with that of those who nearly lost their lives and sanity to the devastation.

The Sunday following the earthquake, I took my girls to a service at a large Protestant church in Little Haiti. I had not attended church for some time and was craving that sense of community and solace that it could offer at moments like this. An earthquake survivor, a Baptist minister, had found his way to us and was telling what had now become the familiar story of hundreds of thousands of corpses, most of them picked up with earthmovers to be carried to mass graves.

As the minister was speaking, the woman sitting in front of me, in her early forties and the mother of two small children, like me, became increasingly upset until she was doubled over and convulsing with grief. That woman had lost twenty-five family members. Because she was not a legal resident of the United States, she couldn't go back to Haiti and try to find and bury her parents, without risking not being able to return to Miami.

There are degrees of trauma and loss, I suppose, and if you get invited on television programs and are asked to write articles about yours, it seems bigger. However, so many people have suffered much more, are still suffering much more, and I surrender all the blank spaces in and around these words to them. I surrender these spaces also to the dead, to the lives unfulfilled, to the stories untold. We will never know all the stories. Mine is only one—and it is from far away, from *lòt bò dlo,* "the other side of the water," three Haitian Creole words which evoke both migration and death. Separation, no matter how it happens, is earth shattering. But even for families accustomed to necessary ruptures, this was the most catastrophic. Like the woman in church, they would never be able to say good-bye and would never even learn the fate of their loved ones who were buried, unidentified, in mass graves.

In the weeks and months following the earthquake, many journalists, visiting dignitaries, and even casual observers praised the extraordinary resilience of the Haitian people. Indeed, that resilience is inspiring. For the first hours and days after the earthquake, Haitians were pretty much on their own. Their government, paralyzed by its own losses, was incapable of assisting them, so they dug their loved ones out of the rubble with hammers and axes and even their bare hands. As food and water became scarce, they divided small rations among themselves.

Haiti, which is often referred to as the poorest country in the Western Hemisphere, had yet another crucial lesson to teach the world: a lesson in resilience. If some of the more sensationalist broadcasts were any indication, the world was expecting something else. Journalists eagerly jumped in the middle of chaotic food and water distributions, allowing themselves to be bumped and shoved for the cameras. Such was the fear of looting that Haitian policemen shot hungry young men to death over bags of rice. However, the massive, large-scale looting that was anticipated never took place. Instead, Haitians buckled down for what will surely be a long and difficult road. They set up temporary shelters with sticks and bedsheets, making public places their homes. When it rained, they stood up and let the muddy water flow between their legs.

After three post-earthquake visits to Haiti, I began to ask myself if this much-admired resilience would not in the end hurt the affected

Haitians. It would not be an active hurt, like the pounding rain and menacing winds from the hurricane season, the brutal rapes of women and girls in many of the camps. Or the deaths from cholera. Instead, it would be a passive hurt, as in a lack of urgency or neglect. "If being resilient means that we're able to suffer much more than other people, it's really not a compliment," a young woman at the large Champs de Mars camp in downtown Port-au-Prince told me.

As friends and leaders both in Haiti and in the international community shape their reconstruction plans for the country, they will be remiss if they misinterpret as complacency the grace, patience, and courage that Haitians have shown for more than a year and a half since the January 12, 2010, earthquake. Haitian history teaches us otherwise. Haitians were resilient against the brutal Napoleonic code of French colonial slavery until they started a revolution that created their republic in 1804. Haitians endured thirty years of the Duvalier dictatorship until they ousted Jean Claude Duvalier in 1986. It is now only a matter of time before their post-earthquake endurance justifiably wears out.

In the meantime, that resilience has shown itself in many homegrown efforts, in the beauty parlors and barbershops in the camps, where people who wake up and go to sleep in the midst of inevitable squalor refuse to let it define them. In the letters dropped in the suggestion boxes in which tent city residents plead for food and water and jobs and schools for their children. In the faces and voices of the men and women who read to, sing with, and draw with the orphaned children in the displacement camps, where they are also living. Often unrecognized, some extraordinary leaders are rising out of the makeshift displacement camps. I know a woman who from one day to the next had a hundred people in her yard. She would never have considered herself a leader before the earthquake. She is sixty-nine years old and has lung cancer. Another man was feeding and organizing an entire neighborhood after the earthquake. He is a painter. Haitian Americans have also stepped up to the plate. Some have rushed to Haiti with larger aid organizations, and others have just picked up and gone on their own. From the young doctors and nurses who arrived that first week to the teachers and therapists for whom going back and forth to Haiti has now become routine. And yes, also the artists, singers, painters, poets, and novelists too.

   For us creative types, especially those who have spent most of our lives outside Haiti yet still consider ourselves bound to it as with the umbilical cords that joined us to our mothers, another Haiti occasionally sparks our imagination. Whenever I am asked to lay out my own personal "vision" for Haiti's future, I think of that place. It is a place where all children (both boys and girls) go to school, where every person eats everyday and has a roof over his or her head. It is a place where women and girls are fully protected, where there is no rape, no kidnapping. In that place, there is no *peyi andeyò*, no insurmountable rural-urban divide. It would be great, however, to see a society emerge out of the rubble that comes closest to the ideal vision that the majority of Haitians, who are mostly poor and marginalized, have for Haiti's future. All of Haiti's children, including my two daughters and all of those who have crossed both earthly and cosmic barriers to *lòt bò dlo,* will be counting on it.

Note

This work was first published in *Haiti after the Earthquake,* by Paul Farmer, edited by Abbey Gardner and Cassia Van Der Hoof Holstein (New York: Public Affairs, 2012). Reprinted with permission from the author.

GOD GIVES, GOD TAKES AWAY!

Myriam Nader-Salomon

I had just arrived home and dropped my bag when the phone rang. It was my friend. Hastily, he said: "Myriam, turn on CNN, there is something happening in Haiti." He did not say what it was, and I, always eager to watch anything about Haiti, didn't ask either. I just immediately turned the television on and could never have imagined what I was about to see. It took me a while to fully comprehend that I was watching the most devastating tragedy that Haiti would endure. I remember that day as if it were yesterday. January 12 changed so many things for those living in Haiti and also for those connected to Haiti all over the world.

I remember watching what was on television with horror. Repeating, "God, God, God! Oh, no, not again, Haiti doesn't need that! O God, protect us!" I wanted to cry but no tear would come out. I could not believe what I was seeing and hearing. So many thoughts flooded my mind. I wondered how my parents, my siblings, my family, my friends were doing. I had to get in touch with them right away, but I also needed to calm down first, as my heart was racing and my head was spinning. What if . . . ? "No, Myriam, everything will be OK," I said, trying to convince myself.

Finally, I grabbed the phone. All lines were down, of course. I had to find a way to get in touch with family and friends by any means possible. "Ah, Facebook," I thought. So I went online and posted on my wall: "If anyone has any news from my family, please post." And I waited, at once listening to the reporting of the tragedy live and looking at my laptop, checking to see if someone had responded to my post. A few minutes later, my sister's sister-in law posted: "Myriam, your family is OK." I could finally breathe, but still I needed to learn more. What did she mean by OK? They are alive but are they wounded? Have they lost their homes? Are they unharmed? She couldn't tell me any more. She was the only one who still had a little electrical power left. She only told me that she spoke briefly with my sister, who said they were all fine.

Little by little I learned all that my family suffered. Although they experienced no death in the family, the destruction to their homes and property was substantial. My childhood home was gone but my mom and dad, who were napping in the house during the earthquake, miraculously survived. I keep repeating to myself that it could have been worse.

My brother lost his entire building in Juvenat, my parents lost their residence along with Galerie Nader and Musée d'Art Nader in Desprez. This was such a cultural loss—so many precious paintings destroyed. The damage was estimated at US$30 million.

This earthquake brought about major life lessons for everyone connected to Haiti. It taught us to never take anything for granted. Material things can disappear any time. What is left is our love for one another, our intellect and memories.

Over the past few years, I have held many fundraisers to help Haiti through the arts. I had so much hope for Haiti after the earthquake. For a long time I cried every time I saw images of the earthquake, and I continue to marvel at how Haitians managed to cope in the face of such adversity. It depresses me that we keep losing track of what is important. This tragedy does seem to have opened many doors for Haiti and yet life has returned to how it was before. This really beats me.

Something else troubles me. More than ever the fate of Haitian women after the earthquake is uncertain and tenuous. Unquestionably, this tragedy hit them very hard, perhaps more so than others. While they are recognized as pillars in Haitian society, serious discussion of progress and development must also address their predicament, vulnerability, and hardships.

SÉISME, ENFER, MISÈRE

Geneviève Gaillard-Vanté

Soudain le soleil se cache et la pluie se met à fredonner sur le toit. Allongée, un livre ennuyeux au nez, je m'assoupis. Tout en n'étant pas tout à fait endormie, une étrange vision de tremblements de terre venant de nulle part frappe à nouveau mes pensées. D'un bond sur le canapé je m'assieds et je hurle presque, *et si un séisme venait à surgir !* Prémonition ? Subconscient en éveil ? Images floues répétitives souvent revenues comme un éclair. Séquences troublantes d'une terre qui s'ouvre pour avaler avant de se refermer . . .

On parlait à peine des séismes dans le temps. Toutes ces histoires semblaient si lointaines . . . Pourtant lorsque j'étais enfant, mon père disait souvent que cela tôt ou tard se répéterait. Aussi, pour cela, il s'était fait construire une maison sur le moins beau terrain du quartier—à la déception de ma mère—car disait-il, quand cela se reproduirait avec l'intensité d'antan, nous serions épargnés grâce à ce sous-sol plus solide qu'il avait choisi sur les hauteurs surplombant le port . . .

Les dernières années précédant le 12 janvier, un géologue soudain alertait. « *La relative quiescence sismique du dernier siècle ne doit pas nous porter à croire que notre pays n'est plus à l'abri de séismes dévastateurs . . .* » Mais qui pouvait mesurer l'importance de ses avertissements ? Plus on se remettait à parler de sismicité, failles et tremblements n'étaient que des mots, simplement jusque-là des mots, dialogue dans de grands livres car « l'inconscient collectif, » les fortes angoisses liées à ces catastrophes historiques n'existaient plus en mémoire. Notre terre, avait bien tremblée de 1750 à 1819, comme toutes les secousses souterraines sur notre île relatées de 1564 à 1789 . . . Mais après ces cycles si éloignés de la réalité, qui vraiment souhaitait attacher de l'importance à un phénomène que nos grands-parents n'avaient jamais connu ? Aussi le 12 janvier 2010, à l'approche de cette heure fatidique où le jour se préparait à se fondre dans la nuit, nul ne s'attendait à vivre la pire des horreurs qui guettait sous leurs pieds.

Le temps est calme et serein où je me trouve si loin d'Haïti avec ma fille et ma sœur. Dans le moment la musique accompagne nos éclats de rires autour d'une histoire pimentée, quand la nouvelle arrive par téléphone dans les courtes minutes qui suivent la tragédie. Sur le coup, cela ne fait pas de sens ce que nous entendons. Tout le reste de l'histoire pour moi ne demeure autre que ce que l'on m'aura raconté, ce que j'aurai lu et ce que j'aurai vu à l'écran. Je bénis le ciel de m'avoir épargné de vivre une telle atrocité.

Une suite de mots insensés donc attachés à cette nouvelle que nous venons d'apprendre. Un collier de mots infinis liés à la détresse, à l'angoisse, au désespoir et au désarroi. Des minutes épouvantables dans l'attente, accrochées maintenant à des écrans çà et là pour mieux comprendre. Une voix déchirante sur les ondes suivie de l'ambassadeur américain dépeint l'apocalypse, invite le monde à la prière. Haïti au loin hurle en détresse le nom de Jésus . . . Et moi, hébétée dans le silence, j'implore. *Seigneur, accueille ceux qui nous ont précédés . . . Envoie tes anges aux quatre coins de nos emplacements, de nos territoires et protège nous contre toutes menaces ostensibles et soudaines à venir . . . Renforce notre foi ébranlée face à l'épreuve, donne-nous le courage de nous relever . . . Apaise nos peines, nos angoisses, nos inquiétudes . . .*

Dans ma foi maintenant ébranlée, téléphone et ordinateur se transforment en bras réconfortants, en seuls brins d'espoir . . . L'internet pour quelques uns dans les hauteurs d'Haïti fonctionne encore. Je sais au moins par voie indirecte que l'un de mes frères est en vie. Par intermédiaire, je suis mise au courant du dénombrement. En bref, le déchirement, les hurlements de la ville, les bruits effrayants des édifices qui s'effondrent dans une nuée blanchâtre coiffent la verdure de la ville et le port. Plus tard je vois les images du séisme captées par mon frère sur le vif dans les reportages de CNN . . . Affolement et hébétude dans les rues, images de l'Horreur du pressant vécu. L'instant du délirium, il filme tout, mon frère. Comment il a fait ? Je me le demande encore.

Huit heures plus tard par un appel du Canada, j'ai la confirmation après mille émotions et angoisses que mon conjoint est en vie. Plus tard, d'autres membres aussi chanceux de la famille sont tirés sous les dalles. Mais il en manque toujours un. Je demande et redemande pour lui . . . Je lui laisse un message via Internet aussi . . . Rien toujours rien de lui . . . Rumeurs, fausses nouvelles . . . espoir . . . puis le choc, dans les mots sous mes yeux, sur mon écran, trois jours plus tard : RIP, Micha. *Rest in peace*, Micha. Repose en paix !

Micha, notre cousin, est tiré des décombres, la cheville broyée tout juste après ses derniers mots. Des familles alliées et amis au Mont-Joli de Turgeau disparaissent aussi à la douzaine. Trente secondes, d'autres disent une minute et trente secondes . . . La majorité de nos demeures familiales sont épargnées comme l'avait présagé mon père, tandis qu'une liste infinie d'amis disparus sous d'autres toits se multiplie. Et les mots, et les mots, rien que des mots. Plus de palais national, plus de cathédrale et églises, murailles et édifices anciens effondrés, visages poudrés de poussière, destruction totale au bas de la ville, milliers de blessés, de cadavres accumulés jonchés le long des rues, rigoles ensanglantées, corps enveloppés de carton ou de tôle mis en terre entre deux portes, enveloppés de nappes brodées ou de draps dans leur arrière cours ou jardins . . . manque d'eau, de victuailles. Les jours et les nuits s'enchainent . . . Et les mots et les mots sur l'écran . . . Les voix dans la nuit s'élèvent dans la clameur au Très Haut pour étouffer les cris dans les entrailles. Une myriade de mots dans le malheur. Partout épreuve et terreur . . .

Durant des semaines, je ne dors plus, je ne mange plus. Avec l'équipe sur notre site social nous devenons reporteurs pour relayer les nouvelles parvenant des quatre coins du monde . . . Pour rassurer ceux qui cherchent encore leurs proches . . . Le 12 janvier 2010, à seize heures cinquante trois minutes, après une minute et trente secondes dans le crépuscule, notre île de misères infinies depuis des siècles chavire dans le plus profond des abîmes. Je repasse en mémoire tout ce qui a disparu. Les lieux où j'ai vécu mes premiers jours sur terre, où j'ai été baptisée, où j'ai été à l'école, où j'ai vécu les plus belles heures de mon enfance, où j'ai travaillé, les maisons et édifices de notre quartier où j'ai joué, là où j'ai évolué. Plus rien. Comme après le passage d'une gomme sur une feuille, une tranche de vie effacée. Plus rien. Des images et scènes de rues effroyables. Membres déchiquetés, amputés dans les plus horribles douleurs par manque d'anesthésie. Des enfants de tous les âges, hommes, femmes et vieillards, fauchés . . . des cris déchirant la nuit. Des mouches aussi, par milliers. Cadavres en putréfaction, empilés sur des terrains vagues, poussés par des grues, toutes classes sociales confondues. Des âmes anéanties par une atrocité inexplicable. Le sol sous nos pieds n'est pas ferme. Et tout passe. Après séisme, enfer, misère. Des milliers encore sous les tentes, sans abris, sans espoir de vie décente pour leur progénitures. Aides éblouissantes extérieures promises et venues, mais rien n'est encore visible. L'avenir de nos enfants et des femmes de notre île, inquiète et préoccupe. Qu'adviendra-t-il de leurs lendemains ? Il faut au moins une vingtaine d'années pour bâtir ou rebâtir un pays. Je ne sais pas pour la génération à venir, mais je doute que je verrai la guérison.

Winter Park, 5 février 2012

Les Femmes, après le séisme : « Tout le monde nous a oubliées »[1]

Lucie Carmel Paul-Austin

D'abord, l'affaissement social

Arrivée le 29 mars 2010 pour une semaine à Port-au-Prince, j'ai vu l'horreur en différé, certes, et j'en ai mesuré l'impact. Au milieu des décombres, ou à travers eux, j'ai vu déambuler les gens, les voitures, les bêtes, et l'humanitaire, partout. Une ville pliant sous les débris, littéralement à genoux, pour une aide qui lui vient par paquets lancés au-dessus des têtes, dans les files où l'assistance se donne ; enfin, une ville ranpant, car tout le monde se trouve logé à ras le sol. Vous me direz, cette ville a toujours été sale, encombrée. Et là où les tentes ont cédé aux structures précaires des bidonvilles, dans le même alignement ou la même organisation chaotique, de quoi s'étonner véritablement ? De tout ! D'une attitude délétère de découragement, et aussi de laisser-faire. Dans l'état de délabrement physique et moral actuel, la ville de Port-au-Prince donne toute la mesure de ce que la faillite des institutions publiques centrales et locales (les mairies avoisinantes) a laissé comme conséquence ultime : l'état de nature.

La cité, dans sa plus simple expression est réduite à l'autogestion. Les autorités, s'il faut les nommer ainsi, sont ailleurs. Soit à recevoir tel dignitaire ou délégation d'humanitaires, soit dans une réunion où se discute le destin des concernés eux-mêmes, soit complètement indifférentes au sort des populations. Plus d'un expriment ce sentiment d'abandon, de *lese grennen* caractérisé : qu'il s'agisse de la salubrité de la ville, du déplacement des personnes en des lieux plus commodes et appropriés, de la disparition des « latrines » au milieu du centre de la capitale, au voisinage des héros de Vertières.

Dans pareille situation, l'individu est livré à lui-même et les lois qui régissent le vivre-ensemble, car il y en a, sont celles ou l'intérêt individuel prime sur celui de la collectivité, quoique imminente et présente en tous lieux. En d'autres termes, pour éviter les conflits récurrents qu'une telle cohabitation à outrance peut causer, les individus s'esquivent dans un véritable chassé-croisé qui évite l'empiètement ou la contiguïté tangentielle, alors que la promiscuité a droit de cité. Les notions de morale, voire de pudeur deviennent relatives et se transforment en un code d'éviction de l'autre. Cette éviction se traduit de manière subtile et diverse, par le mépris des droits de l'autre, par l'indifférence . . .

ET LES VIOLS DEVINRENT MONNAIE COURANTE[2]

Il est clair que si la solidarité a existé, elle ira se perdre peu à peu, ne pouvant plus résister à la tension du quotidien, à la contingence spatiale, et au désarroi des pouvoirs publics. En fait, du jour au lendemain, de nombreuses femmes et fillettes entassées, exposées se sont retrouvées livrées à elles-mêmes dans les nombreux camps de fortune, face à un Etat historiquement patriarcal et autocratique. La faillite avérée des autorités que souligne d'abord la présence des casques bleus onusiens, puis celle massive des ONG ne fera qu'aggraver la situation précaire des populations vulnérables. Tous les rapports de mission convergent dans le même sens : la vulnérabilité des femmes et des enfants en général et des filles en particulier ; l'augmentation des cas d'agressions, de viols et abus de toutes sortes en nette augmentation. Seulement moins de trois semaines après le séisme, le 29 janvier 2010, des associations locales et internationales dénoncent le pillage et les viols dans les camps (www.dailymotion.com). Un an après, la chaîne européenne ARTE, dans un documentaire en date du 13 janvier 2011 confirme cet état de fait. La chaîne de télévision française TF1, dans un reportage, en date du 3 février 2011 décrit une situation de chaos à Port-au-Prince, suite à l'incidence des viols dans les abris de fortune et la défection du gouvernement. Finalement, l'on doit s'en remettre au vieux dicton : *Se mèt kò ki veye kò.*

SE RAPPELER, SE SOUVENIR, AGIR

« Personne ne se souvient de nous ! » Tel est le cri relayé par le rapport de Human Rights Watch sur la situation des femmes et des filles en

Haïti, suite au séisme. Cri, constat ou simple rappel : Il y a de tout
cela pour résumer le mal-être des femmes, en Haïti. Mal-être, car
ne pas se souvenir renvoie à un oubli : « *Yo bliye nou* », « *yo pa sonje
nou* ». Se souvenir, encore moins se rappeler n'est pas l'équivalent
dans notre créole, d'oublier, de négliger, de faire silence, d'ignorer.
Car la trace d'un souvenir, même lointain, oscille dans la mémoire,
dans les gestes. On ne se souvient pas, on a oublié, l'acte est déjà au
passé. Fait accompli, affaire classée. Impression, constat, c'est donc
une vérité révélée à ceux et celles qui ignorent ou ignoraient que la
situation des femmes et des filles en Haïti a toujours été précaire.
Les nombreux chiffres et rapports à l'appui ne font que souligner
les inégalités systémiques auxquelles les citoyennes sont confrontées
dans leur quotidien.

Un tel contexte ne saura être en faveur des femmes, longtemps
maintenues à l'écart des sphères de décision, absentes des politiques
publiques, ignorées des mandataires, sauf en temps de campagne
électorale. Entre-temps, la dégradation socio-économique les
contraint à exiger plus des pouvoirs publics tout en ne leur faisant
pas confiance. L'effondrement physique consomme et recouvre
l'effondrement sociopolitique : la crise de légitimité de l'État est totale.

PLAIDOYER POUR L'ÉGALITÉ DES SEXES

Alors, on comprendra comment la construction sociale des identités
sexuées codifiées a pris des formes diverses et variables selon les
contextes sociaux, économiques, politiques. A travers l'histoire, la
famille, le statut marital, l'appartenance sociale, professionnelle et
religieuse, sont des paramètres qui dessinent un paysage souvent plus
varié que ne le suggèrent les grands modèles narratifs ou explicatifs
fournis par les sciences sociales. Aussi l'épanouissement plénier de
tout individu ne trouve-t-il son fondement que dans la libération
totale, idéale des deux sexes dans notre société.

En d'autres termes, la fin de l'asservissement, des négations de
droit et d'accès aux services de base, à la modernité pleine et entière
ne sera accomplie que lorsqu'il n'existera plus de citoyen/ne/s de
seconde zone, lorsqu'il n'existera plus d'individus dont les libertés
et privilèges sont subordonnés aux préjugés, et autres artifices créés
dans nos sociétés, soit religieux ou idéologique. Comme l'avaient
rêvé les utopistes du dix-neuvième siècle, l'avenir de l'être humain,

sans distinction de classe, de race, et de sexe, ne sera garanti que lorsqu'il n'existera plus de différence sur le plan de l'éthique et du droit, plus particulièrement quand ces différences sont basées sur des conditions objectives que l'individu ne contrôle pas, tel que leur sexe ou la couleur de peau. En bref, rêver d'une humanité plurielle, sans discrimination aucune, l'ultime utopie, une humanité paritaire, à coup sûr.

Les Symboles qui persistent

Apres le tremblement de terre, les pouvoirs, à tous les niveaux de leur représentation, n'existaient plus. L'international, par l'hécatombe enregistrée au niveau de la Minustah, et le national, par l'effondrement des édifices publics. Le séculaire, comme le religieux, aura aussi subi de gros coups. Les églises, vidées, avec leurs croix dressées, continuent de signifier un ordre en décrépitude. Les femmes se sont retrouvées une fois de plus, aculées, dos au mur littéralement . . . Leur seule issue, reprendre le cours de la vie, reprendre leur quotidien saccagé, assumer leur reproduction et la survie de leurs proches, face à la volatilité de leur existence. Continuer à vire. L'on devrait se demander, quel est le sens d'une telle entreprise vouée à la faillite ou la ruine ? Où trouvent-elles le souffle pour tenir si longtemps ? Quel est cet acharnement à vouloir *fè dlo sot nan wòch* ? Il me semble qu'il y a deux raisons envisageables. L'une, c'est l'acte de foi, mille fois répété, dans un quotidien non balisé par les institutions publiques d'Etat et ses services collatéraux. Donc, ces citoyennes n'ont de recours qu'à elles-mêmes ou à la Providence. L'autre raison, c'est la tentative, par l'absurde, de barrer la route aux forces antagonistes auxquelles elles font face : se reproduire et survivre en dépit, malgré et contre des circonstances funestes. Elles repoussent à contre-courant, cette « boule » qu'est la vie. Essayant de la retenir pour ensuite, la faire avancer. Elles ne se préoccupent point de savoir dans quelle direction, à quel rythme. La mesure de cet exercice presque futile—s'il ne s'agissait de maintenir leur souffle littéralement—n'a pas de prix, et n'est pas évalué ni en temps ni en énergie. Notre régénérescence devra partir de là. Les historiennes et historiens ont qualifié, avec autorité, la lutte des femmes pour leur émancipation, comme étant la plus longue que l'humanité ait connue. Une lutte, en continu, contre le servage, l'exploitation, la violence, contre les dénis d'accès de toutes sortes, contre l'obscurantisme. Une longue lutte pour la dignité !

Tout n'est pas dit, et tout reste à faire pour des millions de nos compatriotes, plus particulièrement la moitié, sur qui repose à bon droit : la reprise économique, la (re)construction, l'éducation des générations futures. Tout reste encore un enjeu de taille : l'intégration des citoyennes dans toutes les sphères de compétences, de pouvoir et de décision.

Retournée en Haïti, le 30 décembre 2011, j'ai vu combien et comment le choléra avait changé certaines pratiques de la marchande installée dans nos rues. Alors que j'approchais une vendeuse d'oranges, elle s'est empressée d'enfiler un sachet en plastique à titre de gant pour manier le couteau et tenir l'orange. Question d'éviter tout contact entre elle et le produit . . . Signe des temps, comportement responsable, souci d'hygiène publique. Peu importe ! J'étais surtout ravie de rencontrer dans ce geste un pacte de convivialité, un pari sur l'avenir, un bonheur simple et innocent comme ce pays nous a toujours réservés à mes enfants et à moi.

Brooklyn, 3 février 2012

Notes

[1]   Titre d'un rapport sur la situation des femmes et des filles en Haïti, par *Human Rights Watch (HRW)*, août 2011.

[2]   Consulter à ce sujet les rapports de GARR (Ong haïtienne) et Amnesty International, ainsi que le rapport de HRW, cité précédemment.

CHANGING PERSPECTIVES

Christalie Parisot

Years ago, I watched a very scary movie with my grandfather called *Earthquake*, starring George Kennedy and Ava Gardener. I've learned of bad earthquakes in the news that have happened in various places around the world. I've heard of catastrophic natural disasters that have occurred on every continent. They are all horrible, but nothing compares to a massive disaster that happens at home. In a way, it made me realize how selfish we can be, because, at the end of the day, disasters occur everywhere. Momentarily we feel bad for the victims, but then we quickly move on. Soon enough, it becomes old news.

However, when you witness the church where you used to pray every Sunday with your family reduced to rubble; the school you attended (where so many of your childhood memories were formed) collapsed in front of your eyes; and the house you grew up in disappeared for ever, it is heartbreaking. When you learn about some friends and family having survived the disaster, injured and suffering, or the demise of others you did not get a chance to wish a "Happy New Year," the word "horrible" then seems too weak to describe the experience. It is something that will forever scar you.

I ask myself: Are we really conscious of how lucky we are to be alive? Are we really aware of the pain and suffering that exist in this world? Since the earthquake, I have seen every new disaster through new eyes, with a renewed sense of empathy.

It is so easy for us to move on when we are not directly concerned with a tragedy, so easy to tell someone that we understand their pain when we are not the victims; so easy for us to complain about the petty little things that bother us every day.

I found myself in a city, my hometown, which I could barely recognize. The country I grew up in remains a thing of the past, a memory. Now, what is left are the people trying to leave Haiti, those trying to get back on their feet, others genuinely wanting to assist, and of course, individuals and organizations taking advantage of the situation. It is well known that after every catastrophe, national and international vultures show up at disaster sites under the guise of trying to help.

Despite all this, however, I continue to believe that, as they say in a song written as a tribute to Haiti after the earthquake, "We Shall Rise Again!"

But will I see it?

THE THING

Michèle Voltaire Marcelin

Haitians call it "The Thing." "*Bagay la.*" It is nameless, this monster, like the thousands of lives it stole in one brief moment. It is as if a more precise name would cause it to return. And this is the fear you hear in people's voices when they ask: "What have you heard about 'The Thing'? What are they saying about 'The Thing'? Is 'The Thing' going to come back?"

"The Thing" lasted what seemed like an eternity, zigzagging haphazardly, following a trajectory only it knew, leveling one house, missing the next. How do you measure time when the ground undulates beneath your feet? How do you mark time when the earth shakes and breaks?

There are so many ways it is described, this "Thing" that manifested itself that January afternoon, leaving Haitians in such fear that even those with houses undamaged would no longer sleep inside. When I finally reached Port-au-Prince a month after the quake to connect with friends and family, these are the stories I heard, each a piece of the quilt that forms a whole. I repeat these stories here. Take from them what you will. There is no proof offered. There can be no refutation. The truth is, an earthquake hit my land, and each person experienced this catastrophe differently.

Ramize describes "The Thing" as a dragon breathing fire: a quick flash of light briefly seen, rapidly extinguished. And poor Ramize has never even seen a dragon. I also heard there were places the sea parted in Grand-Gôave, leaving fish flapping loudly on the sand in an insane choreographed ballet. "The earth opened," Magaly said; "The earth opened and swallowed the house and the people as if it were hungry." "I saw my house sway side to side as if it were a branch dancing in the breeze, and then I screamed for my daughter to come out: *Chloé!!!*" Carole relives this moment every time she tells the story. Jacqueline describes it as a bombing even though she has not lived through any wars. She was driving when "The Thing" hit her car, bouncing it like a ball in the street.

Elizabeth was seated on her terrace, crafting a bracelet. Her chair bounced, or was it the street that bounced? "Avenue Christophe was bouncing," she says. Her black and white tiles have burn marks. Where from? Where did this dragon breathing fire come from? She says: "It is not the corpses in the street I will remember, although I have never seen so many dead bodies before; it is the silence that preceded the wailing of women."

The building where Willy was attending a meeting collapsed. He took refuge under a portico. He survived unscathed; one of his friends did not. Someone accompanied Marcel home. He is later found wandering aimlessly in the street, his eyes vacant. "Why are you back in the street? What happened?" "I opened the gate in front of my home and I did not see my house." His entire family had been indoors at the time.

Raymond survived the collapse of the National Palace because he took shelter under a desk. At a street corner, Blanc in a cloud of alcohol was in the middle of a dispute with a man who screamed, "Filthy drunk." This left him unmoved. "The Thing" is what moved him, plastering him with force against a wall. "The other man was hit so hard by falling debris, Mademoiselle Michèle, he died without saying, 'Ah.'"

Romel Joseph, the blind violinist, survived eighteen hours of entrapment with prayer and music to mark the time: forty minutes of César Franck's concerto, forty minutes of meditation. And Janette, whose husband found her after three days under a collapsed bank building. Janette whose eyes were shut and encrusted with white dust, white dust that also filled her mouth, told her husband through a crack: "No matter what happens, remember I love you." Janette, white with dust, white like a statue, sang when she was rescued: "Hallelujah, Jesus is my light, Hallelujah, Jesus is my savior."

A friend's mother, a patrician octogenarian, was found a few days later lounging in bed protected by walls among the rubble, marking her rosary with prayers. How many Hail Marys and Our Fathers did she say before she heard the voices calling her name? "I am here. I am thirsty. Why make me wait so long for a glass of water?" she asked with irritation.

Reggie's office collapsed, and his house was destroyed. How do you start your life over at 60? At the ministry, the building where Marie-Yolaine worked collapsed. She jumped in stilettos through a second-floor window. Not a scratch, not a sprained ankle. Just the trauma. Haitians talk about the trauma of the interior and the trauma of the exterior depending on where you were at the time. Which is worse? On what Richter scale do you measure fear? What is the magnitude of anguish?

Jessie says, "We have had to arm ourselves against the fear, against the pain, against the dead." The morning after the quake, she saw eighty corpses in the street where she had been the afternoon before. I started to cry when I hugged her. "We have cried too much," she said. "We have no more tears."

Josie's brother was hit so hard on the back of his neck that his eyes were projected out of their sockets. She saw so many wounded and dead at the hospital where she brought him. She lost her mind. Another family's maid was found under the rubble. Her poor body, so broken, was placed under a sheet. When it was lifted up, it formed a lump of meat dripping blood through the fabric's weave.

There are things human eyes should not see, human ears should not hear. One should not witness certain things, even secondhand, even a month later with impunity. After visiting the downtown area I returned home and felt feverish. I lay down sick for two days. There was little left of the Port-au-Prince I knew, only rubble, broken buildings, and corpses in the streets. There were entire areas where Godzilla seems to have stomped indiscriminately. That monster, that "Thing" that destroyed my city, leaving the ghosts of more than two hundred thousand hidden among smoke, debris, steel dust, and sand.

Women were fleeing, stumbling out of houses, clutching their children. Men were caught under the rubble. Whether they died in vain, or awakening a new beginning for Haiti, only time will tell. Their deaths are no longer their own.

Let the dead bury the dead.
The living must change the world.

Les Oranges de l'espoir

Jan J. Dominique

12 janvier 2010

Jour de travail ordinaire. Gris, froid, dans cette ville du Nord où je vis aujourd'hui. 17h15, un coup de téléphone. D'abord l'agacement. Un tremblement de terre ? Ridicule ! Il n'y a pas de séisme important en Haïti. J'ai raccroché en promettant de chercher d'autres informations. Pour avoir de la paix.

Entre deux photocopies, je me remémorais mon unique expérience. A la radio, durant une musique, l'aiguille tressaute et l'opérateur rapidement la remet dans le sillon. Je l'interroge sur cette erreur d'aiguillage. Tu n'as rien senti ? L'immeuble a bougé. Un camion ? Je ne crois pas, ce doit être un tremblement de terre. 1995 ou 1996. Vérification faite, c'en était un. Minuscule, à peine ressenti. Je n'y ai plus repensé. Durant mes quarante ans de vie dans mon pays, personne ne m'avait rappelé les séismes antérieurs ou évoqué de futurs. Des cyclones dévastateurs, oui. Des inondations, glissements de terrains après la pluie, oui, oui. Rien d'autre. Personne ne m'avait conseillé de m'abriter sous une table, ou de me précipiter au dehors. J'ignorais les précautions de survie. Comme beaucoup de compatriotes.

En copiant des photographies, en expédiant un fax vers la Colombie, j'imagine à quelle vitesse circule une rumeur de nos jours, grâce au téléphone et internet. Cette histoire à dormir debout a peut-être déjà fait le tour de la Toile, jusqu'au démenti qui déboulera aussi vite.

18 heures. Un client s'approche. Vous avez écouté les nouvelles ? On parle de milliers de morts. En Irak ? En Afghanistan ? Je ne veux toujours pas entendre. Il s'agit d'Haïti. Stupeur et incrédulité. Et ce

sera la nuit blanche, neige et insomnie. Nuit de privilégiée devant l'écran, la télécommande dans une main, le téléphone dans l'autre. Les détails techniques, on s'en fout ! Dis-moi, as-tu des nouvelles de ? Et de. Et de. Égoïste, je pense à ceux que j'aime, durant le décompte des milliers de morts. À l'annonce d'un nom, je me mets à pleurer. Je n'arrêterai plus. Les larmes coulent, coulent, pour ce garçon que j'aimais malgré la distance, pour ceux que j'appréciais, celles qui vont me manquer, et les 200 mille que je ne connaîtrai jamais. Je ne hurle pas comme il y a longtemps, pour d'autres morts que je refusais d'accepter. Pour celles du séisme, je n'ai pas le choix. Personne n'est responsable. Plus tard, on analysera les carences de l'état, les insuffisances de l'éducation. Plus tard, on pensera au futur. Ce jour-là, inutile de chercher des coupables. Le procès n'aura pas lieu. Le tribunal s'est écroulé comme les autres édifices publics. Sur les corps des employés modèles. La plupart des fonctionnaires quittent leurs bureaux vers 14 heures. Passé 16 heures, seuls les meilleurs sont au poste. Injuste nature qui punit la conscience professionnelle. Quelqu'un dira plus tard : S'il s'était produit à minuit, il y aurait eu un million de morts. Comme si il fallait se réjouir de la différence. C'est 200 mille morts de trop. Nous ne saurons jamais le nombre de femmes écrasées. Dans cette ville, de nombreuses familles sont supportées par des femmes. Marchandes, secrétaires, *madan sara*, cuisinières, ouvrières. Toutes chefs de famille. Leur disparition laisse un homme et des enfants orphelins. Lorsqu'il y a un homme.

3 avril 2011

En 2010, devant le désastre et les milliers de victimes, nous n'avons pas marqué la date de l'assassinat de Jean. « Ce serait indécent, » avait-elle dit. Je comprenais, je partageais. Un an plus tard, je suis à Port-au-Prince.

Pendant 16 mois, mes nuits avaient été peuplées de cauchemars. Je vivais à Montréal le jour, à Port-au-Prince la nuit. Ce 3 avril me forçait à affronter mes démons. Un pèlerinage. Seule, dans les décombres de la ville où je suis née qui n'était plus la ville de mon enfance. Trente ans de dictature, des années de gabegie, de bamboche démocratique, d'incurie et de violence l'avaient déjà ravagée. Mais elle était debout. Ce jour d'avril, elle ne tient plus que par morceaux.

Devant chacun de ces morceaux, je serre les dents. Qu'importent les édifices, les quartier rasés, lorsque des humains sont morts, ont été amputés, souffrent encore. Je regarde à peine le Palais National effondré, en remontant la rue des Casernes. Je fixe le Champ de Mars. L'un des innombrables camps de Port-au-Prince en ruine. La promiscuité, les visages fermés, la violence, les yeux vides, le rétrécissement de l'espoir, la faim, les immondices, l'insécurité, le viol des filles et même des garçons. Mais où est la différence ? Cité Soleil et Jalousie étaient-ils auparavant mieux lotis que ce camp ? Les rescapés attendent toujours les maisons promises. En dehors de Port-au-Prince, les constructions érigées dans l'urgence sont déjà abimées. Mauvaise qualité. Les journalistes, las de répéter que les choses n'avancent pas, se tournent vers les dossiers d'aide. Où sont passées les sommes recueillies ? Quel pourcentage de l'aide est arrivé sur le terrain ? La réponse avait été rapide et généreuse après le séisme, et pourtant les camps sont toujours là. S'y sont ajoutées l'épidémie, la lassitude, la permanence de structures temporaires invivables. Les jours qui se suivent et se ressemblent.

À la maison, j'exprime mon découragement. Au désastre du 12 janvier s'est ajouté le retour du dictateur Duvalier. Soudain, j'entends un cri. C'est notre *pratique,* qui amène ses meilleures oranges. Elle admoneste son fils qui arbore un bracelet rose. *Politisyen pa p antre lakay mwen.* Le jeune homme proteste. J'ai le droit de . . . Tant que tu seras à ma charge, tu as le droit de te comporter correctement. Je travaille trop dur pour laisser un politicien tourner la tête à mon fils. C'est ton candidat ? Tu lui fais confiance ? Non, maman, c'est juste un bracelet. Ce n'est jamais juste un bracelet. Nous en parlerons à la maison. Il baisse les yeux.

Je les ai écoutés sans intervenir, pour ne pas le gêner. Mais je me sens ragaillardie. Nous causons, comme d'habitude, du prix des produits, des six enfants de sa sœur qu'elle a recueillis après le séisme, j'ai de la chance, dit-elle, mon fils a terminé son cours d'électricien, il a déjà des contrats, il pourra m'aider avec les petits, ma fille passe son bac cette année. De la chance ! Elle a du courage et de la fierté. Sans elle, j'aurais perdu espoir. Les oranges l'ont fait refleurir.

RECLAMATION

Anne-christine d'Adesky

Everyone has their Haiti earthquake stories—and their pre- and post-earthquake stories—at least those of us who are either Haitian or children of Haiti or have become personally connected to its survival, its history and its future. When it comes to that giant destructive maw of history—January 12, 2010, the day the earth shook for a record 30 seconds and beyond—there is little in our lifetime to compare with it. What remained was an overnight cemetery: a post-apocalyptic landscape of choking dust, broken concrete slabs, and twisted rebar that entombed some 300,000 dead, injured as many, and displaced even more. January 12, 2010, the day Haiti suffered human loss of immeasurable dimensions.

For months afterward, a mere glance at this landscape from any corner of the fallen capital, Port-au-Prince, would cause my eyes and brain to instantly recalibrate, like a camera lens automatically drawing itself back to widen the frame and refocus. I was seeking some clarity amid the chaos, to capture the contours of objects and the contrasts of light and dark.

I was looking as many others were, I know, for what could no longer be seen as easily but remained ever-present: the people who had inhabited a particular house, in a particular neighborhood; their lives and stories; their final conversation; their last breath; their hopes, dreams, and prayers as they lay beneath the rubble. I thought about their terror too, their pain, as I peered within the dim, visible layers of fallen houses, trying to imagine it. I was trying to see them, to hear them, even months and months after this destructive historical event.

I was also looking for something else: for the remnants of the city I knew personally, for the homes and streets and corners where various chapters of my own life had taken place. My ancestral roots are Haitian on my father's side, dating back to the eighteenth century. I have many relatives still living in Haiti. Miraculously, all have survived. Immediately after the earthquake, I realized my own history had been entombed. My history was instantly transformed into memories, the same way that death is a permanent loss. In a moment, it became harder to envision my earlier life as clearly, to hear and see the people and events as vividly. I would stand before a particular mound of rubble and think: *This was there, we did this here, I remember so-and-so there, doing that.* And just as often I would ask: *What was here, before? Who now grieves for this spot?*

Today, more than two years later, I am still searching for what was, seeing at once what has become and is no longer, like two sides of a Janus-faced coin reflecting past and future in a single present moment. I have found a word that best matches my active experience: *reclamation*, a personal quest for repossession that engages my present days in Haiti and personal memories and experiences to help bring the past forward and recapture it. The earthquake, then, has made me a personal historian, one with Janus eyes, looking outwardly on the new Haiti being rebuilt and inwardly on the lost city and its people, steadily emerging to be seen again.

I suspect many others share my experience, especially those like me who are insider-outsiders, with childhood or family roots in Haiti, leading an adult life largely outside it, one marked by important chapters related to Haiti that have profoundly shaped who we are or the direction of our lives.

In my mind's eye, the city of Port-au-Prince as it was before the earthquake is hardly dead or forgotten. It lives even more vividly now, in some ways, than it did before, via this active reclaiming and excavation and sharing with others. Rediscovering its inhabitants, including the people I knew, loved, and now mourn, along with the many new people I encounter, post-mortem. A long list of Haitians and friends of Haiti who lived amazing lives and made important contributions to build its unique national soul. Of course, this deepens my sense of what was lost that day. But it also helps heal the sting of death, because as I reflect on their lives, they live anew in my mind. This, I realize, is an important lesson I have taken away from that terrible day: my own ability, and our collective ability, to not only make the past and our loved ones visible to others, but to make their lives, actions, and spirit impact our present in such a way as to infuse and shape the future. How better to honor them?

There are two people I have yet to reclaim, although the act of doing so has begun. They are among the majority of ordinary, less-visible people who died on January 12. It is precisely the unexceptionable, inappreciable aspects of their lives and especially their deaths that continue to move me and serve as personal touchstones for my present activities and goals in Haiti.

I learned about two girls two weeks after the quake, during the first of my several post-quake visits. The intensity of those early days, overtaken with devastating sights and heightened emotions of sorrow and adrenaline, contributed to my current difficulty remembering what took place on exactly what day. But the exact details are of little consequence when considering what happened to and for me as a result of learning about these two girls.

Like many people, I raced to Haiti as soon as I was able to do so, wanting above all to see and hug and help relatives and friends who had survived the unimaginable. I was personally very lucky: none of my immediate relatives died, and though I lost friends, many also survived and did so without grievous injuries. They were shell-shocked, to be sure, and in profound personal grief, suffering incalculable loss. I knew that nothing I said or did would help much in those initial moments after the quake. So I busied myself to see how I could be of use and where my resources might make a difference, however small.

At first, I focused on networking and reporting, and established a blog to link first responders—humanitarian groups and emergency professionals racing to Haiti—with colleagues I know who run women's groups and organizations. Once I got to Haiti, I began seeing that women, girls, and very young children were especially vulnerable and targeted for sexual assault. This issue remains a key focus of my current activism in and outside Haiti.

Pre-quake, my professional life had shifted from reporting and activism on HIV/AIDS, politics, and human rights to a more gendered approach to these same issues. I was steadily working on sexual violence and its relationship to disaster. In 2004, I launched a program in Rwanda with two medical colleagues to provide female survivors of genocidal rape access to lifesaving HIV drugs. I had learned some important things doing this work and had been planning a book about the experience when the Haiti quake abruptly refocused my attention. Additionally, as a parent of two girls nearing adolescence, I am extremely conscious of possible threats to their safety and attentive to ways I might protect them from sexual violence or other assaults.

During my first week, I spent much of my time navigating the broken city in a jeep, courtesy of a young policeman who did double duty as a driver for one of the businesses run by my relatives. I exhausted him wanting to see every neighborhood I could, pausing every few streets to step outside the car and look more closely at the rubble. We were of course looking for the dead. Although many of the bodies had been carted away to be burned or buried in mass graves at Titanyen—a former killing field for political victims of the Duvalier years—there were many that remained trapped. With horror, we would look and then look again, and then point and say: *Look, there.*

I began my professional reporting career in Haiti in the '80s, covering human rights and political affairs. I have seen my share of dead bodies and the horrors that people inflict upon one another. This was a different kind of looking and seeing, one that called for looking at bodies from a distance, and, like a detective, trying to conjure up a narrative for what had happened to the person in that particular spot. But until I met the two girls, my gaze was still protected.

My friend—I'll call him Victor—asked me if I wanted to see his house. It was in a middle-class neighborhood in Port-au-Prince, one with mostly concrete houses and some paved roads. As we drove up, he told me more about what he and his family had suffered that day. For years, he had been saving up and putting the bulk of his weekly wages into paying the mortgage for the house. All was lost and the bank was still demanding repayment for the loan. His family had lived in this house, along with two teenage girls. One was the child of family friends he had taken in. I'll call her Haiti, as she has come to symbolize other vulnerable, ordinary girls for me. Although he didn't say it, I thought Haiti was likely a *restavek*, a girl sent to live with and do unpaid domestic work for Victor's family in exchange for room and board and schooling. He told me that both girls had died in the house, crushed under the stairway, and that he could not reach their bodies. He felt especially bad because she was in his care and died, while his own children had survived.

All of this was recounted quietly, with reflection. I could see her death was weighing on Victor. *You see,* he said, as we climbed out of the car, *it's because I still can't protect her. Even now. I can't stop the dogs from eating her.*

It was at that precise moment that the shock of the earthquake hit me—profoundly—with a sudden surge of emotion throughout my body. I hadn't seen her body yet, but I could see the horror of this in his eyes, and the sense of helplessness. *It's horrible,* he said.

His house had totally collapsed. What remained was a large square of flattened concrete that now lay like a scrambled puzzle, with big flat pieces on top of each other. We stood at the edge of the road at a point overlooking what had been the roof as he pointed out the layout of the house. *She is trapped,* he said using the present tense as he took my hand to point out the spot, *over there.*

I looked, and then looked again. I couldn't see much. It was too far away. We weren't able to move closer onto the broken roof because it was far from sturdy and might have collapsed beneath our feet. *We can't reclaim her body to bury it,* he explained, clearly troubled. *The parents want us to do that but we can't—not yet. And the dogs have been coming.*

I can't see it, I said to him, still unable to make out her body. *I only see that coconut.* And I pointed to it, an uneven dark roundish shape near a gap in the rubble. And that's when I saw his head shake, imperceptibly, and his grimace. *I don't know what to do,* he said. *She's exposed like that and I can't protect her.* And that is when I felt the second wave of emotion, as physical as the first. I was looking at her head, an almost burnt-looking misshapen object. It had been severed or somehow separated from the rest of her body or perhaps was still somehow attached to the corpse, itself crushed under the slabs.

Oh God.

Later, driving back down and then in the days after, when he returned to see if anything had changed and if the head was still there, I felt all the emotion again, and then again. Shock, disgust, sorrow. It was above all for her that I felt all this emotion, for the unthinkable vulnerability of her head, in such a position of total desecration. And for her life—a life cut short by a horrible catastrophe. Her family now grieved the loss of their daughter from a distance, in the countryside or in a small town. Yet their mourning was incomplete since they were unable to reclaim her body and bury it properly. And for him— the entrusted family friend, the caretaker, the policeman-protector, the father figure—in his eyes, he had failed to protect this girl from harm and was still failing to protect her in death. She was capable and good, he told me. A good girl.

In the months—now years—that have transpired since the earthquake, I have returned several times to the place where she was trapped and perished. Each time, I feel anew the pangs of sorrow that her death brings me. My grief remains so acute because the image of the vulnerability of her exposed head and lost body is etched in my memory. When faced with such horror, it was impossible not to feel such sorrow. *Wrong*, I thought, *so wrong. Horribly wrong.* Her death, the death of an unknown, ordinary girl, the girl I call Haiti, has become emblematic to me of the vulnerability of so many girls like her in Haiti, now as then. So many very young, vulnerable, capable girls are suffering so much in the aftermath of the earthquake. So many restaveks and orphans are suffering. They were in the city that collapsed, and now they fill the city that is being rebuilt. And they remain invisible and in distress.

It has come as no surprise to learn that many of these young girls are among those raped in the aftermath of the earthquake. Or that more young girls, including restaveks, are among the victims of incest that make up increased post-quake reports of sexual violence. The crushing poverty and harsh reality of survival that one encounters daily in Haiti are nothing new to me. If anything, the Haiti I knew as a child was even poorer, and the disparities of wealth and social power were even more glaring to me, a privileged *blan* in the world's first black republic. While newcomers express shock at the living conditions in Haiti's camps for displaced persons, I remind them that many Haitians lived and still live in even worse conditions all over the island. That doesn't make today's reality any less critical, but it's important to understand how serious the problems of poverty and hunger were before, too. So I'm not surprised, and not shocked, but I am newly moved and motivated. The death of that ordinary young girl reflects what was very bad before the earthquake and remains terrible now, and must be rectified.

Several months after that first shocking visit to the fallen house, Victor and I were again together driving around Port-au-Prince. Now the reconstruction was fully underway. Much of the debris had been cleared. He had taken up his old job and was too busy to even drive, but he needed the extra income and so he made time to drive me around and help me in my reporting. We revisited some of the women's organizations for the second or third time, getting updates on how they were recovering. I was reporting on women and still trying to find my place in the reconstruction, where I could be of greatest use. *Let's go there*, he said, and I knew he was talking about her, the girl. Things had become bad, he admitted to me. The family had stopped speaking to him. They could not stop blaming him for her death, even if it wasn't his fault.

Today, this girl remains a focal point for me, a moral compass of sorts. Whenever I think about what I want to do in Haiti now, I think about her and that day; I then think of helping girls and women and Haitians in general to address the inequities of not only gender but also class and privilege. I also want to continue to direct my energy toward supporting the reconstruction. I plan to see Victor and learn more about her and the other girl, her friend, and about their lives. One day I hope to meet her grieving family, to let them know that, even in death, she moved the heart of another, and that with that movement, within me and in my lifetime, a deeper reclamation is taking place. She has taken root and lives. She is pushing me forward, she and other emerging girls. From within Haiti, the new and the old, I can see and hear their voices.

New Orleans
February 22, 2012

SAVED BY SERVICE:
MWEN SÈVI, MWEN SOVE

Charlene Désir

Late one afternoon in January 2010, my phone rang. Normally I wouldn't have been at home at that time, but I wasn't feeling well that day. I was lying on my couch when a co-worker called and told me that an earthquake had struck Haiti. I looked at the clock. My first thought was of my son. He was nowhere near Haiti—in fact, he was only a few minutes away at school. But the news of the tragedy steered my thoughts toward the thing that was most precious to me. I hurried to go pick him up.

I returned home to a wave of bad news. The phone rang nonstop and the television flashed image after image of a devastated Haiti. My immediate family was unharmed, I learned. But every Haitian I knew seemed to know someone who had perished. Close friends would later recount what they had witnessed during those 32 seconds that seemed to last a lifetime. The earth shook. Some felt the ground underneath them rise like a thundering wave. Was this the end of the world? Perhaps God Almighty had finally come and this day was the last, the day of redemption.

Afterward, my friends said, they found themselves maneuvering around scattered bodies with missing limbs, around survivors screaming in pain. Many were on their knees praying and thanking God for having been saved. The stench of dead flesh, the screams, the cries, the wailing would continue for many weeks.

Every story of rescue or destruction, every plea for a dollar felt raw to me, touching a wounded place deep within me that I didn't even know was so tender to the touch. It was a wound that was both literal and metaphorical. It was the island of Haiti itself, the land of my birth. It was also something more than "place" for me: it was the essence of what my people are and have been. I wanted my own redemption.

But who am I? Why do I feel such an overpowering sense of connection to this land and its people?

I was born in Haiti to a mother who had gone back to her home country to escape her abusive husband. For a short time, Haiti was her refuge. My mother would eventually leave me in the care of my grandmother and return to the States. I was granted a visa and a passport when my grandmother, who had already been granted passage, presented herself to the US Embassy, carrying me on her hip, and insisted that she could not depart without her child.

My illiterate grandmother, Mommytom, has been the biggest influence in my life. Many a summer she made sure my US-born brother, my cousins, and I spent time in her beloved Haiti. Always, she wanted us to know Haiti. And she often told me I was a lucky child, protected.

I was a child who always had my face in a book. I received what some call a classical education, comprising a rigorous high school core curriculum that included the sciences, humanities, and the so-called classical languages—Greek and Latin—and then continued on to prestigious universities.

But Mommytom taught me there was more to education than the learning one gets from books. She taught me that *edikasyon* meant, among other things, respecting our ancestors, that *edikasyon* was something deep in our veins, part of who we were socially, psychologically, and spiritually, and that it would manifest itself in the things we did. When I asked why I was the only one of her grandchildren exposed to these teachings, she replied simply, "You were born in Haiti" or *"Kòd lonbrit ou antere ann Ayiti"* (Your umbilical cord is planted in Haiti). Burial of the umbilical cord is a typical Haitian tradition.

Respect for those who had transitioned from this life into the unknown was a major current in the household in which I grew up. Our family ritually held ceremonies to remember those who had died. In that same spirit of service, my grandmother also taught me to serve the living. I was taught to assist others in remembering life, which is sacred and in need for redemption. These ceremonies were a constant reminder of the day when we no long exist in physical form.

In my household, we served. *Nou sèvi*. In response to the earthquake, which took place twenty years after my grandmother's crossing, I reconnected and remembered that I was trained to serve. *Mwen sèvi*.

Prior to the earthquake, I had been working with youth in St. Raphael, a small agricultural town in the northern part of Haiti, miles away from Port-au-Prince. Several of the town's young people lost their lives while at the university in the capital. Many were taking exams when the buildings began to collapse around them. One family lost a son, another lost two daughters, and my husband lost a niece. These losses hit me personally. I wondered, were they lost, sacrificed, eliminated? But I could not respond to my own questions. Instead, I had to act.

I lit my candles in a private place and acknowledged those who crossed, enabling my awakening, my redemption. I surrendered to the source. I went back to my *edikasyon*.

In remembrance of those who died during the earthquake, I opened *Lakou Solèy*, a cultural and academic youth center in St. Raphael. Displaced survivors, students suffering post-traumatic stress disorder, artists, and other community members came together and created a mural bearing images of survival, hope, ancestors, and abstract representations of Haiti as a living Mother.

In my US-accented Creole, I serve my people with passion. It would have been impossible for me to merely consume those images and stories of disaster. In a world that tries to deceive us into thinking that we are less than human, we must fight to believe in the exact opposite, for therein lies the truth. We are all divinely created by the Source. Lives were lost on January 12, 2010. But I was reborn. I directly, defiantly, and deliberately connect to the Source. *Mwen sove*: I was saved.

Nou Se Fanm Tout Bon

Grace L. Sanders Johnson

It seemed like an easy task: Write about your reaction to the January 12, 2010, earthquake and your thoughts on the future of the Haitian women's movement. "I can do that," I thought. And yet for days I found myself sitting in front of a blank screen afraid to think about those first days following the earthquake. Words could not express the full breadth and depth of my emotions *then*, and I have little faith in words *now*. Today, like *then*, I feel an overwhelming desire to say the right thing, to get the story right, to narrate scenes that have no script. So I decided to go back to the place where I began.

A few days after the earthquake, as I searched for answers, I went to a "field," my "mother's garden,"[1] if you will, to "farm some bones,"[2] hoping this would provide me with guidance and insight. I turned to Magali Marcelin, Anne-Marie Coriolan, and Myriam Merlet. I went to Marie Vieux-Chauvet, Paulette Poujol-Oriol, Marie-Célie Agnant, and Edwidge Danticat. I picked up *Amour, colère et folie, Le Passage, Le Livre d'Emma*, and *Brother, I'm Dying*.[3] I took a deep "breath." Their "eyes" demanded that I not disgrace their "memory."[4] I had a "nervous condition,"[5] so I decided to ask these *black, noir, neg*, and *milat* women, the Haitian women activists, writers, these *fanm vanyan*, scholars, artists, mothers, partners, sisters, "What do you have to say about the future of Haiti?" And, as they have always done in the past, they answered me.

On the afternoon of January 12, I was sitting in my parents' home reserving a plane ticket to Port-au-Prince, unaware that the earth was trembling some 1,400 miles away. I was interrupted by my mother's chilling scream and the sound of her feet racing down the hall of our home. This solitary stampede was the beginning of days, weeks, and months of sounds, images, and stories trampling on my heart, body, and consciousness.

In thirty long seconds, the earth moved in Carrefour and shook Port-au-Prince, taking with it many of the leaders of the Haitian feminist movement. Many of these women had welcomed me into their homes and helped me construct my dissertation project during my trips to Haiti in the three years preceding the earthquake. As I received news of these powerful women's deaths, I slowly realized that my last emails would not have responses, and I would never be able to say "good-bye." When I closed my eyes I was haunted by images of their final moments and questions about the future of the feminist movement in Haiti. What did Magali have planned for 2010? How would Myriam have responded to the thousands of Haitian sisters living in makeshift tents with nothing but plastic tarp between them and the unknown state of the nation? Which task would Anne-Marie have suggested we tackle first when so many lives, hopes, dreams, bodies have been amputated?

The earth and the future were unsettled for Haitian women. Likewise, my footing was unsure. My doubts were compounded by fury as I sat numb in front of the television watching the voyeuristic ways the international media hovered over Haiti like vultures, feeding on the images of departed and injured Haitian women, men and children. I wanted to escape the international feeding frenzy. I *could* escape and I felt guilty about this privilege and others. I had the ability to eat, to shower, and to turn off the television when I didn't want to see any more images. Nevertheless, this guilt did not assuage my grief. After several weeks my mother suggested that I go to Montreal. She said that I needed to be in a community of people who would understand the magnitude of January 12.

I arrived in Montreal mid-February in the middle of the Canadian winter. As a "Southern girl," I was sympathetic to the shock of the harsh climate that many of the Haitian women, displaced from their homes and families in Port-au-Prince, must have felt when they arrived in Montreal that winter.The brutal weather, however, was likely the least of our concerns. Although our location had changed, grief, loss, and emptiness followed us, always finding our forwarding addresses. Tears and images of departed loved ones arrived at our doorsteps, hotel rooms, and YMCA cots like delayed luggage we would have rather left at customs or had confiscated by immigration authorities.

Grief followed . . . and remained with me. It needed its time. I was stubborn and wanted to move forward into the future.

I continued to ponder what would become of the future of Haitian women's rights, of feminism in Haiti, and the families that had suffered so many losses. And then, the women answered.

The week after I arrived in Montreal, I received a phone call.

"Are you awake?"

"Yes."

"I had a dream," the voice said.

"Okay, I am listening."

"There are women there with you. They have you enclosed in a circle. I do not know them, but they know you and they love you. They are ebony, caramel, brown-black. Gently caressing your hair. Massaging your shoulders. In the dream they were talking to you, encouraging you. Telling you to move forward with the work."

I wept.

***

Two weeks later, in April 2010, I was invited to the Cercle des Femmes Endeuillées de la Maison d'Haïti. In "the circle," we attended to our pain. We caressed our loss. We embraced our grief. We talked. We shared. We painted. We cried. And we sang:

Nou se fanm tout bon
Nou fè soley leve
Nou fè lapli tonbe
Fòk nou konnen sa
Fòk nou konnen sa
Fòk nou pa bliye sa

Figure 1. "Nou se fanm tout bon." Painting by Grace Sanders. Created in 2011, in honor of the Cercle des Femmes' first anniversary together following the earthquake. Reprinted with permission from the artist.

Nou se fanm tout bon

Se nou ki pote lavi

Tout pitit peyi a konnen chaj nou

Fòk nou konnen sa

Fòk nou konnen sa

Fòk pa bliye sa

Over the next months and then years, we watched each other grow. We took note of the first time someone laughed and the first time no one cried. Our conversations and our art evolved. Narratives that had been about the loss of spouses, children, parents, friends, neighbors became narratives of rebirth. The narratives of goals, dreams, homes, and "home" turned into plans for the future. Each Thursday when we met, we willed ourselves, together, back to life.

In the two years that followed the January 12 earthquake, I took these women with me each time I returned to Haiti. I brought their spirits and stories of survival as I traveled with clothes and medicine. I cannot speak definitively of the future, but I am certain that the spirit of healing that was central to the Cercle des Femmes is also central to Haiti's healing. This healing was born in Haiti. It was conceived in the Caribbean Ocean and incubated in the mountains that adorn the nation. It was birthed by Queen Anacaona and given the breath of life by Erzulie. This healing was reared and walked among us through enslaved women, revolutionary women, suffragist women, activist women, grandmothers, mothers, sisters, and aunts who committed their lives to Haiti's future. The future of Haitian women is in this legacy. This valiant lineage will allow Haitian women to overcome any obstacle, whether it is the devastation of the 2010 earthquake or the daily tremors of domestic violence, sexual assault, and political unrest. Haitian women and the women's movement will prevail.

Nou se fanm tout bon!

Fòk nou konnen sa!

Fòk nou pa bliye sa!

Notes

[1]   See Alice Walker, *In Search of Our Mothers' Gardens: Womanist Prose* (San Diego: Harcourt Brace Jovanovich, 1983).

[2]   See Edwidge Danticat, *Farming of the Bones: A Novel* (New York: Soho, 1998).

[3]   See Marie Vieux-Chauvet, *Amour, colère et folie* (Paris: Gallimard, 1968); Paulette Poujol-Oriol, *Le Passage* (Port-au-Prince: Le Natal, 1996); Marie-Célie Agnant, *The Book of Emma* (Toronto: Insomniac Press, 2006); and Edwidge Danticat, *Brother, I'm Dying* (New York: Alfred A. Knopf, 2007).

[4]   See Edwidge Danticat, *Breath, Eyes, Memory* (New York: Soho Press, 1994).

[5]   See Tsitsi Dangarembga, *Nervous Conditions: A Novel* (Seattle: Seal Press, 1989).

HAÏTI CHÉRIE

Mathilde Baïsez

Quand une amie haïtienne m'a demandé d'écrire une page sur ma perception sur ces deux effroyables secousses sismiques survenues successivement le 12 et le 20 janvier 2010, j'ai répondu affirmativement. Depuis toujours les Haïtiens émaillent le paysage de ma vie qu'il s'agisse d'un cardiologue, d'un professeur remarquable, de collègues, de voisins, d'amis ou de cet inconnu au sourire éclatant qui m'a si gentiment cédé sa place dans l'autobus aujourd'hui. Ces haïtiennes et haïtiens se sont toujours montrés affables, cultivés, spirituels et généreux à mon égard. Par la même occasion, je me suis remémoré ces auteurs magnifiques qui m'ont fait aimer leur île à travers les mots pour la chanter, sans oublier ces musiques à saveur créole qui m'ont fait danser le « kompa » et ces plats parfumés qu'on m'a si obligeamment fait découvrir.

Puis, après avoir vérifié, via Internet, l'avancée des travaux de reconstruction après le séisme, j'ai pu constater que rien n'avait vraiment changé ou si peu; toujours ces mêmes images de ruines et de désolation. J'ai alors essayé de me mettre à la place d'une Haïtienne, dans la soixantaine tout comme moi, vivant dans un environnement insalubre, dans la précarité et la promiscuité la plus totale sous une tente de fortune, sans installation sanitaire décente à sa disposition, souvent mal nourrie sinon affamée, sans distractions aucune pour se remonter le moral, ayant sans doute perdu une partie de sa famille et des amis, craignant pour ceux qui restent, une réalité déstabilisante. Or, quand on sait qu'à un certain âge, l'énergie diminue et que les petits ennuis de santé commencent à se manifester, je me suis demandée comment je survivrais à tous ces stress au quotidien. Je ne peux que m'incliner devant le courage de cette sœur inconnue.

Je l'admire d'avoir la force de simplement continuer à vivre. Elle doit se demander pourquoi la reconstruction de son pays prend autant de temps. Je ressens profondément son chagrin, sa frustration, son angoisse et sa colère devant l'incurie des dirigeants.

Pourquoi elle et pas moi? Je réalise à quel point la vie m'a gâtée. Mes petits ennuis me semblent bien dérisoires après un tel exercice. J'apprécie d'autant plus de vivre à Montréal, malgré le froid qui y sévit en hiver.

Je me rappelle qu'à l'époque du séisme, j'ai passé beaucoup de temps devant la télé, me sentant solidaire de la communauté haïtienne de là-bas et d'ici. (La très grande majorité de la diaspora haïtienne ayant choisi le Québec pour s'y installer.) J'étais frissonnante devant l'ampleur des dégâts: le nombre de morts, de blessés, d'amputés, de sans-abris, les infrastructures scolaires, médicales et politiques dévastées, sans compter les risques évidents d'épidémies, le choléra entre autres, sans parler de la horde éhontée des profiteurs omniprésente dans toute situation chaotique où prévaut la loi du plus fort, et ce cortège de violence, comme si Haïti n'avait pas déjà assez souffert.

Et comment affronter le regard de tous les *ti moun* en pleurs, ces nombreux orphelins, tous ces enfants dont le séisme a englouti des projets de vie?

Alors, comme plusieurs de mes compatriotes, j'ai envoyé de l'argent, des vêtements, des produits de première nécessité, en me demandant anxieusement si l'aide arriverait à bon port. Pour tout dire, je me sentais démunie devant tant de plus démunis que moi, impuissante à répondre à des besoins aussi criants. Une infime goutte d'eau dans un océan de misère.

Cependant le temps poursuit sa course inexorable, une nouvelle catastrophe planétaire estompant l'autre, on se désintéresse malgré soi de la situation. C'est à peine si l'on s'enquiert, de loin en loin, au hasard d'une discussion ou à la lecture d'un article traitant du sujet, de l'état de la reconstruction du pays, des détournements de fonds provenant de l'aide internationale, du magouillage et de la corruption endémique qui se traficotent entre les petits amis des régimes concernées, désireux de se remplir les poches sur le dos du malheur. Et ce, tout en sachant que la tragédie qui se joue en Haïti est la réplique de ce qui se passe ailleurs.

Comment intervenir alors devant de telles situations sinon en se renseignant, en se questionnant encore et toujours sur les causes à l'origine de tels drames, et finalement en gardant l'œil ouvert afin d'être prêts à intervenir à bon escient. Très honnêtement, je n'ai pas de réponse toute faite à proposer; ce serait si simple autrement.

Mais peut-être que ma sœur inconnue est celle qui m'apporte le plus d'éléments de réponse si je suis attentive à sa voix qui résonne en moi. Elle m'assure qu'elle se relève les manches afin de venir en aide à son entourage et ainsi amorcer le véritable redressement de son île, sans attendre le bon vouloir des puissants. Et quand un jour je visiterai Haïti, je la rencontrerai et je la reconnaîtrai j'en suis certaine, cette sœur résiliente, au pays de Toussaint Louverture, au pays de l'indépendance et de la joie de vivre retrouvées.

Le Sort a encore frappé Haïti

Raymonde Maureen Eyi

Très tôt le jour du séisme, j'ai été réveillée par mon amie Adelaïde. C'est rare qu'elle m'appelle dès les premières heures du jour. Les yeux lourds de sommeil, je pris mon portable et toujours dans les vaps, je l'entendis me dire : « Dis Mondy, tu as appris ce qui est arrivé en Haïti ? »

Cette question me fit l'effet d'une douche froide.

« Qu'est-il arrivé ? »

« Tu ne le sais donc pas ? Il y a eu un séisme et beaucoup, beaucoup de morts et . . . »

Je composai le numéro de mon ami à Paris, et pour une fois avec une certaine facilité, je l'avais au bout du fil. Je n'eus pas le temps de lui poser la question. Il confirma la nouvelle macabre que m'avait annoncée Aida.

Encore une fois, le sort avait frappé Haïti et on déplorait des pertes en vies humaines. Je ne suis pas restée longtemps au téléphone, me précipitant hors de ma chambre en tremblant. Je pensais à la famille de mon ami, à ceux qu'ils risquaient de perdre. J'étais hystérique. Je criais dans mon salon à la vue des images que nous montraient les diverses chaînes de télévision. Bien que je ne comprenne pas l'anglais, je n'ai pas hésité à aller sur CNN afin de voir les dégâts causés par la catastrophe. C'était démentiel, irréaliste, impensable, inadmissible. C'était le chaos même. Je hurlais ma colère : « Pourquoi Haïti ? Bon Dieu, que leur reprochez-vous ? Qu'est-ce qu'ils ont fait pour mériter ça ? »

Mon gardien qui m'entendait hurler entre nous un dialogue de sourd.

« Le pays de Monsieur Daniel est en deuil ? . . . Monsieur Daniel est-il mort ? »

Je renonçais à lui faire comprendre les choses. J'étais atterrée. Haïti accumule drames, inondations, séismes, assassinats et autres sinistres. Comment ce pays va-t-il s'en sortir ?

Vers neuf heures, Aida et quelques amis martiniquais débarquèrent chez moi pour m'apporter leur soutien et témoigner leur affection. Ils n'arrêtaient pas de me demander si Daniel avait perdu des parents. Ils posaient mille questions et s'apitoyaient sur le sort du pays de mon ami.

Immédiatement on décida des actions à mener pour aider les sinistrés : collecte de fonds, veillée de prières, concert d'artistes gabonais. Les coups de fil venaient de partout, de tous ceux qui connaissaient Daniel ou mon amour pour ce pays lointain. On disposa des chaises sur les terrasses. C'était exactement comme si j'avais perdu quelqu'un dans la famille, tant ma concession revêtait des allures de deuil.

Fablove, un artiste Gabonais très proche de moi, fanatique de la musique caribéenne, passa la journée à contacter des collègues dans le but de décider des moyens de support à apporter à Haïti.

Le soir à la chaîne de télévision nationale, il eut un tour de table, un débat sur Haïti auquel je n'ai pu participer attendant un appel de Daniel à la même heure. Daniel n'avait toujours pas de nouvelles de sa famille de Port-au-Prince et m'a appris que beaucoup de fonctionnaires haïtiens étaient morts. Sa voix était grave. Je crois qu'il pleurait au bout du fil. Je zappais toute la nuit et pensais à ces mères de famille, à ces gens qui étaient encore heureux la veille, profitant des joies de la vie et que le destin venait de frapper si durement.

Le désastre en Haïti me faisait penser à Hiroshima. J'imaginais la douleur, la détresse de ces milliers de personnes qui se jetaient dans les décombres pour retrouver des parents. Haïti se débattait. Haïti ne fait que cela depuis son indépendance. Aujourd'hui, les années ont passé, les stigmates du séisme sont toujours présents, mais quelque part, l'espoir renaît. Les haïtiens ont besoin d'espoir s'ils veulent croire encore au lendemain. C'est en ces moments là que l'on regarde vers le ciel et que l'on se dit : « Demain un jour nouveau, un jour plus beau avec plein de rires d'enfants. »

THRIVING AMID CHAOS

Carolle Jean-Murat

On Tuesday, January 12, 2010, I got a call from my sister, in tears, telling me a devastating earthquake had hit Haiti at 16:53 local time. They feared lots of destruction in Port-au-Prince, Bizoton, and as far as Jacmel and La Vallée de Jacmel. As I stayed glued to the TV, dramatic pictures were shown repeatedly: dust clouds, destruction, people screaming and dying. I felt like my stomach had been cut open without anesthesia, and each time more bad news came in, it was like a little piece of my insides was yanked out.

For five long days, I could not reach anyone. Finally I learned that all the homes in Lakou Mirabeau, the Bizoton Lakou that belonged to my maternal grandfather, had been destroyed. Now family members were sleeping on the ground, outside, using bed sheets as a roof. They had not eaten for days and thought the world had come to an end. Hundreds of people I knew personally perished during the earthquake, or died afterward because of complications from their wounds. They were friends, relatives, and children that we worked so hard to educate. I also got word that projects I had helped to build were totally destroyed.

I saw on television how every landmark I knew in Port-au-Prince—the churches where I used to worship, including the National Cathedral; the schools I attended over the years; monuments such as the National Palace—had collapsed in the earthquake. In La Vallée de Jacmel, the Lycée had to be condemned; a portion of the hospital collapsed but fortunately, no one died. The people from La Vallée had formed a collective in 1980, an organization called CODEVA (Coude-à-Coude pour le Development Valléen). They first built a small hospital, by asking each villager to bring a rock and a bucket of sand. Later, they built an open market, many primary schools, and the Lycée Philip Jules, which was attended by students from the local areas and even neighboring towns. Some walked long hours to reach the school, often on empty stomachs. These were terrible losses for the community.

I felt powerless and helpless given the immensity of the disaster. Fortunately, because of my close ties to merchants in the Bizoton and Jacmel region, as soon as the lines of communication were opened, I was able to get food and basic supplies, on credit, to feed many while the world helplessly watched food supplies wasting on the docks of Port-au-Prince. I had created a nonprofit organization in 1999 to help La Vallée, *Angels for Haiti*. I had managed to raise funds to hold many programs for health education, art, and music, as well as for the restoration of latrines at the Lycée and building quarters for the custodian. We also offered scholarships each year to hundreds of meritorious students. We had been lucky to find an angel to fund in Bizoton a branch of FONKOZE, a microfinance institution offering a full range of financial services to the rural-based poor in Haiti—but this same FONKOZE branch was totally destroyed by the quake. Desperately trying to assist these communities where Angels for Haiti had done so much, I reached out to the many "Angels" who had helped over the years, asking them for donations to pay for what had already been delivered. Thanks to them help arrived and many lives were saved.

My first trip back after the earthquake was one of the hardest going-back-home experiences I have ever had; it looked like the quake had just happened yesterday. When I visited, as much as 98 percent of the rubble from the quake remained uncleared; there were still over 1.6 million people living in camps with no electricity, running water, or sewage disposal, and the tents were beginning to fall apart. Crime in the camps was widespread, including intimidation from landowners and sexual and domestic violence against women and girls.

There are no words to explain how I felt when I saw the destruction at the Cathedrale, the National Palace crushed and distorted like a pile of pancakes, collapsed buildings, and landslides on the mountainsides. It was like a war zone. I knew there were many family members and friends still under the rubble. Perhaps the most difficult sight for me was looking at this sea of white tents and blue tarps with seemingly no end, under 93° tropical heat with no trees or any type of shade.

As we went through Jacmel, I wept as I passed the many collapsed buildings and the many tent cities. The Hôpital Saint-Michel, the largest hospital and referral center for the region and the people of La Vallée, sustained major damage, sparing only the radiology department. In La Vallée, the destruction was less evident, but still present. Half of the homes were badly damaged and another third were completely destroyed. In Jacmel proper, 70 percent of the homes had collapsed, with the heaviest damage occurring in the poorer neighborhoods. Most of the homes had only one room, with an outdoor kitchen and latrines sparsely placed in the mountainous region. Another problem was that the average household size of five grew to about fifteen or twenty due to the exodus of refugees fleeing Port-au-Prince. There were now over five thousand youths with no place to live, quickly changing the social milieu; many rapes were being reported, and prostitution was on the rise.

Whenever there is a disaster we have to make the best of it all. You can always find the strength within if you look for it. When I heard the news, I felt that the whole world was caving in, but my many years of training as a surgeon, who would respond at any time of the day or night, took over. I now also counsel women who are plagued with emotional symptoms, are feeling stuck, and don't know where to turn. I had to use the same principles for my own survival. Here are the lessons I learned.

Choose your battles: As a gynecologist with no physical trauma training, I decided that I could best serve my country during the first chaotic moments by staying in the United States and coordinating emergency medical teams, being the liaison for those on the ground with no telephone contact with one another, collecting medical supplies, and locating medication and food to be sent to Haiti.

You don't have to wallow in the negative: As the disaster unfolded and images of destruction kept coming in, I stopped watching TV or reading the newspaper. They sapped the little energy I had left.

Be ready to accept help: Many friends and even strangers came along bringing me food or a donation, keeping me company and offering a shoulder to cry on, or helping with fundraising. I received many phone calls and e-mails, some from old patients I had cared for over the years, telling me that they were thinking of me and keeping me in their prayers.

It is okay to mourn: When the pain would be unbearable, I would just pray or weep and was not afraid to do it wherever I was.

You cannot take care of everyone—keep healthy boundaries: Especially while I was in Haiti, many came to me asking me for every type of help and believing that I was their only hope. But this burden took an emotional toll on me, and I came to the realization that it was impossible. I continued to do what I could for whoever I could, making it clear to others whom I was not in a position to support that calling me for help was a waste of precious time and energy. They needed to turn elsewhere.

We still have to celebrate: In July 2010 we celebrated the International Children's Holiday for Peace, an event that I have organized successfully in La Vallée since 2001. Twenty-three hundred children from ten villages participated. We made it a day of celebration where the poor children and orphans could eat, play, sing, dance, and paint murals. We had to continue the tradition. It was important for the children and the community.

Be in the moment: We have the ability to be in the present, and enjoy our surroundings even despite other challenges faced in moments of disaster. Things like watching a bird fly freely in a garden or marveling over a beautiful rose keep me grounded during those times when the memories of the destruction come to mind.

Accept small gestures with gratitude: During my last visit in Haiti, while walking alone in one of the streets, three young girls came running towards me. They kissed me and told me that when they found out who I was, they wanted to let me know how much they loved me. The smallest one handed me a wildflower that she was holding behind her back. After they left, I just stood and cried as this small gesture made it all worth it.

WISHING I COULD HAVE DONE MORE

Evelyn Ducheine Cartright

When I heard the news of the earthquake in Haiti I was instantly filled with dread and sorrow. The heartache that I felt deep down inside was unlike anything I had ever experienced. I was sad and afraid at the same time. I was sad that so many of my countrymen had died in the aftermath of the earthquake, that so many people were still unaccounted for. I was afraid that some of my family members might have died. I was glued to the television set, hoping for another type of news, anything but the awful reality of what had just happened: in just minutes the seismic tremors devastated hundreds of thousands of people.

I had heard of similar earthquakes in other parts of the world, but this one impacted me deeply. Suddenly, I understood the uneasiness I had experienced the day before, a premonition of sorts. On Monday, January 11, around 4 p.m., I was on my to the mall and felt strangely sad; my heart was heavy. I had a weird sensation that something dreadful was going to happen. Wanting to share this heavy feeling with someone, I called my husband right away and told him, "Whatever is going to happen will be huge."

I returned home without going to the mall. I needed to pray.

The earthquake occurred in Haiti the following day. It was, indeed, earth shattering.

I watched CNN in disbelief with tears streaming down my face. We worried about family members still living in Haiti: my brother, his wife and children, as well as my husband's family. We started making calls to inquire about them. My husband was able to speak to most of his family members. They were all safe and their homes unaffected. I was dreading having to go to work the day after the earthquake since I was so preoccupied and upset by not having any news at all about my family. I spent three days praying before hearing that my brother Gerry and his family were safe. A friend had called to say that they were unharmed. Upon learning that the family was sleeping in the yard because of cracks in the walls of their home, we sent food supplies and blankets. Relieved that they were alive, we did not care about the destroyed house.

As soon as I returned to work at Barry University, I was asked to join a task force newly created to help the victims of the earthquake. I was elated to be part of the group because I needed desperately to feel that I was contributing. The people who volunteered to serve on the committee were all dedicated to helping. We met once a week until the end of the semester to plan relief efforts and different fundraising events to help the victims.

Immediate assistance was provided to Barry's students, faculty, and staff of Haitian descent. The Center for Counseling and Psychological Services was also available to them. The Friday following the tragedy, a university-wide counseling session with Creole-speaking counselors was offered on campus and a mass was held at Barry's Cor Jesu Chapel for all those affected by the disaster.

On Friday, January 22, the thirty-five students from the Haitian Inter-Cultural Association (HICA), along with the Office of Student Activities, Alternative Spring Break (ASB), All Greek Council, Campus Activities Board (CAB), Student Government Association (SGA), and the Student Organization Council (SOC) hosted a rally and vigil as well as an overnight student lock-in to compel the university to support the Haiti relief efforts.

The prayer vigil for the people of Haiti was held at 7 p.m. at the Landon Student Union Courtyard. There were presentations and performances by student groups and local Haitian artists and musical groups, including Elie Lapointe and Harmonik. The rally concluded with the lock-in, where students spent the night on campus to raise awareness and generate support for those devastated by the earthquake.

Vigils were held for the people of Haiti on the main campus every Friday thereafter. A special website was created where students could get more information about Barry's Haiti relief efforts. The university subsequently joined forces with the non-profit organizations Food for the Poor and Catholic Relief Services, and students collected food, blankets, medical supplies, and monetary donations on campus, as well as at off-site campuses throughout Florida.

I personally sent out e-mails to try to reach those students affected by the tragedy. Some of the students had lost close relatives in the disaster. A few of them were orphaned and had been left without financial support. After identifying the students, I worked diligently with the task force and registrar's office to arrange full scholarships to support these students in completing their studies to earn their bachelor's degrees.

I wish I could have done more. No matter how involved I got, I still felt that it was somehow not enough because there was so much to be done.

Today I continue to worry about the women and children in Haiti. Thousands of people lost their homes and ended up living in tent camps. The lack of privacy and safety patrols in those camps left women and children unprotected, many of them becoming victims of sexual violence. These attacks went unreported for fear of retaliation. The women who reported these abuses also faced a judicial system that ignored and sometimes even blamed the victims.

Some women unable to secure employment to support their families had to resort to what is referred to as "survival sex."[1] Many women and young girls sell sex to meet basic needs and to support their children. The recovery efforts by the Haitian government and the international community were primarily focused on reconstruction and housing, while the needs of women, young girls, and children were set aside. Though there have been some interventions to protect them, more governmental resources ought to be allocated to support this vulnerable population.

Note

[1] This practice of trading sex for basic necessities is more commonly referred to in the United States as transactional sex.

In Memoriam

Florence Bellande Robertson

In Boca Raton on the morning of March 12, 2012, Florida celebrated nature's beauty and encompassing warmth. As I sat on the manicured green lawn of the Lynn University campus, observing with great emotion the celebration of the unveiling of the Memorial Plaza dedicated to the six members of Lynn's community whose lives were lost in the seism in Haiti, my mind wandered to that equally bright and beautiful afternoon in Haiti two years before. It was January 12, 2010, when the earth roared, swayed, crashed, and swallowed hundreds of thousands of lives and so much of the country's material wealth, historical monuments, and architectural treasures. My country, Haiti, would never again be the same! This horror contrasted with the serenity of Florida that morning and the spiritual experience I was having. The dam of my tears still held after two years, as the harrowing screams echoed from some painful well deep inside. Horror and disbelief at this destructive reality for Haiti remained etched in my memory and heart.

Across the ocean that separates Lynn University and Haiti physically and ideologically, a reminder now stands—an imposing monument of flowing waters whose scintillating prisms invite the viewer to tranquility and reflection. This Memorial Plaza represents a new bridge, heralding a new promise of transnational remembrance, interconnectedness, and collaborative efforts. It is a symbol of hope amid the despair of that catastrophic, apocalyptic moment on that fateful afternoon.

Through the Memorial Plaza, the parents of these "angels of mercy" and Lynn University resolved to immortalize the deaths of the two faculty members and four students who perished in Haiti the

Figures 1 and 2. The memorial plaza at Lynn University. Photos courtesy of Lynn University.

day after they had arrived on a "Journey of Hope" mission under the aegis of Food for the Poor.[1] The living thus chose to transform tragedy and loss into a vibrant testimony to the human spirit of generosity and kindness. In addition to the Memorial Plaza at Lynn University, today, in the neighborhood of Carrefour near Port-au-Prince, now stands an orphanage as the caring gift of a Lynn family who lost their daughter in the quake. The orphanage serves and nurtures some of the country's disenfranchised and parentless youth, giving them the tools to meet challenges with confidence and hope.

Although enveloped in sadness, my buoyed spirit beheld the beauty of the day, the music, and the inspiring words spoken at that moment. I felt comforted by the thought that those "angels of mercy" died trying to pass on their own human privileges and good fortune. They understood and translated into action this verse from the Bible:

"Inasmuch as you have done it to the least . . . you have done it unto Me."[2]

Notes

[1] The names of those from Lynn University who died in Haiti are Dr. Richard Bruno, Dr. Patrick Hartwick, Stephanie Crispinelli, Britney Gengel, Christine Gianacaci, and Courtney Hayes.

[2] Matthew 25:40, King James version.

PART III
ACTIVE FAULTS
RESPONSIBILITY AND BLAME

Mon pays paradoxal

Michèle Duvivier Pierre-Louis

Alors que je ressentais dans tout mon corps endolori les effets du choc, ce soir même du 12 janvier 2010, étendue à même le sol sous un ciel illuminé d'étoiles dans une nuit sans lune, j'ai été saisie par la beauté du chant qui montait de mille voix frappées par la douleur . . . Que dire devant tant de ferveur lorsque des corps mutilés, écrasés, désaxés dévoilent l'étendue de la catastrophe? Que dire aussi devant tant de malheur? Je n'étais pas seule. Nous étions des milliers, des centaines de milliers qui en cette première nuit post-séisme secouée de répliques, faisions, la mort dans l'âme, l'expérience collective du désastre.

Ces voix sorties des ruines en invoquant les puissances divines disaient aussi autre chose. Elles disaient déjà l'espoir. Celui qui naît de la transcendance et permet la reconstruction en ouvrant tous les possibles. Celui qui se veut la négation de la déraison qui nous a conduits au malheur ; celui qui montre notre capacité à rebondir.

C'est dire la manière paradoxale dont nous avons vécu les jours qui ont suivi le tremblement de terre. Lorsque nous apprenions à chaque rencontre que parents, amis, collègues avaient péri souvent sans laisser de traces ; ou lorsque nous avons vu le Palais national cassé, affaissé dans une posture symbolique proche de la génuflexion, comme s'il implorait le pardon des héros de la patrie encore debout sur le Champ de Mars ; ou encore lorsque, en parcourant les rues encombrées de débris huit jours après le 12 janvier, des cadavres décomposés, gonflés et puants, jonchaient encore les trottoirs ou pourrissaient sous les décombres, nous avons pris la mesure de l'univers chaotique dans lequel nous étions plongés. Mais, nous ne pouvions nous empêcher de penser en même temps que tout cela ne pouvait être en vain. Que face à tous ces morts et pour eux-mêmes, le temps était venu de penser, de voir, et par-delà cette vision apocalyptique, d'écouter enfin les voix qui depuis plus de vingt ans s'élevaient d'un peu partout dans le pays pour crier leur désir de vivre autrement, communiquer leur pulsion citoyenne et exprimer leur soif de solidarité.

J'ai pensé en ces moments-là que Port-au-Prince deviendrait une vraie ville, une ville-phare à la hauteur de nos rêves de convivialité et de savoir-vivre dans un espace urbain qui afficherait fièrement son humanité retrouvée. J'ai imaginé les enfants, ceux qui jusque là survivaient dans des bouges immondes, jouant radieux dans des espaces pensés pour eux partout dans la ville ; les jeunes, hommes et femmes, mais les moins jeunes aussi, découvrant l'histoire de leur ville, sa mémoire s'étirant comme un pont entre passé et présent, heureux de pouvoir enfin se projeter dans l'avenir du pays. J'ai pensé, j'ai imaginé . . . Et les jours ont passé. Et les tentes ont recouvert tous les espaces libres de la ville. Et la pluie est venue. Et puis les promesses d'argent, les colloques et séminaires, les illusions, les désillusions, le choléra, la dérision, les élections, la peur. Et encore la déraison, un an après.

Un an après . . . la tension paradoxale souffre de nouvelles crispations. Les voix chantées des premières nuits post-séisme se sont tues depuis longtemps, mais gare à ceux qui se laisseraient croire que ce serait pour toujours. La pseudo normalisation a quelque peu forcé le mutisme, le bruit ayant parasité la parole nue jusqu'à la dénaturer. Mais les faux-semblants et les simulacres finiront par mettre bas les masques maintenant que d'autres voix s'élèvent. Alors, au cœur même du paradoxe, l'espoir renaîtra comme pour conjurer le malheur, et chercher un ancrage dans des convictions neuves.

Je ne peux m'empêcher, comme cela m'arrive souvent, de terminer avec les mots du poète/philosophe : « . . . Quand on se fut endormi, et que vint le milieu de la nuit, un coup de tonnerre éclata, accompagné d'un tremblement de terre, et les âmes, chacune par une voie différente, soudain lancées dans les espaces supérieurs vers le lieu de leur naissance, jaillirent comme des étoiles . . . »[1]

Note

[1] Platon, *La République*, Livre X, 385.

THE FACES OF POVERTY

Jacinthe Armand

I know the mother of a family who lives near a property I own in southern Haiti, in Salagnac, located in the heights of "Les Nippes."

Every day she walks more than two hours each way to the market. She goes there to sell bananas that she has purchased and ripened at home. She has been doing this for years. She suffers from headaches, among other ailments, yet she must continue this arduous routine lest her six children, her husband, and two in-laws not have their one meal a day. Her husband cultivates a small plot of land they own and sometimes, when his health allows, sells his labor to neighboring farmers. Despite the fact that Salagnac experienced only mild tremors during the January 2010 earthquake, the lives of the people who lived there were affected.

For the most part, the women in Salagnac make their living from agriculture. They grow vegetables, spices, and tubers, and sell them in markets far from their homes. They handle the finances and commercial transactions, while the men mostly provide the labor in the fields. However, the women can also be seen planting; that is, when they are not off to the market or taking care of their families. With their homes perched in the mountains, at least twice a week they must saddle their mules, if they are lucky enough to have them, and walk or ride to the market in the wee hours of the morning. The biggest wholesale market near them is in Fond des Nègres. Thousands of middlemen come to this market to buy their produce. These middlemen then resell these products in Haiti's main cities. Their return home is not until sunset.

Since the walk or mule ride is at least two to three hours each way on steep mountain trails, the produce the women bring with them must be sold or left at the market. Knowing this, many middlemen exploit the situation and wait until the afternoon to purchase produce. Consequently, at the end of the day, the women are forced to sell at whatever price they are offered for their goods. These women, now eager to return home with a much lighter load and to make at least enough to buy their families a few staples, practically give away their hard-labored produce at the buyers' offered price. The market prices are not regulated or subsidized by the government, and the result is that many times the sale of vegetables doesn't cover their production cost.

The situation before the earthquake was already difficult for these women, not only because of the aforementioned trek to the market and the dealings with middlemen but also because the weather, the lack of fertilizer, and the costly imported seeds made matters quite precarious and unpredictable. After the earthquake, world attention and "generosity" toward Haiti negatively affected farmers in the countryside because massive imports of donated food decreased the demand for locally grown food. Furthermore, many of the middlemen who purchased from Salagnac farmers died in the earthquake in Port-au-Prince, thus disrupting the established network of distribution. Moreover, the earthquake damage to roads into the cities made transport an added issue.

While things were bad before, they worsened after the earthquake. The women who supported their families through market sales could no longer bring in the same income. Furthermore, more economic pressure was placed on them as many other members of their families who had lost their homes in the capital came to take refuge in the countryside. The folks in Salagnac of course opened their homes to those homeless relatives from the cities, but it was a burden for them to carry. And given that foreign aid prioritized families in the more impacted cities, less attention was paid to those in the countryside. The Salagnac farmers thus felt left out of the post-earthquake assistance.

In 2010, President Michel Martelly ran for office on the platform "Reponse Paysan," which highlights the plight of the rural population, but nothing has yet been done for those in the area of Salagnac. Additionally, the dry weather has not helped matters for the peasant farmers who depend on rain, and not irrigation, as their source of water for agriculture. Life continues, but sadly, the farmers do not have much hope. However, while change is perhaps not yet happening, I am sensing a strong energetic shift that makes me optimistic about Haiti. The earthquake was a strange but forceful wakeup call announcing that the time had come to finally create a decentralized Haiti, encompassing remote regions of the country and improving the quality of life for Haitians everywhere. Participating in this new wave of development should be every Haitian's aspiration if not duty. We will all collectively reap the rewards.

Our people, our women, our children deserve this legacy. We have suffered enough historically. A more enlightened future glimmers on the horizon.

LE SÉISME DU 12 JANVIER 2010 : MES RÉFLEXIONS DEUX ANS APRÈS

Alexandra Philoctète

Au lendemain du séisme, nous étions tous, Haïtiens et autres peuples, en état de choc. Encore une fois, la fatalité frappait Haïti. À l'extérieur du pays, nous avons vu en direct sur le petit écran bon nombre d'enfants, de femmes et d'hommes se faire amputer par des médecins accourus de l'étranger pour porter secours aux victimes. Les rescapés qui avaient pu extirper leurs proches des décombres devaient les ensevelir de nouveau. Le pays ne disposant pas d'équipement d'excavation, c'est à mains nues que plusieurs tentaient de porter secours à ceux que la terre avait elle-même engloutis.

On a vu des gens, qui avaient tout perdu, fouiller dans les ruines pour trouver de quoi bâtir un abri temporaire qui les protégerait du soleil et de la pluie. Parmi ces amas de pierres, on a vu aussi des groupes de femmes haïtiennes errer à travers les décombres tout en scandant des cantiques religieux, demandant pardon, croyant subir les foudres de la colère divine! Croyance cultivée par certains prophètes de malheur.

Au delà de Port-au-Prince et des environs, un vent de détresse frappait le pays tout entier. En revanche, la majorité des femmes, mues par des réflexes de survie, ont pris la route qui les mènerait vers des lieux plus cléments pour échapper au chaos. Quelques personnes ont démontré un sens du partage et de générosité, mais de nombreux palabreurs ont passé leur temps à pérorer, sans mettre la main à la pâte. On ne leur connaît toujours pas de gestes concrets, trop occupés qu'ils étaient à se battre entre eux et à mener leurs intrigues, soit ouvertement soit en coulisses. Trop englués dans leurs magouilles, ils n'ont eu aucun égard pour les habitants du pays qui crevaient de faim surtout pour les femmes qui n'arrivaient même pas à trouver du lait pour leurs petits. Pour ces vendeurs de mots, il n'y avait qu'à compter sur les anges de la diaspora, vaches à lait qu'on pourrait traire à merci, sans aucune reconnaissance.

Puis, l'attente, après l'annonce de l'arrivée de « Pères Noël », ils sont venus, ils ont vu et ils sont repartis ne laissant sur le terrain que des promesses. Voilà qu'une bonne partie de la population démunie croupit encore dans des abris temporaires, sous des tentes données par ceux qui essaient de compenser la trahison de ces étrangers et les discours creux des beaux parleurs. Quant aux femmes, dans ces abris de fortune, elles tiennent toujours le coup malgré tout. Tôt le matin, elle partent du camp et essaient de trouver de quoi nourrir leurs enfants. L'eau potable et l'eau courante n'étant pas disponible, elles sont forcées d'aller la chercher aussi loin qu'elle soit, et si possible avant la chaleur du midi. Faute de sanitaires, elles laissent leurs petits se rafraîchir les pieds dans des rigoles insalubres. Quelques-unes arrivent de peine et de misère à vendre des « fritailles » aux passants.

S'ajoute à l'horreur de la situation, lorsque la nuit tombe la peur pour les femmes et les enfants, sans protection aucune, aux prises avec les attaques de « san manman » qui volent et violent en toute impunité. La cruauté et le cynisme de ces « sans aveux » sont sans bornes. Même les garçons ne sont pas épargnés.

Les femmes qui habitent dans les campagnes, dans les mornes ont repris l'habitude de se rendre en ville pour vendre leurs maigres produits. Leur port est toujours altier, mais la route est devenue plus ardue, plus tortueuse désormais. Elles n'ignorent pas que cette terre qu'elles cultivent avec des moyens rudimentaires, peut encore trembler. Elles ne peuvent s'arrêter à cela, il leur faut continuer. Pour avoir connu tant de fois cyclones, ouragans, inondations et autres caprices de la nature, elles ont appris à se débrouiller seules. Elles n'ont jamais cru à la manne du ciel, ni au beau langage de certains citadins. Leur sens du commerce leur a appris à négocier avec toutes les catégories de gens, les appelant : « ti chérie ou ti cocotte » afin de mieux vendre leurs produits. Leur sympathie va toutefois à leurs consœurs vivant sous les tentes. Il leur arrive à l'occasion de leur vendre des produits à des prix dérisoires, par simple solidarité.

Deux ans après ce jour fatidique du « goudougoudou, » dans les tentes, les femmes ont perdu leur sourire, elles ne veulent plus entendre parler de ces étrangers aux promesses mirobolantes, ni entendre pérorer les beaux parleurs. Certaines d'entre elles portent sur les bras ou en elles l'enfant d'un des viols qu'elles ont subis. Faute de structures et de lois pour les les protéger, elles se défendent parfois avec des moyens dérisoires : manches de balai, pilons ou autres outils précaires. Le système 'D' est en fonction lorsque la solidarité le permet : veiller pendant que les autres dorment et dormir quand les autres veillent. Cependant, malgré cette situation inhumaine, une lueur brille encore dans leur regard, parce qu'elles n'ignorent pas qu'elles ont toujours soutenu ce pays et qu'elles reprendront leur élan tôt ou tard. Par intuition, elles savent que le jour viendra où leurs enfants, filles ou garçons, iront à l'école et connaîtront des lendemains meilleurs. Si elles vivent assez pour le voir, rien ne les arrêtera et ce jour-là, elles danseront toutes sur la place publique et chanteront des chants de leur propre folklore qui, cette fois, ne leur auront pas été dictés par des vendeurs de culpabilité.

Montréal, Canada

"After They Beat Us They Are Like Dogs at Our Feet": An Oral History of Vulnerability and Violence in Post-earthquake Haiti

Claire Antone Payton

Maryse pulled up her shirt and showed me the scars from where she was stabbed. "Here's one. . . . Here's two. . . ."[1] She and I stood together, along with two of her friends, sweating out the afternoon on the concrete steps of the Champ de Mars, the large public plaza in Port-au-Prince's administrative district. It was November 2010. A camp of improvised tarp shelters bloomed in the plaza, housing people made homeless by the earthquake that had ruptured the city ten months prior. According to the IOM (International Organization for Migration) figures, 1,199 such camps across Haiti were housing some 1.06 million people that month.[2] To conduct an oral history project on post-quake life, I spent my days wandering through different IDP (internally displaced persons) camps looking for people willing to tell me their stories.

The Champ de Mars plaza was one of the country's largest camps, with at least 21,000 people sharing a piece of land about one tenth of a square mile in area. Maryse had lived there since the disaster. She was in her mid-twenties. Born in the countryside outside Les Cayes, she had come to Port-au-Prince as a child, at a godmother's invitation, to continue her education. After a few years, she decided she was grown and left school to begin an adult life. To her that meant finding a man, moving in with him, and bearing his children. They lived there until the earthquake forced them onto the Champ de Mars.

Life in the camp was mostly boring. "Wake up. If I have fifty gourdes, I buy a little something to eat. Bathe. Then sit and wait for night again. Wake up, sit and wait. Wake up, sit and wait. . . . I don't do commerce, I don't work. Before the earthquake, I went to work. Now I don't work. . . . Women sit around, make jokes. We talk about our personal lives. We laugh. If there is a radio we listen to some music, but as soon as you lie down you fill with stress."

When the camp wasn't boring it was dangerous. Gender-based violence was a serious threat. The term refers to violence "involving men and women in which the female is usually the victim and which is derived from unequal power relations between men and women."[3] It's difficult to say how common gender-based violence was in the IDP camps because official reports vary so widely. The threat of sexual violence loomed particularly large in people's imaginations, both inside and outside the camps: Maryse described nighttime attacks from masked men she believed came from outside the camp and forced their way into tents to prey on women. Fears of "stranger rape" circulated widely in the months after the earthquake, both in Haiti and in the international press. Although she personally had not been assaulted in this way, she said she knew many who had been, even pointing to a woman near where we stood, saying, "That woman there, they raped her." Maryse avoided going at night to the line of portable toilets that served her camp, preferring to hold it rather than run the risk of an attack.

The person who assaulted Maryse was not a stranger. It was her husband, the tap-tap driver she had lived with since leaving school several years before. He had been away in the countryside seeking medical treatment from an *ougan* when the earthquake struck and did not return to the city until more than a two weeks later. "So, I have my man. . . . He is so jealous! When he came back from *trètman* in the provinces, it seems he heard some gossip. He wasn't even around."

That's when she pointed to her ten-month-old scars. "He did it after January 12. After January 12! He saw everything that was happening; saw that I wasn't hurt at all. You think we'd figure out a way to work together after that." She slapped her hands together for emphasis and her voice rose, seemingly to stress her incredulity at the fact that she survived one of the deadliest disasters in history only to be attacked by the person closest to her.

Indeed, activists working with women in the camps said that cases of gender-based violence among family and acquaintances were much more common than attacks from strangers.[4] Recent sociological research found that following the earthquake, women in devastated zones were at higher risk of intimate partner violence than if the earthquake had not occurred. Factors that elevated women's vulnerability included relationships destabilized by emotional uncertainty and trauma, emotional strain, and increased dependency caused by depleted income and reduced social and familial networks.[5]

The gossip about her, Maryse freely admitted, was based in truth. Without her partner's financial support, she looked for opportunities to exchange sex for food or money. "They told him when he's not around I get dressed up to go out. If I've got no one to help me, I go out and do what I can on the street," she explained.

Maryse's account of the attack implies that she was caught in a socioeconomic bind compounded by the far-reaching destruction. She identified with the Haitian ideal of a male-headed household where the man provided economically. But she also experienced this ideal's limitations, particularly when she was left alone and without financial resources after the earthquake. With limited options, she relied on sexuality to secure a small income. I wondered if she had been using the same methods before the earthquake to gain some financial autonomy, with the lack of privacy in the camp's close quarters making it impossible to prevent her partner from finding out, but she didn't say. Either way, the expectation of female monogamy nearly ended her life. Although gender roles in Haiti are hardly static, it is important to recognize how the earthquake's destabilizing power shifted intimate relationships.

After stabbing her, Maryse's partner took her to a hospital where, she recalled, "the *blan* sewed me up." Yet Maryse did not cut off the relationship. Far from her family in the countryside, and with no social safety net in Port-au-Prince, she depended on her attacker to help her recover from her wounds.

Even the law was no help. "I thought about going to the police. The police said, 'It's your husband that beat you, ma'am, we can't say anything about that. If you leave your husband right now, we'll arrest him.'" The Haitian legal and criminal systems are woefully unequipped to handle gender-based violence, generally affirming men's power to control and abuse their wives.[6] The path to justice the police offered her was not realistic: "I wasn't going to leave him—because even though he hurt me, he'd take care of me after." Although she was referencing her physical recuperation, there was also an implication of continued financial support. The threat of total indigence obliged her to accept—if not normalize—life-threatening abuse. She laughed, acknowledging the cruel absurdity of the situation. Her friend Nadia, who exchanged her own stories of abusive relationships with Maryse throughout the interview, described the cycle of violence vividly, saying that men were so ashamed that "after they beat us they are like dogs at our feet."

I asked Maryse if men would treat women the same way if economic conditions in Haiti were better. "I don't think things would be the same. There are guys who, when they don't have cash, they turn into jerks. When you don't have cash, that's when you should be affectionate with a woman, so she can comfort you. Some guys, when they don't have money, you can't even touch them." Shifting her voice into an impression of an angry man, she continued, "'Woman, get in your own bed! I don't have any money, I can't sleep with a woman today.'" Her friends laughed.

Maryse was frustrated with how the expectation of transactional sex could get in the way of men and women providing each other with emotional support through difficult times. She had compassion for men who felt emasculated by Haiti's dire economic circumstances and believed intimacy and closeness could ease their emotional burden. But she suggested that some were unwilling to accept this gift because for them sex was inextricably bound to the expectation of material exchange.

Conversely, sexual encounters with vulnerable women became opportunities for men to express or reclaim their feelings of power. The process was sometimes humiliating: "Fifty gourdes! Fifty gourdes! ... And then the vagabonds have whatever kind of sex they want." Maryse smacked her hands together with frustration. "For fifty gourdes. However they want it, you have to accept it. If you don't, you won't get the fifty gourdes." She recognized that transactional sex and prostitution put women at risk of STDs and pregnancy and obliged them to do degrading or painful things. Even getting paid was dangerous. "[Women] don't always know if they will get money. Because you have to do it with him so he'll get the money out of his pocket to give you. He finishes doing it, pulls up his pants, he leaves a dollar, goes. But he can just leave, and if you try to stop him he might slap you." The amount she said women got paid was equivalent to $1.25—just enough to buy a plate of food.

Sex was not always about immediate material returns, though. Maryse also mentioned that her personal desires for sex and human closeness motivated her as well. She confided that she sometimes made love even if her partner was unable to provide any assistance at the moment. "Sometimes I'm hungry, but I give them love anyway. Because maybe I'm thirsty for love, he's thirsty for love, and I do it anyway. If he usually supports me but doesn't have it then, I do it anyway. That's not going to kill me." This comment reveals something important that can get lost in talk about transactional sex: sex is not always a commodity. Intimate encounters could also provide Maryse with opportunities to express her own sexual and emotional desires.

In addition to physical abuse, Maryse had to constantly deal with the threat of unwanted pregnancy. With little control over the course of her sexual encounters, it is unlikely she could demand that her partners use condoms. The only options for a woman in that situation, she said, would be to attempt an abortion, or try to leverage the pregnancy into a better living situation for herself. "There are women who pay a little money to drink a medicine and lose the baby, but if you have a husband in the house who can give you food, give you drink, while you are pregnant, then you would keep your baby."

Maryse's account offers a graphic portrait of the interplay of physical violence and structural violence in one woman's life. Her narrative indicates that she clearly recognizes the link between her vulnerability to abuse and her economic precariousness. Her assault connected her physically and emotionally to Haiti's anemic economic situation and to the earthquake's destabilizing power. Without greater material stability, Maryse and women like her are unlikely to disengage from abusive relationships. Transactional sex provided her with some access to resources, but she also chose to take huge health risks to make pathetically small amounts of money.

If listening to her story makes us uncomfortable, it may be because she portrays an uncomfortable reality. Her story is both one of agency and one of extreme limitation. It is about the how the commodification of sexuality mixes with a profound desire to feel human closeness. She shows us how women calculate whether to take long-term risks like abusive relationships, sexually transmitted infections, or unwanted pregnancy because the immediate risks such as not affording food or not recovering from an injury loom so large. Understanding how and why violence and risk in Maryse's life increased after the earthquake is essential for imagining, building, and implementing policies that can better protect women in times of crisis.

If policy change on local, national, or international levels is the goal, we cannot lose sight of the individuals whose lives are on the line. By using one person's account as a privileged vantage point into some of Haiti's most daunting social issues, oral history offers an invitation to compassion. And when it comes thinking about the IDP camps, compassion must be the baseline.

With that in mind, it is worth noting that Maryse's experience was in some ways unusual. For example, research on domestic violence in Haiti before the quake found that although large numbers of women experienced abuse, only a vanishingly small percentage reported being attacked with a weapon.[7] It is hard to overstate the physical and emotional hardship of living in the IDP camps, as several accounts have attested.[8] Yet within that shared experience, there were thousands of unique individual ones. Haitian experience is often framed in the aggregate: the peasantry, the elite, the masses, the displaced. Diluting individual experiences in this way sometimes puts us at a safe distance from the profound messiness of human life. In her interview, Maryse conveyed a multidimensional relationship with sex, agency, vulnerability, and violence. This complexity is an expression of her individuality and humanity, and it needs to be affirmed before any change is possible. Social and economic crises are primarily human crises, and Maryse has the scars to prove it.

Notes

1 At the participants' request, this interview was anonymous, and the names used here are made up. The recorded interview was conducted in Haitian Kreyòl and can be listened to in full on the Haiti Memory Project website, under "Young Woman on Champ de Mars" (http://haitimemoryproject.org/voices/). Translations are mine.

2 International Organization for Migration, "Displacement Tracking Matrix (DTM) Haiti," June 2016.

3 MEASURE Evaluation, "Sexual and Gender-Based Violence," accessed September 1, 2016, http://www.cpc.unc.edu/measure/prh/rh_indicators/specific/sgbv.

4 Anne-christine d'Adesky and PotoFamn+Fi Coalition, "Beyond Shock: Charting the Landscape of Sexual Violence in Post-Quake Haiti" (San Francisco and Port-au-Prince: PotoFamn+Fi Initiative, 2012), 27.

5 Abigail Weitzman and Julia Behrman, "Disaster, Disruption to Family Life, and Intimate Partner Violence: The Case of the 2010 Earthquake in Haiti," *Sociological Science* 3 (2016): 167–189.

6 For more on this, see d'Adesky and PotoFamn+Fi Coalition, "Beyond Shock"; Régine Michelle Jean-Charles, *Conflict Bodies: The Politics of Rape Representation in the Francophone Imaginary* (Columbus: Ohio State University Press, 2016); M. Catherine Maternowska, *Reproducing Inequities: Poverty and the Politics of Population in Haiti* (New Brunswick, NJ: Rutgers University Press, 2006); Mark Schuller, "'Pa Manyen Fanm Nan Konsa': Intersectionality, Structural Violence, and Vulnerability Before and After Haiti's Earthquake," *Feminist Studies* 41, no. 1 (2015): 184–210.

7 Anastasia J. Gage, "Women's Experience of Intimate Partner Violence in Haiti," *Social Science and Medicine* 61, no. 2 (2005): 343–364, doi:10.1016/j.socscimed.2004.11.078.

8 For example, see Beverly Bell, *Fault Lines: Views across Haiti's Divide* (Ithaca, NY: Cornell University Press, 2013); Mark Schuller, *Humanitarian Aftershocks in Haiti* (New Brunswick, NJ: Rutgers University Press, 2016); Pablo Morales and Mark Schuller, *Tectonic Shifts: Haiti since the Earthquake* (Sterling, VA: Kumarian Press, 2012).

We Fall Down, but We Get Up: Calling for Mental Health Intervention for Haitian Women

Olga Idriss Davis & Lyvie François-Racine

The story of the resilience of Haitian women who faced extraordinary adversity in the aftermath of the tumultuous 2010 earthquake is a testament to their courage, strength of spirit, and determination to go on despite the physical blight in their homeland. But what is not often discussed is the psychological impact of the trauma attached to the loss of family or material possessions, or the toll that a handicap may take on their everyday lives.

Our purpose here is to tell a story which centers on the need for intervention in the area of Haitian women's mental health. This story speaks of trauma, depression, and a spirit of survival.

We will also offer some recommendations about the necessity for ongoing conversations about mental disorders and women's mental health around the world.

Maria's Story

This is the story of Maria. Her name has been changed to protect her identity. Co-author Lyvie François-Racine, co-founder and Executive Director of Phoenix Rising for Haiti, was present during Maria's clinic intake. This is Lyvie's recounting of the encounter.

I watched her as she walked into our little makeshift clinic. She was tall and stout—the type of woman whose youthful beauty had turned handsome and noble as she aged. Joining her was a young man in his late teens. Both stood out among our other patients. As

I looked at them, it finally dawned on me why they were there. The boy was missing his right arm. I could not help but stare. The loss of a limb was nothing new, given the mission of our prosthetic and rehabilitation team in Haiti following the earthquake. Yet these two individuals did not seem to fit among the people we had been seeing all day. There was something different about their demeanor. They did not appear to belong in that town.

"May I help you? What brings you in today?" I asked.

Maria briefly closed her eyes, and when she reopened them, her gaze was miles away as she proceeded to tell their story.

She lived in Port-au-Prince and had just returned home from work. She was in her bedroom taking a quick nap before starting dinner. Her son was in his room doing homework and watching TV when the earthquake hit. She felt her entire house shaking and watched things fall off her dresser as she jumped out of bed. Disoriented and in shock, she ran out of the house frantically calling her son's name. She heard him running down the stairs behind her saying, "I'm coming!" Then the house started to crumble around them. By the time she was outside, she looked around and her son was no longer near her. She screamed his name and heard him screaming back from under a wall that had fallen on him. She ran over and started pulling rubble aside until she was finally able to see him.

At first glance, he looked fine except for some gashes on his head and other scratches. Then she noticed that his right arm was pinned under a large mass of rubble. She pulled and shoved as he tried to crawl out from under it. She continued to remove as much rubble as possible. Suddenly, there was a severe aftershock, with tremors that started dislodging additional pieces of the house. As large blocks of cement came crashing down around them and other household items went flying past, she looked up and saw a huge piece of the balcony directly above them hanging by a bent rebar. After each tremor, it dipped lower. Maria knew they had very little time left to act.

As she struggled to free her son, she kept an eye on the balcony, but soon knew she was out of time. Quickly, Maria got up and ran toward the back of the house to the kitchen, where she grabbed a machete. She ran back and told her son, "It is your arm or your life.

I would rather have you alive with one arm than dead with both." As he screamed "No!" Maria cried and started hacking at his arm. She described how much blood there was and how her son passed out from the pain. Finally freed, Maria yanked him away seconds before the balcony pieces came crashing down exactly where they were. She dragged him to the center of the street and laid him down next to other victims hurt and bleeding on the ground. Maria and her son were finally safe.

This incredible woman risked her life to save her son by cutting off his arm.

Yet she has been continually haunted by that horrific moment. At the clinic, she rubbed her arms and hands as if she was still wiping blood and dust from her skin. She finally looked at me, leaving behind the past. She returned to the present. I did not see conviction or resolve in her eyes; all I saw was guilt. She could barely look at her son. Wracked with guilt for the pain and trauma he experienced, Maria failed to see her own heroism and how she risked her own life. She did not recognize that her choice was what had saved him. She could only feel guilt.

I was reminded of an old quote that my mom would always say whenever she heard of tragedy striking young people: "*Manman pitit mare tèt ou sere*," which loosely translates as "Mothers, times are tough; stay strong." We did eventually get Maria's son a prosthetic arm. I hope that this brought her some peace.

TRAUMA AND MENTAL HEALTH

Haiti is a country of strong women. However, they may not recover collectively from the earthquake unless they find ways to deal with the traumatic experience. When I think about Maria and other mothers with similar stories, I know that no matter what we do to fix the body, there remains a need to work on the spiritual and mental health of these women who have lived through tragedy. The mental trauma of Haitian women is simply too deep and too massive to be ignored. But at what point should the focus turn to mental health?

The trauma to which we refer is post-traumatic stress disorder. A type of anxiety disorder, as with the case with Maria, PTSD can follow a natural disaster such as an earthquake, or events such as assault, domestic abuse, rape, terrorism, and torture. PTSD changes the body's response to stress. It affects the stress hormones and chemicals that carry information between the nerves and neurotransmitters.

In particular, rape and sexual violence of Haitian women and girls who lived in the vast network of Internally Displaced Persons (IDP) camps of Port-au-Prince were extreme violations that increased not only insecurity and fear in the country but also behavioral disorders. These atrocities and the prevailing gender-based violence against women not only caused mental health issues but also engendered a downward spiral of deteriorating human rights. After the quake, the government of Haiti, the UN, and global onlookers all failed to address these conditions that exacerbated the mental health of Haitian women. It is imperative that their social and psychological needs be addressed.

CALL TO ACTION

We assert that the conversation about global women's health has failed to address the paucity of health care, education, and access to human rights surrounding women's lives in Haiti more broadly, and their protection in their IDP camps more specifically.

To make others aware of Haitian women's mental health needs, our initial recommendations to consider include:

1. Mandatory consultation with Haitian women on post-disaster reconstruction projects and disaster preparedness;

2. Creation of an infrastructure of mental health programs for immediate and sustainable therapy of Haitian orphans and women;

3. Continuous protection for Haitian women against national gender-based inequity, violence, and discrimination;

4. New regulations requiring that clinicians and researchers working with Haitian women develop culturally competent strategies to communicate with patients and mitigate under-diagnosed or misdiagnosed patients who might not have otherwise come forward. It is imperative that clinicians and researchers view culture as relevant to understanding and providing culturally sensitive and patient-centered approaches to effective therapeutic interventions.

The ongoing conversation of global mental health must engage the stories of Haitian women. As Maria continues to symbolize the indomitable spirit of Haitian women who continue to ask, "Who will comfort me?" we hope we can offer this resounding reply: "The international community of sisters will."

Quel est mon mêle ?
Le Manfoutisme haïtien

Florence Etienne Sergile

Entre 1985 et 2005, je produisais du matériel didactique pour promouvoir la passionnante histoire naturelle du pays. A la fin de cette période, les professionnels des sciences naturelles menaient une compétition déjà perdue avec ceux des sciences politiques pour obtenir des fonds de manière à développer du matériel de vulgarisation. Haïti avait besoin de démocratie, pas de production agricole, ni de conservation de son patrimoine naturel, ni de protection contre sa vulnérabilité aux cataclysmes naturels. Entre temps, malgré le populisme, la décentralisation et l'investiture de la gouvernance locale, les sécheresses suivent encore les cyclones et leur cortège de désastres comme si c'était un hasard, toujours comme si c'était la première fois. Je ne suis pas convaincue que les sciences et le populisme fassent bon ménage. Après vingt ans de lutte pour la promotion de l'éducation environnementale, fatiguée de prêcher dans le désert ou de dépeindre les mêmes scenarios, j'ai enterré ma palette de vulgarisateur environnemental, séché mes larmes et pris mon deuil restant déterminée que ce qui est politiquement correct est trop souvent techniquement incorrect.

En effet, il y a des lois de la nature, et des codes de construction et de gestion des ressources naturelles, développés pour faire valoir richesses et infrastructures, mais qui, comme par enchantement, ne s'appliquent plus depuis longtemps à la République d'Haïti, d'où nos désastres répétés.

J'aurai pu me trouver aplatie sous les décombres d'une quinzaine d'institutions écroulées avec des amis ou collègues ou pire, coincée avec une tasse de café ou devant une affiche d'oiseaux endémiques à protéger. J'ai une rétro-peur qui me fait encore frémir. Je m'estime chanceuse d'avoir été à la rue Clervaux au moment du séisme, mais jamais n'avais-je pensé voir, entendre et sentir ce que j'ai vu, entendu et senti. En 40 secondes, je me suis trouvée en enfer en plein Pétion-Ville. On connait l'histoire : un grondement souterrain, un pesant silence, des volutes de poussière malodorante, des gens sortant de leur courte torpeur, paniqués, courant dans tous les sens, des structures publiques écrasées, la Place St. Pierre envahie, aucun plan urbain ou communal d'évacuation, dans un pays aussi fragile. L'avantage de militer dans les sciences naturelles et de connaître l'histoire géologique du pays enseignée au lycée est de pouvoir prédire les événements subséquents et d'être en mesure de garder son sang-froid ; pas de panique et pas besoin de réinventer explications et stratégies. Le pire est d'écouter les fausses rumeurs de houle et de tsunami, et d'être envahi par les cris hystériques des très religieux et leurs incessantes invocations à l'Eternel à chaque tremblement.

Un peu après, j'ai ressorti mon cahier d'ébauche pour produire du matériel de prévention et mitigation des désastres. Je voulais profiter de mon élan mais pour m'entendre dire que ce n'était pas une priorité et ensuite observer que malgré la tangible réalité de 2010, pas grand-chose n'avait changé. Les racontars séismiques vont bon train, le laisser-faire c'est encore réinstallé pour faire place au laisser-aller, mes collègues géologues se démènent sans répit pour se faire entendre, et nos décideurs mettent leurs œillères pour s'occuper tranquillement de leurs petites affaires. Au moment où j'écris, des tempêtes se forment sur l'Atlantique et je suis préoccupée par leur trajectoire.

A ce sujet, je partage de grandes inquiétudes avec très peu de gens. Quels sont les codes de construction, les plans de prévention pour le prochain cyclone, la prochaine rupture de faille ? Les canaux de drainage sont-ils curés ? Chaque cataclysme qui passe sur Haïti m'amène un profond chagrin car il dégénère toujours en catastrophe dont nous subissons tous les conséquences. Après le tremblement de terre, tout était paralysé : les enfants ne pouvaient pas aller à l'école, les champs étaient dévastés et les récoltes perdues, les magasins fermés ou pillés, les sans-abris innombrables et j'en passe. Si nous ne pouvons pas freiner un cataclysme (séisme, cyclone, volcan, tsunami), nous pouvons mettre des garde-fous pour minimiser les dégâts de manière à protéger les citoyens et leurs investissements. Je suis ennuyée de voir que poser de simples balises devient alarmant et monstrueux.

Les secousses, tant physiques, que morales du 12 janvier 2010, désormais date fatidique dans les annales haïtiennes, m'ont donné les réponses aux questions que j'avais enfouies loin dans ma mémoire : Que faisons nous de ce qui nous est enseigné à l'école ? à l'université ? Faut-il jeter des passerelles entre les mythes et la réalité ? Comment intégrer l'enseignement des sciences naturelles à la culture haïtienne pour créer et préserver nos richesses ? En quelle langue produire ? Il me manque encore beaucoup de données, mais j'ai de nombreux brouillons que je finirai dans un proche futur.

Insoutenables secondes

Viviane Nicolas

Le 12 janvier 2010, dans plusieurs régions d'Haïti, il y a un vrombissement saisissant, inattendu, durant trente cinq secondes insoutenables. En moins d'une minute, en une fraction infime et interminable de temps, l'Ancêtre Taino assiste à l'ébranlement, l'effondrement incoordonné des principaux symboles de pouvoir érigés sur sa terre profanée, dénaturée.

Par centaines, par milliers, environ trois cent mille vies sont anéanties, brisées, et ne sont maintenant que des corps mutilés. Des espoirs s'évanouissent, dans un paysage alourdi par le béton armé qui, en moins d'une minute, s'affaisse impitoyablement en gros blocs lourds dispersés à l'ombre d'arbres à la stature imperturbable.

L'hydre de malheur poursuit encore son cours en 2010. Pluies diluviennes, vents bruyants, divisions et troubles politiques, puis choléra, jalonnent à nouveau de déboires et de cadavres cette terre anciennement luxuriante et belle.

Par surcroît, de *saints apôtres* dans leur zèle civilisateur, aliénés, fous et dans leur ignorance tordue, notoire et criminelle, ont sauvagement taillardé à mort et à coups de machettes, au vu et au su de tous ainsi que des familles concernées, plus d'une cinquantaine de Vodouisants, les accusant de jeter dans leurs localités, sorts et poudres de choléra.

Les riches caciquats d'hier, dépouillés par les colonisateurs, de l'or, des joyaux, des représentations des Xémès et autres créatures de Dieu ; les somptueux caciquats aujourd'hui parsemés d'immondices, de détritus et de matière fécale humaine, puissants vecteurs de mal-être, de maladies et du choléra récemment introduit en Haïti ; les splendides cités des caciques, rois, reines, butios, thérapeutes, artistes et créateurs invétérés d'Ayiti Bohio Quisqueya ; les cités, domaines fleuris et finement décorés, de nos jours, majoritairement déboisés et trop souvent inondés par les eaux en furie ; le Xaragua, royaume de la Reine Anacaona, l'épicentre du tremblement de terre ; la ville de Léogâne et ses environs croulant sous le béton et les décombres, pavoisée de camps de réfugiés et de tentes et abris précaires.

Ces dons de nos ancêtres, les potentiels artistiques, savoirs thérapeutiques et philosophiques ancestraux, prégnants, intenses et forts au pays, doivent s'assumer pleinement et se développer contrairement à l'attentisme illusoire, stérile et improductif que génère le piétinement des valeurs nationales et l'abandon de la terre. La conscience collective Haïtienne, malgré différences, appartenances spécifiques, ignorances respectives et mutuelles, peut encore se décloisonner, s'ouvrir et requestionner les préjugés, les limitations confessionnelles et politiques exclusives, discriminatoires et pénalisatrices qui ont laissé une terre exsangue et vulnérable au effets du séisme. Il est temps que les damnés de la terre trouvent leur place au soleil, fatigués qu'ils sont, d'être diabolisés et inférisés. Il est temps que la mort virtuelle et physique cède le pas à la reconstruction collective en Haïti, une reconstruction qui retournerait à la source et à la terre léguée par nos ancêtres Tainos.

Les nombreuses cultures et religions d'Haïti nous disent que les valeurs ancestrales ne meurent pas. Les fondateurs Afro-Amérindiens de la patrie attendent que leurs descendants, métissés avec d'autres populations établies au fil du temps au pays, s'imprègnent des lumières de l'Haïtianité, dans leur jonction à celles des civilisations sœurs, capables de mener à la décolonisation du mental nécessaire à la reconstruction d'Haïti, nation unique, savante et fière, et à l'épanouissement de ses ressortissants.

Port-au-Prince, le 11 Janvier 2011

Je suis fatiguée

Dolores Dominique-Neptune

Près d'onze mois après avoir mis mon fils en terre, je me refuse toujours à accepter cette horreur, pour moi, pour les autres, pour cette nation.

Le 12 janvier 2010, nous avons chacun perdu notre innocence. Plus d'amnésie collective.

Le 12 janvier 2010, nous avons gardé notre profonde capacité de déni ! Nous dansons sur le pont du Titanic !

Les premiers jours après le séisme, dans les rues de Port-au-Prince effondrée, on assistait à une solidarité incroyable entre les Haïtiens. A mains nues, une population s'entraidait ! Montrant à tous et surtout à elle-même, que la grandeur d'une nation pouvait s'exprimer dans les moments les plus difficiles.

Depuis lors, la vie a repris et l'on a le sentiment que cette solidarité a disparu, que nous avons oublié tout ce qui nous unissait. Que le poids qui nous entrainait vers la mésentente et la discorde a reparu et est devenu encore plus lourd.

Les petites querelles ont repris, les politiques se chamaillent pour des élections qui auront ou n'auront pas lieu, pour la possession d'un fauteuil bourré, dans un palais cassé, dans une ville-cimetière effondrée, pour un pouvoir inexistant, pour des millions qui arriveront ou n'arriveront pas.

Pendant ce temps, les réfugiés sont dans des camps, les disparus ne sont pas listés et les morts n'ont pas eu de sépulture décente. Je n'arrive pas à me remettre de cette année, ni de ce pays, ni des actions des dirigeants. C'est la chronique d'une catastrophe annoncée.

Depuis plusieurs années, l'ingénieur géologue annonce qu'il y aura un tremblement de terre ici et que le bilan en sera très lourd. L'État et le gouvernement n'ont rien fait pour le prévenir. Nous n'avons rien fait !

Depuis le 12 janvier, on SAIT qu'il y aura des pluies et des cyclones. L'État et le gouvernement n'ont rien fait pour en prévoir les conséquences. Nous n'avons rien fait ! Et les pluies sont arrivées. Et les cyclones sont arrivés, emportant avec eux combien d'entre nous.

Depuis le 12 janvier, on dit qu'il y a un risque de catastrophe sanitaire. L'État et le gouvernement n'ont rien fait pour l'empêcher. Et le choléra est arrivé, emportant et continuant d'emporter nos concitoyens. Tout en ne faisant rien, on a préparé des élections à quarante quatre millions de dollars pour l'organisation seulement, sans compter les millions dépensés soit par le candidat du pouvoir soit par les autres candidats.

Je ne sais pas combien de maisons auraient pu être construites ni de vies sauvées avec ces millions, mais ce n'était pas la priorité. Ce n'est pas la priorité. Je me demande combien d'entre nous devrons mourir pour que NOUS, la population, le peuple, soyons enfin la priorité de cet État, de ce gouvernement ? Nous ne sommes pas la priorité ! Notre priorité ! De toutes les façons, nous savons maintenant le lourd tribut de nos deux dernières catastrophes : Trois Cent Mille et Mille Six Cents ont respectivement péri, et ce n'est pas encore assez cher payé. Je me demande quel serait le nombre acceptable ?

Chaque mort que l'on compte est un épieu enfoncé dans les entrailles de toutes les mères car chacun d'entre eux est notre enfant. Il est à nous ! Il est à MOI ! Et j'en ai marre de les compter ! Marre ! A bout !

Je suis fatiguée de cette année 2010 qui n'en finit pas de nous anéantir. Mais je suis surtout fatiguée de ces candidats dont les discours sont vides et creux, faits de banalités et de lieux communs. De ces candidats et de leur entourage qui n'ont qu'un seul but : prendre le pouvoir. Quel pouvoir ? Un pouvoir de rien, dans un palais cassé, une ville-camp et des millions de sans-abri. Ils n'offrent rien. Ils ne proposent rien. Ils n'ont donc d'autre ambition que de le prendre et de le garder tel quel ! S'ils s'arrêtaient un moment pour voir combien ils sont tous minables de courir après ÇA, ils verraient que ÇA indique leur niveau de médiocrité. Mais aussi et surtout, leur niveau d'inconscience et de manque d'empathie pour une population et un pays qui se meurent.

C'est cela pour moi l'enfer : cette incapacité qu'ils ont TOUS d'avoir de l'empathie pour nous, le Peuple, nous qui souffrons. Comment voir ce pays et ne pas se dire : ils sont en enfer TOUS et nous avec.

Je les plains et nous aussi.

Comment passer devant ces camps et ne pas avoir le cœur qui saigne ? Comment voir ces enfants qui pleurent et ne pas avoir envie de les soulager de leurs maux ? Comment voir ce pays et ne pas se demander à quand le changement ?

Il ne mérite pas cela : ces énormes tout terrain blindés en cortège de plus de cinquante, ces personnes politiques qui promettent sans même savoir les besoins et les possibilités réelles de ce pays, ces enfants qui deviennent de la chair à canon, ces adultes que l'on paie pour qu'ils aillent voter et qui le font parce que cela leur permettra de nourrir leurs enfants pour un temps et parce qu'ils manquent d'ambition pour ce pays !

Je les regarde tous avec leurs sourires : certains triomphateurs déjà, d'autres narquois, et je me dis qu'ont-ils compris de nous ? Je les regarde avec leurs slogans bidons et je me dis : allons-nous passer encore cinq ans à patauger dans les excrétas et la crasse ? Ceux qui ont dépensé ces millions dans cette campagne-là ne sont pas capables d'avoir ni empathie, ni sympathie, ni compassion pour eux, pour nous. Sinon, ils auraient demandé à leurs commanditaires, leurs donateurs, de les aider à soulager les vrais maux de cette population souffrante, mourante. Mais, et c'est la quadrature du cercle, les donateurs ne donneraient pas pour cette cause-là. Cette cause-là n'a aucun retour sur investissement.

Dimanche. Je n'irai pas voter. Mesdames, Messieurs les Candidats, vous n'avez pas su gagner ma confiance, vous avez gagné ma méfiance et, considérant les circonstances et les catastrophes vécues, je suis fatiguée de vous. Je viens de faire dormir dans mes bras l'avenir de ma famille et peut-être de cette nation. Je pleure de n'avoir qu'un pays sans avenir, qu'un peuple sans ancrage et qu'une société divisée à lui offrir! Alors encore une fois . . . Pauvre Petit Pays !

In Haiti, Two Years after the Earthquake

Josiane Hudicourt-Barnes

On January 12, 2010, those of us who were in Port-au-Prince, Pétion-Ville, Delmas, Léogâne, Jacmel did not really understand what was happening around us. It was incomprehensible. We could not accept what we were seeing, hearing, feeling. For many of us, our entire world was crumbling before our eyes. For others, only part of their world collapsed. Yet we realized that this tragedy affected all of us; neither the amount we earned nor the shade of our skin nor our level of education shielded us from the horrors of the earthquake that day. Our everyday lives had radically changed. We were all sleeping outdoors; our fears of thieves and bad spirits were now less important than our fear of roofs collapsing, walls crumbling, and ground shaking. Nothing was for certain, not even the earth we stood on. We could no longer count on the solidity and stability of the world around us.

It was so sad, so ridiculously awful, that we could not even cry. Many of us prayed and sang; others fled. And, as is often said in Haiti, when a person loses a very close family member, things will never be the same again. Many of us spent our days helping one another, scrambling for resources for ourselves and for our neighbors, digging the wounded and the deceased out from the rubble. People came from all over the world to help us. Many lives were saved because of those who volunteered and those who sent supplies.

Others were completely hard-nosed. One funeral-home owner was inflexible about the fee he charged for his burial services. The price for a no-frills burial was US$6,000 cash, no exceptions. No credit, no checks. The exorbitant amount of cash needed for a funeral service is just one example of opportunists using this disaster to make money. With all the banks closed, what was a family to do with a loved one's body? They resorted to burying some in backyards, while other bodies were left in piles to be picked up by trucks going to Titanyen, an area north of Port-au-Prince that became a designated mass grave for earthquake victims. Another example of financial hardship is that rental prices for houses still standing doubled and tripled. And to compound matters, two major insurers in Haiti refused to pay the insured for their losses. These are all instances of the lack of justice in the country.

We thought that things would change completely in Haiti. Things had to change. We do so many things so poorly in our country. All aspects of our lives, community, and government are unstable. Many thought that this earthquake would be a chance to start over and force us to rebuild a better society, a better country; this was the hope.

I believe I might have predicted this catastrophe. Two months prior to the earthquake, I worked in the office of the then–Prime Minister of Haiti, Michèle Pierre-Louis, who was, at the time, being vilified by the Haitian press and the legislature for no valid reason. Her administration had done stellar work, in particular, following the March 2008 food riots and the four hurricanes that struck the country that summer. There was great confidence in her integrity and her capacity to produce positive change. On October 31, 2009, when she was voted out of office, I told one of my co-workers that I thought something really bad was going to happen to Haiti because we do too much wrong. I had this strange feeling that every destructive political move in Haiti was followed by a "natural" disaster.

The threat of natural disasters is very real in Haiti. Yet we lack the ability to respond and react to them in ways that reduce the loss of lives and livelihoods. We haven't yet learned from science or from experience. We don't plan ahead. We don't live for the common good. Public service and the welfare of the community are not motivators in Haiti. There is instead a concept called "degaje" whereby every person wants to find a way to make money, regardless of the legitimacy of the activity. How could there be ten million people trying to survive with no social services, no urban planning, no enforcement of regulations, no preventative measures, no justice?

We talk about our problems. We discuss what should be done, but those in charge of the governmental machinery rarely care and are most often incapable of efficient work. Ironically, "degaje" also produces genius, enterprise, and creativity; but personal ingenuity and drive cannot take the place of good management, planning, and fiscal responsibility in government.

Today we are not "building back better," as many had hoped. Makeshift homes, improvised neighborhoods, and schools and universities housed in temporary structures often located on steep slopes function and serve the population as well as they can. Our mountainous, hurricane-exposed land continues to lose its protective vegetation and topsoil, making it more prone to landslides. Our medical facilities and public health policies remain inadequate. Citizens of the country are not educated in preventative measures and health habits. Leaders talk persistently about petty issues while most of the population lives under precarious, difficult, and life-threatening conditions. After the *catastrophe* of 2012, some of us are more aware of safer ways to build, but the country continues to be just another disaster waiting to happen.

CRI DU CŒUR POUR HAÏTI : CHANGEMENT ET RECONSTRUCTION SONT-ILS DES UTOPIES ?

Marlène Racine-Toussaint

Le 12 janvier 2010, la date de l'effroyable séisme, restera sans nul doute inoubliable dans les annales de l'histoire de notre chère Haïti. A la vue des images projetées par les chaines de télévision à travers le monde, aucun être humain, haïtien ou pas ne put se permettre de rester insensible à un tel désastre. En effet, nous avons vu accourir à notre secours plusieurs pays du monde, des organisations internationales et privées et un nombre incalculable d'individus répondant spontanément à l'appel de leur cœur. Ce fut très beau et émouvant.

LA RÉACTION HAÏTIENNE

Quant à la réaction haïtienne, elle fut extraordinaire. Dans mon esprit, elle s'apparente aux efforts de solidarité, d'union, d'entente et de respect mutuel qu'ont fait nos ancêtres pour arriver à l'indépendance. Puisque je n'étais pas sur le terrain lors du séisme, les rapports d'amis victimes (ou non) ont en quelque sorte confirmé qu'à ce tournant de la vie nationale, nos frères et sœurs sont enfin arrivés à s'entendre, à se serrer les coudes, sans distinction de clan, de couleur, de classe. Un front uni a été formé pour faire face à ce nouvel état de choses. Des images que projetaient la télévision et la presse parlée et écrite permettaient de croire que le jour était enfin arrivé où les mots de notre emblème national « L'Union fait la force » allaient vraiment prendre corps.

On a vu hommes, femmes et mêmes des adolescents braver le danger pour porter secours aux sinistrés et chercher à sauver ceux qui étaient ensevelis sous les décombres. On a vu les employeurs dormir côte à côte, avec la domesticité, à la belle étoile, sur les trottoirs ou dans la cour de leurs grandes demeures. Cette proximité ne gênait personne dans ces moments de dure épreuve. On n'y pensait pas tout simplement.

Mais une fois ces premiers moments passés, la nature égoïste, méchante, répugnante, revancharde, profiteuse de la grande majorité a repris ses droits. Cette mosaïque infiniment diversifiée que représentait notre peuple, a reçu plusieurs brèches. Les préjugés de clan, de couleur, de classe et même de race ont repris le dessus. Cette plaie profonde qui ronge les cœurs et les esprits est réapparue encore plus béante.

LES ZONES D'OMBRE DE LA SOCIÉTÉ

Bien que les images du pays et de la catastrophe étaient répandues dans tous les medias du monde, j'étais toujours assoiffée de nouvelles fraiches et sures. Les gens se refugiaient aux États-Unis, ou bien parce qu'ils avaient perdu leur avoir, en biens meubles et immeubles, ou bien parce qu'ils avaient subi des pertes de vie humaine, ou encore parce que ils étaient traumatisés par le désastre. J'ai retenu, particulièrement, les paroles horribles de certains qui m'ont laissée abasourdie par leur méchanceté et leur manque d'humanité et de compassion pour les êtres humains.

Plusieurs racontaient en riant qu'ils payaient leurs domestiques pour rentrer dans la maison effondrée pour quérir certains objets. Ces fidèles serviteurs revenaient en courant, le visage rempli d'effroi craignant que le « goudougoudou » recommence et que l'immeuble ne s'effondre sur eux. Comment pareil spectacle ait pu causer des réactions de joie, de rires ou être des sujets de blagues? Que devenons-nous ? Où donc est passé cette soudaine et circonstancielle solidarité?

Le tremblement de terre a durement frappé les femmes, ce « poto mitan, » dont les conditions de vie n'ont pas toujours été très brillantes. En particulier, plusieurs des têtes de pont du mouvement féminin ont péri sous les décombres. Quelques années après, on les trouve encore dans une posture courbée sous le joug de la domination masculine. Elles ont été violées et abusées sous les tentes et les criminels sont restés impunis. Sur leurs visages ternes se lisent encore les reflets de la résignation et du désespoir. Plusieurs d'entre elles disent n'avoir aucun espoir de lendemains meilleurs. Malgré les promesses, elles ne voient pas encore la lumière au bout du tunnel.

Séjour en Haïti après le séisme

Je suis partie assez jeune d'Haïti pour aller étudier à l'étranger. Mon grand rêve était de retourner après avoir terminé mes études supérieures et mettre les connaissances acquises au service de mon pays. Les années terribles de l'époque duvalièrienne, les changements opérés au pays durant mon absence, les situations politique familiales, et mon changement d'état civil ont contribué aux affres de l'exil volontaire qui m'a gardé en otage à l'étranger. Les facteurs impondérables de la vie et les circonstances indépendantes de ma volonté ont conduit à cette triste réalité. J'étais devenue une « diaspora » et j'ai franchement ressenti du remords d'avoir si longtemps quitté mon pays.

Après le séisme, la nécessité de retourner au pays pour prêter main forte, dans la mesure de mes moyens, s'est fait sentir. Il y avait en moi ce besoin incompressible d'aller voir de mes yeux ce qui restait de ma ville natale. Servir sur le terrain était devenu une hantise et l'obligation de porter secours à mes frères et sœurs s'était tournée en obsession.

Quelques mois après le tremblement de terre, j'ai accompagné un groupe de professionnels étrangers qui ont exprimé le désir d'aider à la reconstruction et à la restructuration du pays. J'ai cru en la véracité de leur démarche. Malheureusement, j'ai vite réalisé que tout un chacun avait son agenda personnel. Cela m'a broyé le cœur. Je me suis alors dit qu'il est bien loin le temps où on verra notre rêve à tous se réaliser—une Haïti rénovée. D'aucun me jugeront certainement pessimiste mais les faits semblent me donner raison.

Les étrangers, comme des vautours profitent du désastre. Ils achètent tout, emportent nos ressources minières sous les yeux ahuris et incrédules des Haïtiens. Ils ont des plans extraordinaires qui ne sont pas adaptés à nos réalités. De toute évidence, le point de mire est Port-au-Prince. C'est naturel. L'épicentre était dans cette région qui a enregistré d'énormes pertes de vies humaines et de dégâts en biens meubles et immeubles. Après avoir visité quelques villes durant mon séjour avec ce groupe : Saint-Marc, Léogâne, Mirebalais, Saut d'Eau, Hinche, etc., force a été de constater que ces endroits bien que n'ayant pas été très fortement touchés par le séisme étaient dans un état tout à fait délabré. La misère qui sévissait est affreuse. En plus de tous ces maux, les politiques s'entredéchirent, c'est la lutte sans merci dont l'enjeu est le fauteuil bourré. Tandis que nous nous entredéchirons, il est clair que nous avons perdu notre souveraineté. Mon pays est vendu et je n'y puis rien.

Unforgotten

Claudine Michel

Vignette 1: Ertha, Port-au-Prince, Haiti, 1980

On a hot summer day in 1980 I found myself in a poor neighborhood of Martissant, waiting in the street for electricity to return before resuming filming a program I was then producing for the Télévision Nationale d'Haïti. While I was sitting on the curb, I had an encounter with a young girl that I remember vividly. She was from a modest background, perhaps even a *restavèk*,[1] and must have been about ten. I will call her Ertha.

It was the time of the "Réforme Bernard" advocacy for Kreyòl instruction in the school system, and resistance was strong in many sectors of Haitian society. I had asked Ertha whether she went to school, and if she enjoyed it. With none of the innocence that we know children to have at that age, a smirk appeared on her face. Her gaze signaled a level of awareness and cynicism that harsh poverty plants in the heart of the youth. Ertha, who attended a small neighborhood school, announced sassily: "*Matmwazèl la di m pale fransè. Egal, li di m pa pale!*" Those were hard words to hear from this frail little body, forced by life circumstances to grow up too soon. Clearly, she had already come to understand the meaning of being silenced.

Not unlike other children from impoverished nations—or from rich countries that relegate them to neighborhoods where it is intended that they should perish in jail or in the streets—Ertha had been handed the worst of life. The literal translation of what she had verbalized was powerful in and of itself—"The teacher telling me to speak in French [a language I do not know] amounts to her telling me that I am not allowed to speak."

This young girl was fiercely denouncing the rejection and silencing she felt subjected to—that *she mustn't be heard*, that *what* she had to say did not matter, and that ultimately, *she herself did not matter*.

I was at the time a student in the language and culture program at the École Normale Supérieure at the State University of Haiti. I had been learning about the need to reform our school system and the scientific theories that justified the Réforme Bernard, and also about desirable teaching methods and pedagogical techniques. That particular day in Martissant, I received instruction not from Piaget or Vygotsky, or even from esteemed linguist and early Kreyòl proponent Dr. Pradel Pompilus, one of the first Haitian scholars to receive a doctoral degree, but from young Ertha. Her lesson revealed matters that the regular curriculum had neglected to teach us—matters that children themselves understood when they felt ostracized and excluded: language opens doors but it also silences. Language is political. It is power.

REFLECTIONS: UP FOR GRABS

"Up for grabs!" A country up for grabs. Children up for grabs.

[Children] whose lives are put in brackets. Rejected, unloved. Forgotten.

I have used this expression often since the 2010 quake as it fundamentally captures some of my sentiments and frustrations *vis-à-vis* the international community. Six years after the seismic cataclysm that ravaged Haiti, as I prepared to write this piece, and while a bit of the same phenomenon is already happening following Hurricane Matthew, I finally looked up the meaning of that phrase.

"Up for grabs" means "available, obtainable, to be had for the taking; for sale, on the market; informal: for the asking, on tap, gettable."

To this day I am profoundly grateful for the genuine humanitarian help that arrived in Haiti after the earthquake. I honor, as much as those Haitian lives cut short, the lives of those foreign nationals who also perished on that fateful day, some of them far too young, like the six students from Lynn University in Boca Raton. I honor the soul sisters and brothers who respect and serve Haiti—some love Haiti as a second *Patrie*. But I also resent the takeover of my birth country and abhor the state of an occupied Haiti. Whatever happened to Haiti for Haitians? Whatever happened to raising children in Haiti with a bright future in a nation *"en voie de développement,"* the phrase I so often heard when I was a child growing up in Haiti? Even this phrase that we hated so much at the time seems to carry more promises of hope than the current reality.

Since the earthquake of January 12, 2010, this expression, "Up for grabs," has come to my mind repeatedly. It has haunted me as I witnessed the 11,000 NGOs that displaced grassroots projects and small neighborhood organizations that had been faithfully attending to community needs for twenty or thirty years. Foreigners everywhere. Many of them young and idealistic, some of them talented and some perhaps even well-meaning.

A country up for grabs. These young and not-so-young opportunists build careers through global networking, climbing social and economic ladders on the back of Haiti, looking for fame and political appointments as world experts in global poverty. There were job opportunities to be had, and the vultures arrived in full force.

Did it ever cross their minds that young Haitians would be suitable applicants for the kinds of positions they were given as so-called experts (sometimes trained in a week)? Does equivalent salary for equal work mean anything to racketeers who earned as much as ten or twenty times more than Haitians for the same labor? Did they ever consider that Haitians would have welcomed the option to learn a new trade and the possibility to work in their own sector with integrity? Haitians who owned successful community libraries, educational and social programs, agricultural co-ops, or small neighborhood clinics, or who fed thousands of children in small home cantinas did not see the money raised for Haiti by the international community. Might it have been too much to dream that Haitians would have the first pick at the opportunities to rebuild themselves? Would it have been too much to dream of new life rising where the ashes lay?

Up for grabs! Aid money up for grabs. A country up for grabs. A people up for grabs. A little girl up for grabs as her country has failed her, as the international community has let her down. A child, obtainable, to be had, for the taking, gettable!

VIGNETTE 2: ERTHA, SUN CITY, CALIFORNIA, 2010

Thirty years have passed and equity and access to schooling are still not a reality for all of our youth; despite a number of small advances,[2] some of our Haitian children still do not have the privilege to speak or learn in their native tongue, Kreyòl, in school.

This second story is also about language—or lack thereof. It is the story of another young girl, a five-year-old earthquake survivor, who traveled a few months after *Goudougoudou* to be adopted by a family in the United States. I will also call her Ertha —a child up for grabs.

***

On January 29, 2011, I was an invited panelist at the UCLA Fowler Museum at a one-day symposium marking the first anniversary of the quake. We were asked to tell *"Ti istwa Ayiti"* (little stories from Haiti), recounting the untold stories of people who might not have had the opportunity to be heard.

I told your story, Ertha

That day, Ertha, I told what I think is your story.

As an educator and as a Haitian mother, I said, I hurt today in a way I never have in the course of making a presentation. *I shared your story, Ertha, as I imagined it to be.* This is a story of poverty if I ever encountered one, I told the audience as I dried my tears, composing myself to speak.

> *Precious Ertha, I don't mean to speak for you, I don't mean to take away what in Haiti was for you suffering and pain, though you most likely did not know that it was that, except perhaps for the pouncing of hunger you might have felt those days you did not have enough to eat, or when you longed for a caretaker who did not return, or the friend who would no longer lie next to you on your* nat *made of straw, that makeshift bed where forgotten children try to catch some sleep at night.*

> *I don't mean to take away the joy you encountered in what was a loving transitional family in Sun City, in a home where there were three other lovely young Haitian girls, adopted themselves and held dear by their new family. It was obvious that these girls and their mother shared a lot of affection with you for the month you spent with them—in transition.*

Child of sunshine, I don't want to take away your joy of meeting your new mother, your new siblings in that cold state where you went to live. I don't want to take away your joy of entering this paradise of a bedroom that they had prepared for you with so much love. A Minnie Mouse outfit laid out on this dream bed (perhaps an outfit sewn by your own birth mother in Haiti).

Ertha, I don't want to take any of that away or the love that your adopted parents will have for you.

For loving you even before meeting you, I honor them.

I don't want to take away the love that you will return to them as a loyal daughter. Your joy of being an American—a Haitian American—and all that the future holds for you. I don't want to take any of this away. These are your joys to keep.

Ertha, I continued . . . Be happy. Be healthy. Be loved. Be proud of yourself and of your two countries. These are the wishes I have for you.

And know that I only tell your story so others may learn what happens to the forgotten children of this world.

Ertha's story is that of a young girl, neither disabled nor impaired in any way, who simply did not know language. She had not been nurtured through language. Like the story of the wolves who raised a German boy. Almost like the story of Romulus et Remus, the twins saved by the wolf.[3] You did not know language, as your innate linguistic abilities had not been reinforced. This is what extreme poverty does to some of our children. This is the work of racism, imperialism, greed, and corruption. Children left behind who are silenced in deep ways. Children who don't even have access to the tool of language.

In Sun City, the woman who served as mother figure for you during the month you spent in their home, your auntie I would call her, thought you were speaking Kreyòl as you made those unintelligible sounds she could not understand. As the date was nearing when your 'real' adopted parents were to come and fetch you, your auntie had called me to translate for her. She wanted me to explain to you that this new home where you had found solace was not your permanent home. She wanted me to tell you that they will always love you in Sun City. That she will remain your auntie.

That you had three cousins in this town. And that your new home was in a far away, very cold state. Your new mommy's name was Esther. She was waiting for you. She loved you already. She had sent photographs that you later proudly showed me. She had prepared a nice cozy room for you, had laid beautiful clothing on the brand new pink comforter awaiting you, and had toys everywhere ready to welcome you in your new home.

Little sweet Ertha, you ran to greet me at the door when I arrived. Your smile and warmth enraptured me. You gave me the biggest hug. I felt instant love.

But I soon discovered that my Kreyòl belle knew no language. She only made sounds. This is what I heard coming from your lips, expressed with confidence and style:

> *Men da pa ti di . . . Li tou en* [pause] *ma ka pi tou . . . Da wi nout do ka lè . . . Pa ti ka to . . . To lo wè . . . Bon pa m ak . . .* [smile] *Chen pi ay ban toto fi dò . . . dan dan dan . . .*

You would say it quickly with the right intonation, smiling, making eye contact as if you were having a full conversation with me, in your first language, giggling and cuddling with me, happy to relate to someone who seemed to care and who spoke to you in that language, the sounds of which you vaguely remembered. Clearly my Kreyòl made you happy—viscerally. I had brought home to you. Haiti was there with you. You felt it. I did too.

Chen pi ay ban toto fi dò . . . dan dan dan, you said . . .

All Kreyòl sounds you would utter with meaning only to you, while others thought we were speaking the same Krèyol.

⋆⋆⋆

Dan dan dan . . . dan dan dan . . . dan dan dan . . .

In my heart I heard the *ddddddd . . . dddddddd . . . dddddddd* of Èzili Dantò, whose tongue was cut off during the revolution. Èzili Dantò, mother archetype par excellence, perhaps was watching over her forgotten child.

Ertha, was your tongue cut off? Cut off like Èzili Dantò's? Why were you silenced? Like Èzili, did you try to displace forces that wanted to hold on to their power?

You uttered sound patterns recognizable to a Kreyòl speaker, but these were not Kreyòl words. For the uninformed ear, this sounded like Kreyòl. You were speaking. You simply did not know English. But while the sounds, syllables, and intonation of the language meant something familiar to a Kreyòl speaker like myself, this was not grammatical speech.

Remarkably, you had generated your own language system. Like a baby, you showed an infinite range of sound patterns, but unlike children with better opportunities, you had not been led to organize and channel those sounds into meaningful syntax.

***

You said "dog" in English when you saw the furry animal run with the other children in the house. At some point, in the midst of your *tou a si pa ma bag a re don pi ta lou . . . dan dan dan . . .* I heard you say an actual Kreyòl word when you showed me the photograph of the bed that awaited you in the cold city . . .

You said "KABANN," "bed" in Kreyòl. I heard it.

The word became my anchor.

I held onto it. KABANN, you repeated.

KABANN, KABANN, KABANN, KABANN!

The sound was familiar to your ear. You repeated it ad nauseam as you circled the dining room furniture, running, smiling, giggling . . . Haiti had visited you.

I knew it . . . The way you related affectively to me, hugging me, stroking my hand and caressing my hair, and smiling with your missing tooth and your *dent cariée,* a tooth with a cavity in front . . . The way you played with the other children . . . You were a vibrant little girl, smart, waiting for the world to embrace you.

I knew it. *I knew you had language in you, Ertha.*

Your language instinct had simply not been nurtured.

***

What kind of poverty prevents children from learning to speak their first language, and to relate *with* language with other human beings? Wretched poverty to an extraordinary degree. Occupied land where poor children are disposable commodities, up for grabs, at times adopted by monsters who rape and kill little girls from other countries, but most often by loving hearts who rescue these angels from this country where the arid sun dries lands that no longer produce.

I was so gratified—truly—when after about three hours of interaction with you, you did learn some words—real Kreyòl words that were added to the few English words that you had learned during your month in Sun City.

***

Action-oriented pedagogy tells us that a word is not yours, it is not mine, it is of the group. Language is, in many ways, relational. We learn in sociolinguistics that major aspects of language are apprehended through society and the community. These language elements are situational and contextual. They open doors to a system of knowledge, a system of relating to others. Language, in this way, is linked to opportunities or, in other cases, the lack thereof. This use of language signals that we inhabit a particular space, a particular social context; we read it, understand it, step into it, and relate.

Similarly, I will never forget that encounter I had with the other young Ertha thirty years earlier in Port-au-Prince; it was then that I first learned about the power of language. That was also when I was confronted with the *languages of power* in this world.

Language is relational. *No one related to you, Ertha. You sat in the orphanage all day on the floor, in a corner of the* galri *waiting for the bowl of* diri ak pwa kole *or* mayi moulen, *which would be your only meal for the day and would sustain your body. No one talked to you, precious little girl, no one interacted with you. No sustenance for your mind was offered. No sustenance for your soul.*

At five, Ertha, you spoke no language. Your language instinct had not been nurtured and was left, like a "dream deferred," to dry up like a grenn zanmann *in the sun.*

You had not been loved, forgotten little girl.

REFLECTIONS: DREAM OF REVOLUTION

Before beginning to share your story that day at the symposium, I paused. Wondered if the story was for me to tell as I pasted it together armed with my knowledge of psychology and sociolinguistics. Will my words ever get at the heart of this little Haitian girl's harrowing experience in her native country and her right to that other future? A future outside Haiti, away from her birth family, away from the sun that bathed her brown skin as a young girl, away from the trees that surrounded her, away from the *grenn kenèp* she might have chewed on if someone thought of giving her a taste of this delightful local fruit, away from her drums and stories, snatched away from the land of her ancestors. I still wonder. Is it my story to tell?

That day, I also read a poem that I penned in your honor, a poem titled "Unequal Distribution." The words spoke of what was happening to other little girls who remained in Haiti; it was a poem about haves and have-nots, about *moun an wo, moun an ba*, about dreams that never were. You had escaped, Ertha. I am glad that you left poverty behind but my heart continues to bleed as other little Erthas have not. My heart aches because you had the right to live free of poverty in your *own* country. When will this stop, I asked? How many children of poverty will continue to be taken out of their country, away from their own family, language, and culture—those forgotten children up for grabs?

I then began to speak: "I am grateful for this space to begin to tell your story, Ertha—you, this little frail five-year-old Haitian-born girl, whom I met in Sun City, California, while you were in transit to your adopted home in this cold northern state." What really is Ertha's story? Who could speak for her? Why was my encounter with this young girl so important to share? And what is even more poignant: will we ever really know her true story?

A psychologist friend in the audience at the Fowler Museum told me how much she was moved by the story. We discussed an alternative: the child had had language that she lost, traumatized by the quake. I did think about this alternative, I assured her. But in the grander scheme, I told her, frankly, to me the story is not that different. The poverty, corruption, and mistreatment of Haitians are what led to the devastation in Haiti during and after the quake. It is not the quake alone that killed and destroyed. When one considers that earthquakes with a similar magnitude in other parts of the world have killed 100 to 300 people versus the carnage that happened in Haiti—over 300,000 killed, 1.5 million displaced, 10 percent of the population now disabled— it is clear that while the quake caused damage, poverty is what killed.

So the quake is not what silenced this child. In either of those cases, *se lamizè ki fè ti moun nan pa pale!* Poverty shut her up.

For Ertha, for our other Haitian girls, let us end this cycle of poverty so these children can speak, literally and figuratively.

Let us build Haiti in a new way with Haitians at the center of the equation as both agents and beneficiaries of change in a land where the joyous sounds of happy children can fill our ears and hearts.

I dream of a new Haiti where young children will have a healthy future, loved by parents who can afford to feed them, who have work that they can accomplish with dignity, who want to build a future with and for their offspring, and who long to rebuild their country.

I dream of a bright future for our girls, Ertha, under the shining Haiti sun, *dans une Haïti heureuse.*

Maybe you will return to Haiti someday, grown, accomplished, perhaps in search of your birth mother's grave, hopeful and ready to share a future of hope with those who have remained.

> *Men da pa ti di . . . Li tou en ma ka pi tou . . . Da wi nout*
> *do ka lè . . . Pa ti ka to . . . To lo wè . . . Bon pa m ak . . .*

These were the sounds made by a little girl I will never forget. These were the sounds of poverty, neglect, abuse. These meaningless syllables are a *lanbi*[4] sounding a call to action to save our girls and the future of our country—ourselves, the Haitian way.

Ertha, here are the closing lines of the poem

I wrote for you soon after I met you.

> How many cups of revolution
> will it take to reconstruct and rebuilt Haiti?
> How many cups of revolution will it take for little [Ertha]
> to throw away her whistle[5] and dream of a new Haiti?

I now add:

> Indeed, what type of revolution is needed for Ertha to
> have equal chances in her own country, to enjoy the right
> to live with her own parents, who would earn a decent
> living in a nation that would allow them to raise their
> children with dignity, free of fear, in joy and happiness?
> What type of revolution will it take for Ertha to have
> access to an education, a relevant education, in her own
> language, an education *qui lui permettra de s'épanouir*,
> that will maximize all her life chances, that will open
> gates, *k ap louvri baryè a pou timoun yo*,[6] as mandated by
> the Declaration of Children's Rights?

VIGNETTE 3: A GROWN ERTHA, PORT-AU-PRINCE, HAITI, 2040

After thirty years of a happy life in the United States, Ertha returns to Haiti for a visit. She is grateful she can make the trip. She has learned Kreyòl. *Mèsi Jezi*, she says. *Mèsi Granmèt. Mèsi Zansèt yo.*[7]

She is accompanied by her young daughter, Ertha-Lynne. She wants to introduce her to the country of her birth. But more importantly she is there to reclaim her past, her native land, her language, and the people she never forgot—in her flesh and soul.

Unforgotten.

Notes

I struggled greatly in writing this story as I ventured into an arena in which I am not an expert. Emotionally, this was also heavy since I have been thinking about this first little girl for over thirty years now. I want to express my most sincere appreciation to *Tokay* Michel DeGraff for his helpful comments and insights, for pointing to the exact terms, and for his reassurance about the linguistic claims I was making. Kyrah M. Daniels offered invaluable suggestions about the question of voice that I was grappling with and noted that she had been deeply touched in reading an earlier version of the essay; she, along with others, gave me the confidence I needed to continue writing. Nadège T. Clitandre and Rose Elfman made several key suggestions and, along with LeGrace Benson, Florence Bellande Robertson, and Marlène Racine-Toussaint, convinced me that the story needed to be told in this volume. Thank you also to Anne Charity Hudley and Mary Bucholtz for verifying my use of the term "syllables." Lastly, a salute to Régine Michelle Jean-Charles who also dreams of a bright future for Ertha.

[1]   A term with deeply scarring connotations, *restavèk* is *yon ti moun ki rete ak granmoun*, an unpaid child worker, often abused and neglected. The fortunate ones may at times receive some schooling, while many remain bound to the house as unappreciated laborers who never really become members of the family.

[2]   See Michel DeGraff's response to Danielle Allen, "What Is Education For?," *Boston Review*, May 9, 2016, http://bostonreview.net/forum/what-education/michel-degraff-michel-degraff-responds-danielle-allen. More generally, DeGraff's work with the MIT-Haiti initiative has already created significant shifts in educational outcomes with Kreyòl STEM instruction, while also emphasizing the liberatory potential of instruction delivered in Haitian Kreyòl. Children's stories such as *Fabiola Goes to School* (2016) and *Fabiola Konn Konte* (2012) by Katia D. Ulysse offer hope for Haitian *restavèk* and the possibility of language instruction in Kreyòl as a viable solution. *Epitou, chapò ba* for the extraordinary contributions of EDUCA Vision, the sole publisher of Haitian educational material in the United States, which has consistently produced reading material and software in Kreyòl and in bilingual format for over twenty years.

[3]   Beyond various stories and mythological tales of children raised by wolves, apes, and bears, there seems to be evidence of several "feral" children: victims of neglect, abuse, and social isolation that resulted in a lack of language acquisition. Genie, born in California on April 18, 1957, is apparently one of the last cases, studied until her mother finally forbade any more scientific observations of her in 1978.

[4]   *Lanbi* is the large conch shell used during the Haitian revolution to call and rally the troops and organize community. It has become a symbol of liberty and freedom in Haiti and in other parts of the world.

[5]   After the quake in Haiti, young girls in tent cities were given whistles to wear around their necks and alert others to avoid the pouncing hands of assailants wanting to sexually assault and rape them. See Claudine Michel, "Unequal Distribution and Other Poems," in *Pawòl Fanm sou Douz Janvye, Meridians* 11, no. 1 (2011): 159.

[6]   Claudine Michel, "Louvri baryè pou timoun yo," address delivered at a conference on Haitian Children's Education, Bronx Community College, May 17, 2013.

[7]   Thank you, Jesus. Thank you, Creator. Thank you, Ancestors.

PART IV
FORESHOCKS
REPRESENTATION AND IMAGE

Haïti ou la santé du malheur

Yanick Lahens

À 4 heures 53 minutes, le mardi 12 janvier 2010, Haïti a basculé dans l'horreur. Le séisme a duré une minute trente secondes. Debout dans l'embrasure d'une porte, pendant que les murs semblent vouloir céder tout autour, le sol se dérobe sous vos pieds, une minute trente secondes c'est long, très long. Dans les secondes qui ont suivi, la clameur grosse de milliers de hurlements d'effroi, de cris de douleur, est montée comme d'un seul ventre des bidonvilles alentour, des immeubles plus cossus autour de la place et est venue me saisir la gorge jusqu'à m'asphyxier. Et puis j'ai ouvert le portail de la maison. Sur le commencement de l'horreur. Là, déjà, au bout de ma rue. Des corps jonchés au sol, des visages empoussiérés, des murs démolis. Avec cette certitude que plus loin, plus bas dans la ville, ce serait terrifiant. Nous avons tout de suite porté secours aux victimes mais nous ne pouvions pas ne pas pleurer.

Et dans ce crépuscule tropical toujours si prompt à se faire dévorer par la nuit, je n'ai pas pu m'empêcher de poser cette question qui me taraude depuis : pourquoi nous les Haïtiens ? Encore nous, toujours nous ? Comme si nous étions au monde pour mesurer les limites humaines, celles face à la pauvreté, face à la souffrance, et tenus par une extraordinaire capacité à résister et à retourner les épreuves en énergie vitale, en créativité lumineuse. J'ai trouvé mes premières réponses dans la ferveur des chants qui n'ont pas manqué de se lever dans la nuit. Comme si ces voix qui montaient, tournaient résolument le dos au malheur, au désespoir. J'ai parcouru le lendemain matin une ville chaotique, jonchée de cadavres, certains déjà recouverts d'un drap blanc ou d'un simple carton, des corps d'enfants, de jeunes, empilés devant des écoles, des mouches dansant déjà autour de certains autres, des blessés, des vieillards hagards, des bâtiments et des maisonnettes détruits. Il ne manquerait que les trompettes de l'Ange de l'Apocalypse pour annoncer la fin du monde si le courage, la solidarité et l'immense patience des uns et des autres ne sont pas venus nous rattacher au plus tenu de l'essentiel . . .

UNE LONGUEUR D'AVANCE

A ce principe d'humanité, de solidarité qui ne devrait jamais faire naufrage et que les pauvres connaissent si bien. Pour dire la puissance de la vie. Ces vivants si farouchement vivants dans une ville morte. Patients jusqu'à l'extrême limite. Les quelques inévitables pillards systématiquement relayés par la presse internationale ne font pas le poids face à tant de vie et de dignité revendiquées.

Et je tirai ma leçon en pensant à un mot de Camus envoyé par un ami écrivain : « Nous avons maintenant la familiarité du pire. Cela nous aide à lutter encore. » Cet acharnement m'a semblé non point le fait d'une quelconque fatalité (laissons cela à ceux qui voudraient encore par paresse ou dérobade évoquer le cliché d'une Haïti maudite) mais celui d'une suite de hasards qui nous ont propulsés au cœur de tous les enjeux du monde moderne. Pour de nouvelles leçons d'humanité. Encore et encore . . .

Hasard géologique qui nous a fixés sur la faille dantesque des séismes, hasard géographique qui nous a placés sur la route des cyclones en nous sommant, en sommant le monde de repenser à chacune de ces catastrophes, les causes profondes de la pauvreté. Hasard historique qui nous a amenés à réaliser l'impensable au début du XIXe siècle, une révolution pour sortir du joug de l'esclavage et du système colonial. Notre révolution est venue indiquer aux deux autres qui l'avaient précédée l'américaine et la française, leurs contradictions et leurs limites, qui sont celles de cette modernité dont elles ont dessiné les contours, la difficulté à humaniser le Noir et à faire de leurs terres des territoires à part entière. A la démesure du système qui nous oppressait nous avons répondu par la démesure d'une révolution. Pour exister. Exister, entre autres, au prix d'une dette à payer à la France, au prix d'une mise au ban des nations. Ce qui ne nous a pas soustraits du devoir de solidarité agissante envers tous ceux qui, comme Bolivar en Amérique latine ou ailleurs, au début de ce XIXe siècle, luttaient pour leur liberté. Et puisque nous avons ouvert la terre d'Haïti à tous ceux-là, nous avons une longueur d'avance dans ce savoir-là. Savoir qui se révèle d'une brûlante actualité dans ce moment où, à travers la catastrophe qui frappe Haïti, devrait se jouer la réciproque et pourquoi pas la redéfinition sinon la refondation des principes de la solidarité à l'échelle mondiale.

La Révolution américaine et la Révolution française, contrairement à la nôtre, ont, elles, su faire avancer la question de la citoyenneté. Nous n'avons pas su user de la constance et de la mesure qu'exigeait la construction de la citoyenneté qui aurait dû mettre les hommes et les femmes de cette terre à l'abri de conditions infra-humaines de vie. Parce que la démesure a ses limites, la glorification stérile du passé comme refuge aussi. Qu'on se souvienne de Césaire qui fait dire à l'épouse du roi Christophe, dans la tragédie du même nom, de prendre garde que l'on ne juge les malheurs des fils à la démesure du père.

SUR UN PIED D'ÉGALITÉ

En dépit de ces limites-là, en dépit de sa pauvreté, de ses vicissitudes politiques, de son exiguïté, Haïti n'est pas une périphérie. Son histoire fait d'elle un centre. Je l'ai toujours vécu comme tel. Comme une métaphore de tous les défis auxquels l'humanité doit faire face aujourd'hui et pour lesquels cette modernité n'a pas tenu ses promesses. Son histoire fait qu'elle dialogue sur un pied d'égalité avec le reste du monde. Qu'elle oblige encore aujourd'hui à la faveur de cette catastrophe à poser les questions essentielles des rapports Nord-Sud, celles aussi fondamentales des rapports Sud-Sud, et à ne pas esquiver les questions et les urgences de fond. Qu'elle soit aussi plus que jamais ses élites dirigeantes à changer radicalement de paradigme de gouvernance. Tous les symboles déjà faibles de l'État se sont effondrés, la population est aux abois et la ville dévastée. De cette *tabula rasa* devra naître un État enfin réconcilié (même partiellement) avec sa population.

Mais Haïti donne une autre mesure tout essentielle du monde, celle de la créativité. Parce que nous avons aussi forgé notre résistance au pire dans la constante métamorphose de la douleur en créativité lumineuse. Dans ce que René Char appelle « la santé du malheur. » Je n'ai aucun doute que nous, écrivains, continuerons à donner au monde une saveur particulière.

Port-au-Prince, Haïti, dimanche 17 janvier 2010

When I Wail for Haiti: Debriefing (Performing) a Black Atlantic Nightmare

Gina Athena Ulysse

> *We wonder . . . if it is the sound of that rage which must always remain repressed, contained, trapped in the realm of the unspeakable.*
>
> —bell hooks, *Killing Rage*[1]

> *And if that rage is not uttered, spoken, expressed then what becomes of it? So much has been written deconstructing the mad white woman relegated to the attic. Less is known of black female rage for there is usually no place for it. Its very articulation is a social death sentence especially in mixed company. Her rememories stay crushed in her body, her archive. She dare not speak. Shut your mouth. Careful. There is a place for unruly little girls like you who do not know when to be quiet. When not to offend white sensibilities. When not to choke. When to submit. Shhhhhh—Take a deep breath. Swallow. There is no safe word.*[2]
>
> —Gina Athena Ulysse, "(4) Her Rage"

Days after January 12, 4:53:10 p.m. when the earthquake ravaged my birth country, I told one of my dearest friends that part of me secretly wished I could just go on top of Wesleyan University Foss Hill, get on my knees, raise both arms in the air, and scream at the top of my lungs until I was totally spent.

Just don't let anybody see you, he warned me. We laughed it out and talked about consequences of being deemed unhinged. Indeed, the last thing I need is for people to think I have come undone. I am already outside the box and something of an endangered species. I am a tenured black woman. A black Haitian woman at that. A black Haitian woman who has always spoken her mind way before tenure. A black Haitian woman without a recognizable last name, as I like to say to those unfamiliar with my birth country's class and color politics. I have ascended to and made a space for myself in a new social world that in many ways eluded generations before me who lacked such access or had other freedom dreams. As Bill T. Jones has so aptly put it, I have had as much freedom as I have been willing to pay for. That said, I am an "established" faculty member at a small but well respected university, albeit one whose expressive breadth and professional maneuverings upset disciplinary lines to create "nervous conditions"[3] among purists. Though I was trained as a cultural anthropologist, I cannot afford to lose it, and certainly not in public. I am also an activist, a poet/performance artist, and a multimedia artist.

So, I did the next best thing: I consolidated all my energies and exposed my pain and rage on stage.

I had been performing my one-woman show "Because When God Is Too Busy: Haiti, Me and THE WORLD" for several years now. In one of its earliest renditions, I describe this work as a dramatic monologue that considers how the past occupies the present. In it, I weave history, theory, and personal narrative in spoken word with Vodou chants to reflect on childhood memories, social (in)justice, spirituality, and the incessant dehumanization of Haitians.

My first full post-quake performance was on February 4 at the chapel of my home institution. Although I was on sabbatical, I volunteered to perform in part because I simply needed to let it out. This work, which contains musings on my relationship with Haiti from the aftermath of migration in my early teens through a grueling graduate school experience, is part coming-of-age, part conscientization, and part hollering.

It was during the early years of my graduate training that I began to actively perform, in part to retain my childhood dream of wanting to be a singer, to ground myself and allow my creative spirit to breathe through a restructuring process that threatened to desensitize me. Performance for me then was a cathartic act of defiance. It became a platform to express my newfound acceptance of the fact that silence is just another structure of power that I simply refused to recreate. A rejection of docility. It was a determination to disclose That Which

Must Be Kept Private if we are not to disrupt the order of things and reap the rewards of playing along. Complicity is condemned. After earning the doctoral degree, and once I began teaching full-time, performing became a lifeline, a space to exercise an opposition to the contained or bifurcated self required by professionalism. Most importantly, it has always provided me with the space to continually engage my commitment to Haiti.

Performance for me is what I call an alter(ed)native—"a counter-narrative to the conventionalities of the more dominant approaches in anthropology. . . . It connotes processes of engagement from an anti- and post-colonial stance, with a conscious understanding that there is no clean break with the past. With that in mind, alter(ed) native projects do not offer a new riposte or alternative view; rather, they engage existing ones, though these have been altered . . . co-opted and manipulated to 'flip the script' and serve particular anti-and post-colonial goals."[4] Hence, I begin with the unequivocal premise that colonialism had fractured the subject. Determined to not leave the body behind, the alter(ed)native is a mindful and loving attempt at a gathering of the fragments in pursuit of integration. In that sense, the alter(ed)native is unapologetically a political project.

On the stage, I am motivated by a sheer will to step into and confront the growing and gnawing web of a recurring black Atlantic nightmare with unspoken gendered dimensions that remains archived in our bodies. It is trapped in aspects of what Carl Jung calls our "collective unconscious,"[5] for lack of a better term.

I did not intend to do this, but neither was it completely *par hasard*. Rather, the auto-ethnographic process of deconstructing the personal, in which I engaged in my first book on Jamaica (where I did my doctoral research), spilled into my internal dialogues about Haiti. As a result, I found myself using my past to make connections to the social that further revealed national and international trends that have been inscribed *ad infinitum* and could still benefit from more visceral explorations.

The more that I perform, the more it has occurred to me that in fact, we actually know very little of the primordial of Haitian experiences. Though we have seen countless images and heard the cries, the wails, especially recently. Random women covered with dust roaming the street. Searching for their loved ones. Screaming. These are roving disoriented beings historically perceived as devoid of logic.

The *show* always begins with me chanting somewhere on the premises or in the audience (never back stage). The chant becomes a loop as I walk through the parameters of the space (often to form a circle) until I face the audience and then take center stage. Prior to the earthquake, I chanted the original lyrics I remember from childhood:

> *Noyé nape noyé*
> (Drowning we are drowning)
> *Noyé mapé noyé*
> (Drowning I am drowning)
> *Ezili si we'm tonbé lan dlo, pranm non*
> (Ezili if you see us fall in the sea, take us)
> *Métres, so we'm tonbé lan dlo, pranm non*
> (Goddess if you see us fall in the sea, save us)
> *Sové lavi zenfan yo noyé napé noyé*
> (Save the lives of your children, because we are drowning)

After the quake, I changed the words. By the time, I performed on February 4, there had been over fifty aftershocks. Estimated death was being reported then at 200,000, and the mass graves were being filled with the unidentified. So then drowning became trembling. Trembling the earth trembled. Trembling we are trembling. Ezili should we tremble again, hold us. Save the lives of your children because the earth is trembling.

I used repetitions of this chant as a portal—to access the body and keep it present. It is interwoven between pieces as a reminder of the ultimate aim of the work. We had gathered here to process and discuss a major catastrophe. I stopped the performance halfway through to present a dispatch from Haiti. I closed the show with words of a conversation with a friend.

After that night, I began to improvise in other performances. I shortened the "me" parts of the original text (and analyses of past moments of conflict in Haiti as these were becoming less immediately consequential given the urgency of the current situation) and began to include voices of people in Haiti. By the time, I did my last performance at LaMaMa on December 13, all the original pieces were abruptly interrupted with dispatches from Haiti, from people whom I had either encountered online or interviewed during my two post-quake trips. Their voices made the performance current. Most importantly, the stage became a platform to give *immediate visibility* to those without. The show then became a hybrid living newspaper.

With each performance I did in the past year, I became increasingly aware of the fact that we do not know or have never confronted Haiti's pain. We have talked about it. Written about it incessantly. Some have actually engaged with it. Still we have never sat with it in its rawest form and let it be. It has always been smothered. Shhhhhh. Not in public and certainly not in mixed company. Somatic theories tell us that in many ways some of it is still there. Trapped. It remains unprocessed trauma.

This past year, in light of the impact of the earthquake at home and abroad, I began to think more and more about the absence of discussions of psychoanalytical explorations of the experiences of Haitians in the aftermath of the Revolution. We have no substantive record of those moments of fracture, of pain when screams stemmed from deep within before they found constructed expression, sometimes in rage. The little we know of those moments comes from the fearful gaze of colonizers. What did we sound like to ourselves? I keep wondering what could Ayiti—this land where spirits inhabit permanent resting places in nature—tell us about the collective and individual sounds we made in the aftermath of the Revolution.

The earthquake for me is another pivotal moment of collective horror that must not be smothered, especially since we have so many tools with which we can record and are recording it. In the latest installment of the show, I interrupt the personal with individual quotes and statistics about post-quake conditions. The Vodou chants are there as signification of the ethical that is to highlight the moral imperatives at play. Coupled with history, this weave is now deployed to foster more textured and multivocal possibilities. This approach is particularly relevant since daily life is not compartmentalized. Indeed, people live, make, and remake themselves in a messy world that continuously begs for interdisciplinary crossings. I begin with the premise that theory alone simply cannot enclose the object of study, as anthropologist Michel-Rolph Trouillot has succinctly put it.[6] So I go deep within. I collect what I call my ethnographic collectibles (excess bits unfit for publication because they were too personal, too raw, or seemingly trivial) and recycle them. I shut out the world to access that which I have been socialized to repress. Trained academic. Repress. Digging deep to find ways to express a history of violence. Repress. I consciously and rather expertly manipulate my voice and let it out knowing I am crossing boundaries. Re-sowing seeds that caused white fears of a black planet. Exposing bourgeois attachments to the restraint. Trading with different forms of capital. Undoing reason. More specifically undoing enlightened reason.[7]

To perform a reassembly of the fragments Toni Morrison insists needs to occur in a clearing,[8] I select the stage to confront the visceral embedded in the structural. Performance becomes a public clearing of sorts, a site to occupy and articulate the embodied. The primeval. Releasing sound bites of the horror. Unhinging the raw. That which for black women must too often remain unspeakable.

Wailing is my chosen method of intervention.

Notes

This article was originally published on February 13, 2011, in *Postcolonial Body Performance Narratives*. Reprinted with permission from the author.

1   bell hooks, *Killing Rage* (New York: Henry Holt, 1995).

2   Gina Athena Ulysse, "(4) Her Rage," excerpt from "VoodDooDoll, What If Haiti Were a Woman: On ti Travay sou 21 Pwen Or an Alter(ed) native in Something Other Than Fiction," *Because When God Is Too Busy: Haiti, Me & THE WORLD* (Middletown, CT: Wesleyan University Press, November 2016).

3   This is the title of Jean Paul's Sartre's introduction to Frantz Fanon's *Wretched of the Earth* (1961), which was reiterated by Lisa Malkki and Allaine Cerwonka in "Nervous Conditions: The Stakes in Interdisciplinary Research," in their book *Improvising Theory: Process and Temporality in Ethnographic Fieldwork* (Chicago: University of Chicago Press, 2007).

4   Gina Athena Ulysse, *Downtown Ladies: Informal Commercial Importers, A Haitian Anthropologist and Self-Making in Jamaica* (Chicago: University of Chicago Press 2008).

5   C. G. Jung, *Civilization in Transition (The Collected Works of C. G. Jung, Volume 10)*, 2nd ed. (Princeton, NJ: Princeton University Press, 1970).

6   Michel-Rolph Trouillot, "The Caribbean: An Open Frontier in Anthropological Theory," *Annual Review of Anthropology* 21 (1992): 19–42

7   I thank Gillian Goslinga for pointing out the qualification. Indeed, it is enlightenment that is at stake.

8   Toni Morrison, *Beloved* (New York: Alfred Knopf, 1987).

VESSELS FOR HAITI

Anna Wexler & Catherine Tutter

VESSELS FOR HAITI II and III were interactive, community-engaged performances initiated by Catherine Tutter and Anna Wexler with healing intentions for Haiti in response to the catastrophic earthquake of 2010. The focal point of these events was a co-created memory vessel with reference to such forms used in the practice of Haitian Vodou. In an earlier participatory event responding to the earthquake, Catherine spun individual written contributions of poetry, stories, drawings, and prayers for those who perished into paper yarn, splicing them all into one continuous skein. Anna and Catherine then affixed this encoded yarn to the bottle in a ritual binding action to centralize the authentic power of each participant's expression of sorrow for the loss of each life, known and unknown, and hopes for recovery in Haiti.

As an object of spiritual remembrance and compassionate response, our vessel continued to birth a field of expression in the production of hand-worked materials during VESSEL FOR HAITI II, in November 2010, at the Mobius Artists Space in Boston, Massachusetts. Participants engaged one-on-one with individual artists in intimate acts of reflection and creation of embellished bottles, sequin-illuminated textiles, spun paper yarn, and other forms to enhance and extend the healing intention of the bottle (Figure 1). In this twelve-hour performance event, meditative conversations and artistic actions explored the ethics of shared loss and compassionate action in response to the ongoing suffering in Haiti.

VESSEL FOR HAITI III was impelled by Edwidge Danticat's text "A Year and a Day" (*The New Yorker*, January 17, 2011), in which she invokes Vodou traditional belief that the souls of the dead dwell

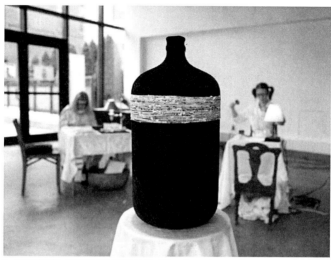

Figure 1. VESSEL FOR HAITI II. The bottle and yarn, with participants sewing in the background. Photo courtesy of the authors.

under the water for this amount of time, after which they are ritually reborn into the community of the living. As Danticat writes, "I heard one of the survivors say, either on radio or television, that during the earthquake it was as if the earth had become liquid, like water. That's when I began to imagine them, all these thousands and thousands of souls, slipping into the country's rivers and streams, then waiting out their year and a day before reemerging and reclaiming their places among us. And, briefly, I was hopeful."

Imbued with the hope emanating from this transformation, the site-specific performance actions in VESSEL FOR HAITI III took place on a pier in the Hudson River as part of a Mobius event at New York City's 2011 Fountain Art Fair (Figure 2). With the bottle as a focal point and driver, Catherine and Anna engaged audience participants in the ritual construction of a ceremonial raft filled with offerings, including flowers around which were wrapped paper strips inscribed with the names of those who perished. The same names were etched into the Memorial Wall. The raft was launched into the river in honor both of those experiencing the spiritual metamorphosis of rebirth, and of Agwe, the Vodou spirit of the sea, believed to transport the souls of the dead under the water where their ancestors dwell.

Figure 2. VESSEL FOR HAITI III. Participants contributing to the raft's construction. Photo courtesy of the authors.

HAITI: THE PRICE OF FREEDOM

Carolyn Cooper

In the days when BWIA (British West Indian Airways) used to fly to Haiti, I once sat next to a man named François. François asked me to help him fill out his immigration form. His occupation was "painter," and as he was about to get off the plane, he gave me an unexpected gift—one of his paintings. I'd mistakenly assumed he was a house painter. To be honest, I thought the painting rather touristy. It was a landscape, with clouds, birds, trees, and houses all lined up symmetrically. Only the people were placed randomly.

All the same, I was touched by the gesture. The painter's generosity far exceeded the small service rendered. But dismissively setting it aside, I took more than a decade to frame the painting. I was amazed to see how the defining border transformed what I'd thought derivative into vibrant art. By investing in a frame, I'd decided that the painting was worthwhile, that it was, in fact, art. It makes you wonder about how perception is altered by the ways in which we frame reality.

"A PACT TO THE DEVIL"

Take, for instance, Pat Robertson's lunatic perspective on the catastrophic earthquake in Haiti. Founder and chairman of the Christian Broadcasting Network, Robertson, a former Republican candidate for the US presidency, makes Sarah Palin look like a certified intellectual. In an interview on January 13, Robertson made a preposterous declaration. He said: "You know, Kristi, something happened a long time ago in Haiti and the people might not want to talk about it. They were under the heel of the French. Ah, you know, Napoleon the 3rd and whatever. And they got together and swore a pact to the devil. They said we will serve you if you'll get us free from the French. True story. And so the devil said, 'OK, it's a deal.' And ah they kicked the French out. You know, the Haitians revolted and got themselves free. But ever since they have been cursed by one thing after the other."

Where do you start to unravel the knots of confusion? First of all, I just love that eloquent "whatever." Wikipedia defines the slang word as "an expression of (reluctant) agreement, indifference, or begrudging compliance." As used here by Robertson, "whatever" signifies a total suspension of thought. The brutality of enslavement by the French is reduced to mindless indifference.

PAYING FRANCE REPARATIONS

In Robertson's "true story," the devil and the Haitian freedom fighters are in cahoots. In their pact, the devil promises to liberate the people. But in the next sentence Robertson uses "they": "and ah they kicked the French out." Is this "they" the combined forces of the devil and the Haitian people?

Or is Robertson unconsciously conceding that the people, more than the devil, had a hand (and a foot) in their emancipation? He does go on to say that "the Haitians revolted and got themselves free." But that rather peculiar turn of phrase "got themselves free" takes us right back to the claim that freedom was a gift from the devil.

Furthermore, Robertson asserts that in exchange for this devil-rendered freedom, Haiti is cursed. Here this simpleminded Christian minister edges away from the lunatic fringe and right into the arms of the "mainstream" analysts of the plight of the Haitian people: Had Haiti remained a colony of France, like the overseas Departments of Martinique, Guadeloupe, and French Guyana, how blessed the people would now be! But no. The Haitian people dared to declare their independence. And just look at how pauperized they are.

It is still not widely known that Haiti was forced to pay 90 million gold francs in reparations to France for its independence and for the value of its slaves. This vast sum is equal to more than US$21 billion today. Haiti had to borrow the money from French banks to pay it off. The repayment of this debt stretched out over decades and had a devastating impact on the Haitian economy. At the end of the nineteenth century, 80 percent of Haiti's national budget was still being spent on debt repayment and interest. Sounds like an IMF (International Monetary Fund) agreement, a truly devilish pact.

The US refused to recognize the new Haitian republic and imposed an embargo that lasted until 1862. In 1915, the US invaded Haiti to protect its economic interests. The US occupied Haiti until 1934. Local Haitian leaders were no less predatory than foreign forces, as demonstrated in the truly terrifying reign of Papa and Baby Doc. But there was also the redemptive Aristide who affirmed social justice as an essential Christian principle. He was deposed in a military coup.

HAITIANS IN PORTMORE

As crazy as Pat Robertson's explanation for the Haiti earthquake was, it's not that different from the account I got from a man who works in construction in my neighborhood. He said: "Is because of all a di gun dem weh di Haitian dem a bring inna Jamaica. Whole heap a AK47. Dem exchange di gun fi ganja." To my vain attempt to reason with this man, he responded: "A through you don't know. Nuff Haitian inna Portmore."

This is a classic example of how other Caribbean people still demonize Haitians. We forget about our shared history. It was a Jamaican, Boukman Dutty, who spearheaded the Haitian Revolution. In August 1791, Boukman/Book Man, so named because he was literate, conducted the religious ceremony at Bois Caïman in which a freedom covenant was affirmed, Pat Robertson's so-called "pact with the devil." Whatever.

When I think of Haiti, it's not the poverty that first comes to mind. It's the magnificent art created by these resilient people. I know that out of the rubble of this earthquake the Haitian people will rise yet again. And they don't need the help of the devil.

Note

First published in the *Sunday Gleaner* (Jamaica) on January 17, 2010. Reprinted with permission from the author.

THE USES OF VODOU: HISTORICAL AND POST-EARTHQUAKE REFLECTIONS

Kate Ramsey

The international response to the January 12, 2010, earthquake in Haiti was strong, but in the days and weeks that followed it became clear that the greatest initiative and leadership in the face of the catastrophe were coming not from international relief agencies and organizations, nor from the Haitian government, but from the survivors themselves. This was particularly true in impoverished areas in and outside Port-au-Prince where aid was slow to arrive, if it ever did at all. Stories of self-organization, mutual aid, and solidarity became a mainstay of international reporting on the disaster and a welcome counterpoint to the disempowering and patronizing images of the Haitian poor that were ubiquitous, including in fundraising solicitations and other well-intentioned appeals.

In the early days following the earthquake, there was renewed interest outside Haiti in a question that the US media often posed like this: Why is Haiti so poor? Alongside the analysts who addressed that problem in its complexity,[1] there were also commentators who in high-profile editorials located the root of Haiti's poverty in its "culture," and particularly in the religion that they called "voodoo." David Brooks in the *New York Times* contended that Haiti suffered from "a complex web of progress-resistant cultural influences," including "the voodoo religion, which spreads the message that life is capricious and planning futile." As an authority on Haiti, Brooks cited Lawrence Harrison, a former official in the United States Agency for International Development in Haiti, who now runs the Cultural Change Institute at Tufts University.[2] A few weeks later, Harrison made his own intervention on the subject in the pages of the

Wall Street Journal, declaring that Haiti had "defied all development prescriptions" because its "culture is powerfully influenced by its religion, voodoo," which he described as devoid of "ethical content." Both Brooks and Harrison asserted in their respective editorials that "voodoo" was a progress-impeding force, and Brooks made that contention the partial basis for his conclusion that a more "intrusive paternalism" was called for on the part of the United States and the international community toward Haiti, asserting that this would represent a break with the "same old, same old" approaches to development.[3]

In fact, there was nothing new in Brooks' prescription of such a solution, nor in his and Harrison's claim that "voodoo" obstructed progress and contributed to or even produced poverty in Haiti. To take a few examples, in 1796, five years after the start of the massive slave revolts in northern Saint-Domingue and nearly three years after general emancipation, France's commissioners in the colony legally prohibited for the first time what they called "the dance known by the name of *Vaudou*" on the grounds that it was contrary to republican institutions, good morals, public health, public safety, and, implicitly, the strict plantation labor regime to which most of the formerly enslaved were subject.[4] In the late 1890s the French bishop of Cap-Haïtien, who led the first major Roman Catholic "crusade" against "*le vaudoux*" in Haiti after the return of the church in 1860, anticipated both the assertions of Brooks and Harrison and the televangelist Pat Robertson's much-publicized interpretation of the 2010 earthquake as the consequence of a revolutionary-era "pact with the devil." The bishop charged that "*le vaudoux*" both cursed Haiti in the eyes of God and was impeding national economic progress: "a dancing people," he warned, "degraded by savage orgies, will never be a working people."[5] During the US occupation of Haiti between 1915 and 1934, American civil and military officials claimed at one time or another that "voodoo" was an obstacle to the rule of law, foreign investment, economic prosperity, and the moral and physical welfare of the Haitian population. It served as both an explanation for Haiti's problems and a pretext for an earlier "intrusive paternalism" that disrupted the lives of the Haitian rural poor in myriad ways, not least through the repression of their religious practices.[6]

As these historical antecedents make clear, Brooks's and Harrison's pronouncements were rooted in the long-standing assumption that (among other ills) Vodou is not just unmodern (and thus, in the logic of modernist development, destined to decline), but actively anti-modern, obstructing the linear course of progress in Haiti. Both assumptions have been challenged by a host of scholars and practitioners in recent years who argue that Vodou and other African diasporic religions were born of the forces and process of modernity under slave regimes across the Atlantic World and are today, as Stephan Palmié has put it, as "modern as nuclear thermodynamics."[7] For any semblance of plausibility, the idea that Vodou is a chief cause of poverty in Haiti depends on the denigrating way the religion has long been represented by outsiders, the political force of which is clearly far from being exhausted and has always materially impacted the Haitian majority. That in the immediate wake of the January 2010 catastrophe the charge was given new credibility in the pages of two of the world's most widely circulated newspapers is a sign that the scapegoating of the religion could become stronger in the present conjuncture unless vigilantly challenged.

Beyond perpetuating falsehoods about Vodou, the most immediate problem with the assertion that "voodoo" keeps Haiti poor is, of course, that it effaces the complex of geopolitical factors that actually have impoverished the country at the same time that it conveniently absolves or minimizes any international role in that historical process. However, depictions such as Brooks's and Harrison's are arguably even more insidious in that they also work to authorize and empower the externally imposed development policies and programs that many on the receiving end of aid regard as having exacerbated the desperate conditions they were ostensibly meant to alleviate.[8] In this light, the contention that the Haitian poor are cultural agents of their own immiseration could not be more serious for the course of Haiti's post-quake recovery. If the Haitian majority is held responsible for the country's low standing in human development indexes on account of (at least in part) their deficient or actively pernicious religious culture, then clearly they cannot be entrusted with setting the terms of development agendas in their own communities, much less with helping to shape the vision of a new Haiti. Such logic is particularly egregious in the face of the self-determinism to which impoverished communities have owed their survival before and certainly since the earthquake. In the weeks that followed some argued that the catastrophe could and must be made into an opportunity to "build Haiti back better."[9] One prerequisite of that project is deconstructing images of Haitian popular religion that have long served as a pretext for denying the Haitian majority full civil capacity and agency.

Notes

This essay is adapted from Kate Ramsey, *The Spirits and the Law: Vodou and Power in Haiti* (Chicago: The University of Chicago Press, 2011), 20–23. Reprinted with permission.

[1]   See, for example, Alex Dupuy, "Beyond the Earthquake: A Wake-Up Call for Haiti," and the essays of other contributors to the Social Science Research Council's online forum "Haiti, Now and Next," http://www.ssrc.org/features/pages/haiti-now-and-next/1338/1339/ (accessed 22 March 2010).

[2]   Harrison is the author of such works as *Underdevelopment Is a State of Mind: The Latin American Case* (Lanham, MD: Center for International Affairs, Harvard University, and University Press of America, 1985), and *The Central Liberal Truth: How Politics Can Change a Culture and Save It from Itself* (Oxford: Oxford University Press, 2006).

[3]   David Brooks, "The Underlying Tragedy," *New York Times*, January 14, 2010; and Lawrence Harrison, "Haiti and the Voodoo Curse: The Cultural Roots of the Country's Endless Misery," *Wall Street Journal*, February 5, 2010.

[4]   See Jean Fouchard, *Les Marrons de la liberté* (1972; Port-au-Prince: Éditions Henri Deschamps, 1988), 280–281.

[5]   François-Marie Kersuzan, quoted in Carl Edward Peters, *La Croix contre l'asson* (Port-au-Prince: Imprimerie La Phalange, 1960), 248.

[6]   See Ramsey, *The Spirits and the Law: Vodou and Power in Haiti*, 147.

[7]   Stephan Palmié, *Wizards and Scientists: Explorations in Afro-Cuban Modernity and Tradition* (Durham, NC: Duke University Press, 2002), 15.

[8]   See Jennie Smith's analysis of such programs: "Experiences with aid undermining the interests of the aided are now familiar to Haitians. This has led many Haitians, particularly those involved in the popular

movement, to see foreign-sponsored development and democratization
initiatives as inherently exploitative strategies—as being aimed primarily
at breeding dependency and undermining grassroots efforts directed at
real change." Smith, *When the Hands are Many: Community Organization
and Social Change in Rural Haiti* (Ithaca, NY: Cornell University Press,
2001), 30–31.

9   Testimony of Paul Farmer before the U.S. Senate Committee on Foreign
Relations, January 27, 2010. Full text at http://standwithhaiti.org/haiti/
news-entry/pih-co-founder-paul-farmer-testifies-at-senate-foreign-
relations-committee/ (accessed March 21, 2010).

An Unnaming:
The Haitian Earthquake Metaphor

Danielle Legros Georges

In 2010 Haiti suffered a devastating earthquake, which nearly destroyed its capital city, Port-au-Prince. An extraordinarily large number of men, women, and children lost their lives. Additionally, more than one million quake survivors were rendered homeless, and remained so for a long time. Everywhere in Port-au-Prince were signs of the devastating disaster. The government did not pick up much of the debris for some time. Many interior walls were exposed. Furthermore, the blue and white tarps and tents that continued to house many people were places where girls and women were especially vulnerable to violence. Many houses bore such stamps as *MTPTC 4* or *MTPTC à démolir*, painted by the Ministry for Public Works to indicate the degree of a building's structural solidity or compromise.

Haitians have come to refer to the earthquake as *bagay la*— that thing. If a metaphor is a transfer, then the shift from the term *"earthquake"* to *"that thing"* has us leaping from a precise and measurable natural phenomenon to an unnamed zone or space. Whether speaking English or Haitian Creole or French, we know what an earthquake is. It is a trembling of the earth, when seismic waves propagate in fluid or solid materials. The Haitian-created metaphor, however, does not signal what an earthquake *is*, or what the January 2010 earthquake *was*, but what this earthquake has meant, and will continue to mean to Haitians.

The figurative *thing*—because of its generality, its indistinctness— serves as an inclusive field which can accommodate the heartbreak and horror experienced and witnessed by Haitians: the lost family members, neighbors, and colleagues; the profoundly affected Haitian institutions; smashed supermarkets and outdoor markets; the crushed schools; as well as the lost sites of memory and community, of everyday living.

While metaphors often rely on images, *that thing* is marked by the absence of an image. Perhaps this responds to the overproduction of visuals relating to the earthquake, a saturation of horrific images that created a pervasive sentiment from having seen too much. Moreover, which one image would serve, could serve, to describe all that has been experienced and seen? And all that *has* happened?

To live and move forward with their lives, Haitians must first contend with the structural, social, and environmental challenges existing prior to (and after) the quake. These issues contributed to Haiti's poverty, leading to the scale of death and damage seen in affected cities and areas. There is the historic tension between the Haitian state and the citizenry it is meant to serve; another concern is the large presence of the international community in Haitian political and economic affairs. Add to this a proliferation of non-governmental organizations on the ground (some effective at providing needed services, some not); the still highly visible presence of armed United Nations security forces in a country not at war; and the nation's continued public health and ecological challenges. These are a daunting set of circumstances, exacerbated by an external gaze often propagating Haiti as "the poorest nation in the Western hemisphere," despite what Haitians know to be an infinitely more complex reality.

How can an image accommodate all these truths? With *bagay la*, Haitians have chosen not to choose an image. What image could hold what the earthquake has meant to them? Is it possible, too, that the creators of the metaphor were reflecting a sense of being unmoored, unnamed by the earthquake which affected the lives of the poor, rich, old, young, disabled, and able-bodied alike? Perhaps they thought: the earthquake unnamed us, and so we must unname *it*. Same for same. *Kif Kif.*

Seamus Heaney provides a definition for poetry as an order "true to the impact of external reality and . . . sensitive to the inner laws of the poet's being."[1] Haitians are known for the poetry and sophisticated wordplay in their everyday interactions with one another. The

Haitian sensibility is poetic and quick-witted. Haitians, for instance, employ proverbs, networks of metaphors, to help illuminate political, economic, social, and familial situations. Many of these proverbs are rooted in Haitian oral culture, and echo the incisive comparative and inventive abilities of their authors, unidentified poets—like the originators of *bagay la*.

> *Ravet pa janm gen rézon devan poul.*[2]
> *Sé kouto ki konn kè yanm-nan.*[3]
> *Bourik chajé pa kanpé.*[4]
> *Yon sèl dwèt pa manjé kalalou.*[5]
> *Jodia pou ou, demain pou mwen.*[6]

On poetics, Aristotle writes, "The greatest thing by far is to have a command of metaphor." He adds, "This alone cannot be imparted by another, it is the mark of genius, for to make good metaphors implies an eye for resemblances."[7]

Haitians have given and continue to give birth to metaphors grounded in Haitian external realities, mirroring and refracting them. *Bagay la* is another example of just such a creation. It is a term both singular and sweeping, one that wrestles with something the likes of which we've never seen before. It could just be a sign of poetic genius.

Notes

[1] Seamus Heaney, "Creating Poetry," Nobel Lecture, December 7, 1995, http://www.nobelprize.org/nobel_prizes/literature/laureates/1995/heaney-lecture.html.

[2] "The cockroach is always wrong when it argues with the chicken" provides us with one mighty big chicken that, by virtue of its sheer size in relation to the roach, will always win an argument.

[3] "It's the knife that knows the heart of the yam" encourages us to have a healthy skepticism with regard to appearances.

[4] "A loaded donkey can't stand still" shows us a beast so burdened that running with its crushing load beats standing inert under its impossible weight.

[5] "You don't eat gumbo with one finger" emphasizes the need for two fingers in order to nourish oneself—and our dependence on one another.

6   "Today for you, tomorrow for me" envisions a future in which what goes
     around has come around—and justice has prevailed.

7   Aristotle, *The Poetics*, translated by S. H. Butcher, http://classics.mit.edu/
     Aristotle/poetics.html.

UNDER THE PHOTOGRAPHER'S GAZE

Toni Pressley-Sanon

Immediately following the 35 seconds of violent tectonic upheaval that Haitians euphemistically call "the event" or *goudougoudou* (the onomatopoeic approximation of the sound the earth made when it shifted so violently) journalists, military personnel, aid workers, and laypeople descended on the island nation. Until those fateful moments Haiti was, in many ways invisible to the world even though it rests just 681 miles from the coast of Miami, Florida. However, at least for a short time, what we all saw on TV, on the internet, or in the newspapers changed all that.

Here, I briefly reflect on the work of photo-journalists who took up their cameras after the earthquake and, through their images, extended the work that colonizing nations began centuries ago. Many photographs were circulated on the internet immediately following the quake. I discuss two such photos to highlight what I see as the perpetuation of the profoundly imbalanced relationship between the first-world journalist and the third-world subject/object of his/her story who is repeatedly subjected to the first-world gaze. This contemporary relationship is the latest incarnation of that which has existed historically between the colonizer and the colonized. I contend that without a radical intervention to disrupt this dysfunctional relationship, the same colonial ideology that put them in place will continue to be perpetuated.

IMAGES AND REPRESENTATION

The images that surfaced immediately following the earthquake through various media are part of a larger cadre of ideologically charged images that have come to represent Haiti and its people. For my purpose here, specific individual realities in the iconographic images represent perceived attributes of the class into which the individual has been placed. Many of the images that define Haiti are negative—violence, voodoo, and disease, for example. Yes, there is violence in Haiti, but the history behind that violence is both long and complex. Yes, Haitian people do practice a religion that honors spirits and requires sacrifices, but the image of cannibalism that is the stuff of Hollywood is far from the reality. And yes, there is disease in Haiti, but disease is everywhere, and while the FDA blamed Haiti for spreading AIDS in the United States, it was later revealed that the origin of the pandemic was the reverse. For the viewer who does not know Haiti and is fed these images along with the rhetoric of Haiti as a "carnival of barbarism," the challenge becomes how to resist the ideological bias.[1]

In terms of the colonial project, the image is placed in the service of creating the "anonymous collectivity" in which the colonized is "designed to drown," as Alfred Memmi tells us.[2] There is a way out of this conundrum: that is by reading, viewing, and listening critically with an eye toward what is outside the frame or hidden. This critical way of viewing the image helps the viewer challenge the devices that are also at work to Other certain people pictured in photographs, such as labeling them savage, barbaric, or evildoers.

In the process of rejecting this voyeurism and the many misguided analyses, I have deliberately left the photos out of this essay as a way of engaging the content of the photographs without doing further damage to the subject. By not showing the photographs, I explore the possibility of alternative ways of talking about these images without, at least, visually perpetuating the violence that I argue was originally done to their subjects/objects.

PHOTOGRAPH 1

The shot is taken from an aerial view; it is at first difficult to know what the viewer is looking at. The objects on the ground can be easily mistaken for just another view of the trash that clogs the streets of Port-au-Prince, bits of debris clumped together, piled on top of one another. In other places the debris is scattered, perhaps blown by the wind. Splashes of blue and red jump out at the viewer. It is perhaps only when the viewer reads the caption, which informs him/her that what is pictured are bodies that have been dumped in front of the city morgue which is filled to capacity, that he/she takes a closer look in an effort to decipher what exactly is on display.

PHOTOGRAPH 2

The second photo is a close-up. A photographer is on the ground, just a few feet from a woman who is walking around among those bodies that the viewer has just seen from a distance. She wears a white scarf on her head, a light blue skirt and white blouse, plastic flip-flops on her feet. She seems oblivious to the photographer, focused as she is on trying to locate her loved ones among the dead. The bloated bodies all around her, contorted into various positions, in various stages of decay, some alone, others piled on top of each other, strewn amongst the Styrofoam containers that now also litter the streets of Port-au-Prince. The viewer may wonder if the smell of decaying bodies bothers the young woman as it so clearly bothered Anderson Cooper as he reported from Titanyen, or how is it that the white upper-class American man's nose is more sensitive than a poor black Caribbean woman's? And also what does this tell us about the uses and misuses of Haiti?

Photos, with their ability to capture several images in quick succession, are used for a myriad number of reasons, not the least of which is to act as what Susan Sontag labels "vehicle(s) of voyeurism."[3] The photos that surfaced on the television screens, on the internet, and in print media (and many since) are examples of how the medium of photography allows people to view photos of atrocities that happen in other countries from a distance.[4] Both the photographer and the viewer are implicated in this voyeurism. It makes a consumer of news also a kind of consumer of others' pain.

When the bombardment of news puts pressure on the journalist to hold the attention-deficit interest of the reader/viewer, then the journalist must hunt for more dramatic images in order to stay relevant. A brief survey of TV news programs, the newsstand, or the supermarket check-out line confirms Sontag's assertion: "If it bleeds, it leads."[5]

While the photograph may be accompanied by text, the immediacy and accessibility of the image make it central to the journalistic endeavor. In contrast to a written text "which, depending on its complexity of thought, reference and vocabulary, is pitched at a larger or smaller readership—a photograph has only one language and is destined potentially for all."[6] "When it comes to remembering, the photograph has the deeper bite."[7] Photographs are also used as part of larger ideological processes because they have an immediate effect with a long-term resonance.

PHOTOS' OBJECTIVITY/SUBJECTIVITY

Photographs bear witness to the real—since a person who was there took them.[8] But the act of focusing on what is depicted in the photo privileges the photojournalist's ideological perspective. The question of what is not photographed (what is outside the frame) is very often not asked by the viewer.

People in the throes of disaster are not afforded privacy or dignity. For example, in the photo of the young woman searching for her loved ones, even though she is alive, she does not speak for herself. She is the object to be seen and her consent is not sought. Information about what she is really doing, just like her consent, is not important, nor is it desired because it would detract from the power of the photographer and, by extension, that of the viewer.

With regard to Haiti in the aftermath of the 2010 earthquake, photography became a political tool that empowers people from the West while disenfranchising and silencing others, Haitians in this case.

Notes

This is an excerpt from a longer work: Toni Pressley-Sanon, "Lucid Cameras: Imagining Haiti after the Earthquake of 2010," *Journal of Haitian Studies* 17, no. 2 (2011): 6–32. Reprinted with permission.

1 "Haiti and Its Regeneration by the United States," 500.

2 Memmi, *The Colonizer and the Colonized*, 85.

3 Sontag, *Regarding the Pain of Others*, 18.

4 Ibid.

5 Ibid., 17.

6   Ibid., 20.

7   Ibid., 23.

8   Ibid., 26.

Bibliography

Chomsky, Noam (2010). *Hopes and Prospects*. Chicago: Haymarket Books.

D'Amico-Samuels, Deborah (1992). "Undoing Fieldwork: Personal, Political, Theoretical and Methodological Implications." In Faye V. Harrison (ed.), *Decolonizing Anthropology: Moving Further Toward an Anthropology of Liberation*, 68–87. Washington, DC: Association of Black Anthropologists American Anthropological Association.

Danticat, Edwidge (2010). *Create Dangerously: The Immigrant Artist at Work*. Princeton: Princeton University Press.

——— (1996). "We Are Ugly, but We Are Here." *The Caribbean Writer* 10. http://www.thecaribbeanwriter.org/index.php?option=com_content&view=article&id=602&catid=13:volume10&Itemid=2&section=volume. Accessed August 24, 2010.

Gilman, Sander L. (1986). "Black Bodies, White Bodies: Toward an Iconography of Female Sexuality in Late Nineteenth Century Art, Medicine and Literature." In Henry Louis Gates, Jr. (ed.), *Race, Writing, and Difference*, 223–261. Chicago: The University of Chicago Press.

"Haiti and Its Regeneration by the United States" (1920). *National Geographic* 38 (July–December).

JanMohamed, Abdul R. (1986). "The Economy of the Manichean Allegory: The Function of Racial Difference in Colonialist Literature." In Henry Louis Gates, Jr. (ed.), *Race, Writing, and Difference*, 78–106. Chicago: The University of Chicago Press.

Memmi, Albert (1991). *The Colonizer and the Colonized*. Boston: Beacon Press.

"Pat Robertson Says Haiti Paying for 'Pact With the Devil'" (2010). *CNN U.S.*, January 13. http://articles.cnn.com/2010-01-13/us/haiti.pat.robertson_1_pat-robertson-disasters-and-terrorist-attacks-devil?_s=PM:US. Accessed September 25, 2011.

"Paul Shirley to Haiti: Maybe Use a Condom Once in a While" (2010). *The Huffington Post*, March 28. http://www.huffingtonpost.com/2010/01/26/paul-shirley-to-haiti-may_n_437725.html. Accessed September 25, 2011.

Pratt, May Louise (1992). *Imperial Eyes: Travel Writing and Transculturation*. New York: Routledge.

Rogers, Molly (2010). *Delia's Tears: Race, Science and Photography in Nineteenth Century America*. New Haven: Yale University Press.

Rony, Fatimah Tobing (1996). *The Third Eye: Race, Cinema, and Ethnographic Spectacle*. Durham: Duke University Press.

Said, Edward (1978). *Orientalism*. New York: Vintage Books.

Sontag, Susan (2003). *Regarding the Pain of Others*. New York: Farrar, Straus and Giroux.

Yancy, George (2008). "Colonial Gazing: The Production of the Body as 'Other.'" *The Western Journal of Black Studies* 32, no. 1: 1–15.

IN A ROOM WITHOUT WINDOWS: SEEING HAITI BEYOND THE EARTHQUAKE

Manoucheka Celeste

Most people who lived through major events can tell you where they were at the time. For example, many remember 9/11, and the assassinations of President John F. Kennedy and the Reverend Dr. Martin Luther King Jr. For me, as presumably for many Haitians, I will never forget where I was during the 2010 earthquake in Haiti. I was in Seattle, far away from Port-au-Prince, in a room with no windows at the University of Washington, with my phone turned off. It was not until I left that room and turned my phone on that I learned that the earth shook my childhood home, leaving mothers crying and children searching for their families, and requiring a nation to once again be defined by its ability to survive and overcome adversity. Much of that night was a blur. I do remember my mentor suggesting that I not watch the news. Don't watch the news? I study the news, how could I not watch? But I took a day off.

When I finally turned on the news, I was overwhelmed by what I saw and was quickly filled with anxiety, anguish, and anger. Phone calls, emails and web surfing in search of news about my neighborhood and my family filled that day. I should not have been surprised by the images of injured, bleeding, and sometimes dead black bodies. The racialized coverage of Hurricane Katrina almost five years prior, and years of international coverage marking Haiti and other nations or neighborhoods with black people as "other," should have prepared me. But the surprise still came, and this time I fully grasped what it meant to be black in this world. I write now in an attempt to make sense of this catastrophe.

RESPONDING TO THE NEWS COVERAGE

The coverage of the earthquake was the first time that I saw myself outside of my *self*. The news coverage was not only about my country but also about my family, my people, and me. From Anderson Cooper's awkward attempt to speak French to a young girl who spoke Haitian Creole to the bloodied young women shown in numerous photographs, I saw myself everywhere. A few days after the earthquake I was interviewed by a local news channel; at the time I still had no news about my own family. When I watched the segment that included the interview, I noticed that I was no longer the expert or researcher, I was an eyewitness, a victim, as evidenced by the camera zooming in on the cell phone that I held in my hand all day and all night, waiting for news.

In order to reclaim my position as subject, rather than just object, I wrote. On January 26, the *Seattle Times* published my editorial, where I reflected on how the catastrophe turned into a missed "opportunity for media to respond in an unprecedented [humane] way."

> Videos of dead bodies, including children and the elderly, filled our television screens. For those of us who tuned in for information about friends and families, it was and is unbearable and despicable. . . . The focus on poverty, with the repeated tagline "the poorest country in the Western Hemisphere" and references to crime and unrest, make it hard for viewers to imagine any other aspect of life in Haiti. People were called looters for taking food from collapsed buildings after not having eaten for days, framing their survival as a crime. The humanity needed in this moment is clearly missing. . . . The question that plagues me and hopefully all audiences is: Who is able to die with dignity?[1]

I sought to appeal to what I believed to be a universal right: to be treated with dignity in life and in death. I associated the media coverage of the earthquake to other recent events because it was necessary to illustrate how we are all connected by tragedy. Most importantly, it was vital to point out that the coverage of the earthquake and Haiti spoke more broadly to problems with how the black diaspora is represented in Western media.

This editorial led to more emails and phone calls, mostly from people who could relate to the story I told. Yet for me as a media scholar, the most impactful responses came from those who reminded me of the urgent need to study representations of Haiti and blackness. These responses revealed problematic portrayals of Haiti by authors who used the very stereotypes that I sought to challenge to defend the supposed accuracy of US media coverage. Stereotypes, according to Hazel Carby, serve "not to reflect a reality but to function as a disguise or mystification, of objective social relations."[2] Patricia Hill Collins also asserts that "the authority to define societal values is a major instrument of power," one that elite groups use to manipulate ideas.[3] One need not be in a particular position to exercise power, as demonstrated by the comments of two especially motivated individuals, one whose Letter to the Editor appeared in the *Seattle Times* and another who mailed me a typed letter in response to my editorial about Haiti in media. In that letter the person who identified herself as Carolyn wrote:

> I have never seen an image of Haiti that is not disturbing. The same can be said about vast areas of Africa, which like Haiti, never seem to have any functioning government except roving gangs of thugs.
>
> AIDS is a new disease, only about 30 years old. And in most areas of the world, it is under control. But in Africa, we see endless AIDS orphans. Africa's astoundingly high rates of rape and promiscuity have given it the highest AIDS rate in the world.
>
> Instead of facing this, you blame the messenger. The appalling behavior of people in Haiti and Africa is not the fault of the media. They only report it. The people of Haiti and Africa have created it.
>
> Haiti has been there for 500 years and independent for 200 years. It shares an island with the Dominican Republic, with the same climate and natural resources. But while the DR has, by Latin American standards, a reasonably functioning government, economy and society, Haiti has always been the worst basket case in the Western Hemisphere, just like Africa...
>
> In more than two weeks of watching tv reports of the quake, I have never seen a Haitian government official. Apparently there is no functioning government in Haiti,

except for roving thugs with machetes, robbing and
looting.

Carolyn's words illustrate one of the most common rhetorical
strategies used in coverage of Haiti, which is to relate the nation
to the continent of Africa as a way to justify the sordid images and
stories. This connection has been made previously in different ways,
including, for example, by Stuart Hall (2001), who argues that in
some ways Haiti "is the symbolic island of Black culture, where one
feels closer to the African inheritance than anywhere else."[4] African
inheritance may be affirmative in contexts such as Hall's, but in
instances such as Carolyn's derogatory statements, the connection is
created to situate Haiti as further away from the US white mainstream
and closer to this mythic and monolithic blackness that Africa has
come to symbolize. Haiti is linked to Africa as a means of marking
"Otherness," one aspect of this African inheritance. Haiti becomes
equivalent to an entire continent—the continent Western media use
to mark poverty and backwardness.

To Carolyn, Haiti is a "basket case" and uncontrolled "except for
roving thugs with machetes, robbing and looting." Yet, if we recall
Hurricane Katrina, the US government was also visibly missing, and
black inhabitants were also identified in media coverage as looters,
while their white counterparts were deemed to be survivors. With
Haiti's earthquake, as with Hurricane Katrina, blackness is once
again connected to violence. Carolyn adds that people of "Africa"
have AIDS, as do the people of Haiti, and that "these people" created
this epidemic. In her commentary, Carolyn weaves a narrative of
primitivism, illness and dysfunction across the black diaspora.

In the Seattle Times on-line "Letter to the Editor" section, writer
Steve Krueger deems these representations as necessary for democracy.
Kruger, who identified himself as a retired journalist, is the Seattle
President for the American Federation for Radio and Television
Artists, an organization that represents media professionals. He
writes:

> The job of a reporter is to present reality, not spin.
> Accurately telling a story—even a distasteful one—is not
> part of some great social experiment. It is a service to a
> democratic society.

> Even before the quake, Haiti was a wretched place that
> the world ignored—I know. I spent time there in the early
> 1980s as a reporter. That history cannot be changed by
> simple wishful thinking.[5]

We wonder, whose democracy is he referring to? Who are these images servicing? Much of Kruger's argument is focused on the role of journalists in telling an objective truth, reporting the story without spin. But media scholars have long challenged the idea of objectivity in news coverage, acknowledging the ways that one's positionality impacts stories and images. The choice to cover one particular story and not another is evidence of the subjective nature of news.[6] There are, indeed, many choices that are made throughout the editorial process, choices made by individuals with various ideological commitments and life experiences that influence their judgment.

It is the very claim to objectivity that makes Steve Kruger's opinion of Haiti so essential to dissect. To him, Haiti is indeed a "wretched place." It was a "wretched place" when he spent an unknown amount of time there thirty years ago as a reporter. One must ask, what was Steve's opinion of Haiti before he arrived? How did his perception of Haiti thirty years ago impact what he reported and how he framed his stories at the time? His views certainly informed his stories about Haiti and continue to do so. Steve thus undermines the very objectivity that he claims to have as he reveals his opinion of Haiti. Steve argues that journalists tell the truth without bias, but his words exemplify just that—bias— and reinforce the need to rethink the way we interpret truth and reality as they are represented to us.

The "wretched place" that Kruger saw in the early 1980s was the same place where I was born around the same time. It was where I learned the importance of community and the value of education. It is the place where my grandmother indulged my spunk and gave me the self-esteem needed to take on a world that, as I later learned, devalues the body into which I was born. Haiti is that very place I wanted to run to after the earthquake. Once I finally made it there that April, it is where, during my attempt to haggle for a piece of art, I heard the words that made me feel whole for the first time since leaving Haiti at age nine: "Don't offer her a foreign price. Se moun peyi-nou li ye." I am the child immigrant who wanted her home to claim her, the home that Steve calls wretched.

Haiti is not an easy place to conceptualize or to study. For almost three years in my doctoral program, I had to repeatedly explain why Haiti was important in communication scholarship. To be frank, I had to explain why black people in general were important. So the earthquake became an unfortunate incident which caused me to no longer have to explain the importance of Haiti. For many scholars, the decision to study Haiti, black people, blackness, or difference is a radical one. We challenge the Eurocentrism that defines much of Western scholarship. This scholarship requires a level of reflexivity that many other scholars may not practice. We must often grapple with how to write and teach about Haiti without valorizing the very structures of knowledge that limit the ways we understand this complicated place. As a Haitian scholar, now living in the United States, I continually ask, how do I speak about Haiti without speaking "for" Haiti? Sociologist Carolle Charles offers some insight on this, asserting that we must consider the internal and external factors that shape the nation and its people.[7]

New Visions of Haiti

After January 2010, I never again want to be in a room without a window in fear that I might miss something. In a way, I understand the window to be a theoretical one, a radical, and critical one.[8]

In addition to considering Haiti in the context of internal and external factors as Charles suggests, Haiti must also be understood in its relationship to the black world. Haiti and black liberation ideology have long threatened a global social order that is needed to justify racism and black exploitation. Situating media as an ideological apparatus for the maintenance of political ideology and interests[9] allows scholars studying US media to identify and dissect controlling images of Haiti and Haitians. It also permits us to articulate the ways that a "basket case" Haiti is necessary to construct and justify an oppressed black America. Scholars including Michel-Rolph Trouillot and Doris Garraway[10] have written about this relationship between Haitians and black Americans. For white supremacy to continue, it is necessary for Haiti and its blackness to be represented as backward and for its peoples to be denied their humanity.[11]

Patricia Hill Collins's analysis of controlling images also offers a framework to comprehend the ways that US black women have been represented since before slavery, but this theory also helps in understanding representations of Haiti and Haitians. Controlling images, according to Collins, justify oppression and are "designed to make racism, sexism, poverty, and other forms of social injustice appear to be natural, normal, and inevitable parts of everyday life." She further contends that "others," or those deemed strangers, "threaten the moral and social order."[12]

In many ways Haiti and Haitian liberation continue to pose a threat to the stability of US racial hierarchy, beyond the country's history as the first free black Republic. Haiti today remains a place that requires us to think about blackness, liberation, and equality on a global scale. The nation continues to offer radical possibilities. These possibilities will be realized not through "wishful thinking" or "rewriting history," as Steve Kruger wrote caustically. They will be realized when Haitian voices become more central as scholars, journalists, writers, and activists, work that many of us are now doing. We must no longer see Haiti as an object. Haitianists can be a part of actualizing Haiti's radical potential by doing what US media outlets failed to do after the earthquake: employing the radical act of compassionate researching and recounting of stories.

Notes

1 Celeste 2010.
2 Carby 1987, 22.
3 Collins 2009, 76.
4 Hall 2001, 27.
5 Celeste 2010.
6 Entman 1993.
7 Charles 2011.
8 See Virginia Woolf's *A Room of One's Own*.
9 Celeste 2011.
10 Trouillot 1995; Garraway 2008.
11 Diaz 2014.
12 Collins 2009, 77.

Bibliography

Carby, H. (1987). *Reconstructing Womanhood: The Emergence of the Afro-American Novelist*. New York: Oxford University Press.

Celeste, M. (2013). "Framing Haitians and Cubans in *The New York Times*: Enduring Imprints of Political History." *Journal of Haitian Studies* 19(1) 66–94.

Celeste, M. (2011). "Media Construction and Representations of Legitimate/Illegitimate Citizens." Dissertation. University of Washington.

Celeste, M. (2010). "Disturbing Media Images of Haiti Earthquake Aftermath Tell Only Part of the Story." *Seattle Times*, January 26. http://old.seattletimes.com/html/opinion/2010897834_guest27celeste.html?prmid=op_ed.

Charles, C. (2011). Keynote Lecture. Bridging the Antilles: Caribbean Conference. Seattle: University of Washington.

Collins, P. H. (2009). *Black Feminist Thought*. New York, NY: Routledge.

Diaz, S. P. (2014). Personal communication, February 5.

Entman, R. (1993). "Framing: Toward Clarification of a Fractured Paradigm." *Journal of Communication* 43 (4): 51–58.

Garraway, D. L. (2008). "'Légitime Défense': Universalism and Nationalism in the Discourse of the Haitian Revolution." In D. L. Garraway, *Tree of Liberty: Cultural Legacies of the Haitian Revolution in the Atlantic World* (pp. 63–88). Charlottesville: University of Virginia Press.

Hall, S. (2001). "Negotiating Caribbean Identities." In B. Meeks & F. Lindahl, *New Caribbean Thought: A Reader*. Kingston, Jamaica: The University of the West Indies Press.

Nwankwo, I. C. (2008). "'Charged with Sympathy for Haiti:' Harnessing the Power of Blackness and Cosmopolitanism in the Wake of the Haitian Revolution." In D. L. Garraway, *Tree of Liberty: Cultural Legacies of the Haitian Revolution in the Atlantic World* (pp. 91–112). Charlottesville: University of Virginia Press.

Trouillot, M.-R. (1995). *Silencing the Past: Power and the Production of History*. Boston: Beacon Press.

DEAD CITIZEN

Jerry Philogene

A t 4:53 P.M. on Tuesday, January 12, 2010, for thirty-five seconds, a catastrophic 7.0-magnitude earthquake devastated Haiti's capital, Port-au-Prince. An estimated 300,000 lives were lost, nearly 1.5 million homes were destroyed, neighborhoods vanished, government buildings toppled, and historic sites were decimated. For a country that engaged in a long and bloody struggle for freedom and continues to battle the ramifications of enslavement—underdevelopment, neoimperialism, and internal political conflicts—this was yet another disaster.

I watched the images on the television screen as a member of the Haitian *diaspora*—one who feels Haiti deeply in her heart and celebrates its people, history, arts, literature, music, dance, food, and language in her private life and academic work; one who is shielded by US walls from Haiti's precarious economy and random violence; one who is pained by its bittersweet past, its tumultuous present, and its unknown future. I made frantic calls hoping and praying, making sure that family and friends were okay; some were, some were not. I remained safely in my house, staying informed by the modern phenomenon that is twenty-four-hour media coverage brought to me by the "specialized tourist," the journalist and the photojournalist.[1] How was I to make sense of these images, repelled yet fascinated to see more, know more? How was I to make sense of what these images *told* me had happened?

For weeks afterward, the North American news media was inundated with images of Haitians being rescued from the rubble of destroyed buildings. An unprecedented outpouring of North American and European aid amounting to nearly $1 billion was promised to Haiti. As days passed, more images of mangled, dismembered, and dead bodies appeared in the national and global news media. Stories of bodies buried under buildings, rescued by Haitians and international teams, captivated the global community. They accompanied images that captured the confusion, pain, and trauma launched on that horrific day. While most of the news coverage was filled with compassion and sympathy, it was also peppered with narratives that reinforced the well-known and persistent stereotypes, misrepresentations, and pernicious clichés about Haiti and its people.

The descriptive words and images paired with these narratives further emphasized a sense of perpetual hopelessness for Haiti. Posting on the blog of the Social Science Research Council, Colin Dayan wrote:

> In their coverage of the earthquake, the media represented Haiti as a passive, neutered object of disaster, with no history, no culture, nothing except images of rubble, pain, dirt, and misery. How did the news dare to show piles of bodies being bulldozed into mass graves after the earthquake? To talk about the smell of urine? To focus on women in postures that could only be called abject?[2]

SOCIAL DEATH AND FLAWED CITIZENS

These images circulated in the dominant US public culture as representatives of a grand narrative of the "shadowy specters of death" that, according to former presidential candidate and Christian televangelist Pat Robertson, permanently loom over Haiti.[3] Something systemic, deeply rooted, and profound was revealed in the wake of the earthquake: the fact that such graphic images and descriptive vocabularies have a sustained historical legacy. They are part of longstanding narratives and stereotypes that constitute Haiti as a permanent ward of the global community, incapable of being rehabilitated due to its inherently flawed nature. While we may have heard and read stories of Haitians helping Haitians (through friends, family, and Caribbean-based media) what we *saw* in the popular US and international media were images that dehumanized individuals and rendered them anonymous beings to be pitied and aided, yet again.

Despite the fact that Haiti's nation-state formation began with a calculated and strategic struggle for freedom and liberation, it is perceived as a lawless nation filled with powerless people and flawed citizens. Haiti has been constructed, in part through a visual discourse, as a socially dead space, entangled in postmodern enslavement. Building on the pioneering work of Orlando Patterson on the notion of social death as denial of personhood, I coined the term "dead citizen" to refer to the politicized Haitian body visually framed to symbolize individuals perceived as being ineligible for personhood. The historical visualization of Haiti, coupled with the more recent images of dead Haitian bodies shown during the 2010 earthquake, languishing in the sun and piled on top of one another, further contributes to the notion of "dead citizen."

HISTORY REPEATED: DEAD BODY OF A MARTYR

Here I cannot help but recall the 1919 black-and-white photograph of the dead body of François Borgia Charlemagne Péralte, a major leader of the oppositional fighters known as *cacos,* who was murdered by US marines during the 1915 occupation of Haiti. The photograph (Figure 1) has emerged as an iconic symbol of martyrdom in Haiti's history of resistance. The display of Peralte's half-naked corpse on one of the most sacred and holy days of the Vodou religion, *Fèt dè Mò* (Day of the Dead), and the dissemination of the image of Péralte's body, propped like Christ on the cross, offer an opportunity for a rich analysis of the power of the visual field and its complex relation to violence and resistance, citizenship and domination. While alive, Peralte's active body represented the combative citizenry; once dead, his passive body came to represent the complexity of lives that struggled against coercive material and political forces.

The photograph provides a historical context for the contemporary images of victims and survivors of the earthquake as well as those associated with other social and political circumstances. There are similarities between the public display of Péralte's corpse and the images of the dead and injured bodies of the earthquake victims. I argue that both were left open to voyeuristic fascination. These dead bodies were imprisoned in a regulatory gaze of the global world that confirmed the notion that Haiti is not viewed as a space of viable citizens; this visual discourse reinforces the assumption that the country is a cursed nation pathologically destined to its history

Figure 1. Photo of the body of François Borgia Charlemagne Péralte, November 1919. Courtesy of the US Marine Corps.

of suffering. Indeed, the 2010 post-earthquake media images have further concretized the understanding of Haitians as impoverished, lawless, unruly, and disposable people.

For centuries, as a neocolonized nation, Haiti has been figured as one large, unruly, racialized body marked by disease, poverty, and contamination. Nowhere was this truer than in the 2010 images of dead rotting bodies laid out for public viewing. The images that inundated the global mainstream news media were of individuals haphazardly buried in massive shallow, makeshift, communal graves, individuals unable to obtain the appropriate rituals of burial normally granted to citizens due to the destruction caused by the earthquake and the mayhem that followed. Like that of Péralte, their death was a public event. Many of the anonymous dead were buried in a sparsely populated area north of Port-au-Prince called *Titanyen* (loosely translated as "little nothing"), which has historically served as a site of mass graves. Their carelessly discarded Black bodies stand in for the metaphorical death of Haiti.

Figure 2. "Haiti Apocalypse," by Patrick Corrigan. Toronto Star, January 15, 2010. Reprinted with permission from Torstar Syndication Services.

LIVING AS "DEAD CITIZEN"

Among the visual images that commented on the devastation caused by the earthquake, many newspapers and magazines featured cartoons that reified the relation between Haiti and an ever-looming presence of death. One of the most striking to me is a cartoon published in the *Toronto Star* a few weeks after the earthquake (Figure 2). In the drawing, we see four skeletal figures, shrouded in black, riding horses. One carries a scythe (for harvesting the soul); two carry banners signaling their arrival; the fourth figure carries a rod with a skull on top. On the lower left-hand side of the image, on the dry, barren earth, are two young Haitian boys who note the arrival of these figures in an indifferent manner. One notes, "Here they come again . . ." and the other responds, "They never left!" In this morbidly sardonic image, the cartoonist confirms the constant presence of the specter of death on Haitian soil.

How might the generative tensions between the living and images of the dead offer an understanding of what it means to live as "dead citizen"? If violence is part of Haiti's historical landscape, the foundation of its freedom, then why is the discourse of death sewn into the fabric of its national identity? How might we employ the figure of the dead body to suggest a narrative that does not ubiquitously revolve around suffering and death, but presents the redemptive possibilities of social death, attempting to create a visual discourse that suggests that the livability of "dead citizen" is a central ethos by which Haitians on the island *and* in the diaspora survive? What sorts of generative power reside in the image of Péralte's slain body? In the bodies of the earthquake victims? How might we employ the figure of the dead body to suggest redemptive possibilities for those earthquake victims? How can we create a visual discourse that suggests the livability of "dead citizen" as a means of survival? I am not offering celebratory conclusions; instead, I hope for a space, perhaps a condition, where "dead citizen" can exist *within* and *against* historical and political conditions of impossibility and create opportunities for Haitian subjectivity. I assert that "the voices of the dead may speak freely now only through the bodies of the living."[4]

Perhaps it is through a rearticulated visual historicity that an understanding of the subjectivity and transformative powers of "dead citizen" can allow for an understanding of the dead in relation to the living, not only in the ways they live but also in the ways they die and the reasons *why* they die. It is then that we can fully understand the agency of those earthquake victims who fit the bill of "dead citizen," the livability of a social death, and their relations to the cultural logic and material conditions of history, heritage, and image making.

Notes

This is an excerpt from a longer article: Jerry Philogene, "'Dead Citizen' and the Abject Nation: Social Death, Haiti, and the Strategic Power of the Image," *Journal of Haitian Studies* 21, no. 2 (2015): 100–126. Reprinted with permission.

[1] Sontag, *Regarding the Pain of Others*, 18.

[2] "The Immanent Frame" is a blog of the Social Science Research Council that publishes "interdisciplinary perspectives on secularism, religion, and the public sphere." Colin Dayan, "What Is a Metaphor a Metaphor for?," March 24, 2010, http://blogs.ssrc.org/tif/2010/03/24/a-metaphor-for/.

3   Ellis, *If We Must Die*, 12.
4   Roach, *Cities of the Dead*, xiii.

Bibliography

Ellis, Aimé J. *If We Must Die: From Bigger Thomas to Biggie Smalls.* Detroit: Wayne State University Press, 2011.

Roach, Joseph. *Cities of the Dead: Circum-Atlantic Performances.* New York: Columbia University Press, 1996.

Sontag, Susan. *On Photography.* New York: Farrar, Straus and Giroux, 1973.

———. *Regarding the Pain of Others.* New York: Farrar, Straus and Giroux, 2003.

ART, ARTISTS, AND THE SHAKING OF THE FOUNDATIONS

LeGrace Benson

Unspeakable. Giving voice to it, a father keens over the body of his little girl. Unimaginable. A BBC photographer cannot feel anything: it is like looking at a movie that will not end—unreal. Haitian photographer Danny Morel stands in the street: "I cannot believe what I am seeing. I cannot believe this." An architect finally reached when the cell phones are working again says,

> I was right there a few hundred yards from the National Palace and it was unimaginable. We would try to run outside and the floor would come up to meet us. Finally we got out. I am back here now. I see the rooms we sat in open to the sky and resting over rubble and underneath the dead. It is unimaginable.

A woman cradles a forelimb in her arms. "I hold on to this," she moans. "This is all I have left of my child." Far away in Cap Haïtien, Bertelus Myrbel goes into a dream. He has lost a cousin. He has to do something. He paints three scenes of Port-au-Prince tumbled into pandemonium. Still and silent, the three canvases come out to show those outside the dream and outside Haiti that the event is terrible beyond imagining. People who have been inside a war would understand.

It had happened before, but long ago. In Cap Haïtien, situated athwart another of Haiti's tectonic fault lines, the Cathedral of Our Lady of the Assumption, newly sanctified in consequence of the Concordat with the Church at Rome, crashed in 1860 along with most of the houses and many of the public buildings. In the previous century there had been three quakes: in 1751, 1761, and

1770. Uprisings that led to the open revolution of 1791 eerily track these dates, beginning with François Makandal's proto-revolution of 1751. Earlier, Louis XIV had authorized the French slave trade in 1670 and by 1685 was obliged to sign the Code Noir with its strictures against the most heinous abuses. In between there were two earthquakes, 1673 and 1684, devastating some plantations and thus reducing economic gains.

Even minor constraints against brutality in the Code Noir were ignored in the interest of restoring profitability. By 1697 slaves initiated a revolt. Small and failed for the moment, it was sign of things to come: Makandal's revolt and the ultimately successful efforts of Toussaint and Dessalines.

The 1770 quake wrenched the ground along the same fault line of the 2010 event, running through Port-au-Prince east to west. Haitian historian Thomas Madiou wrote that the tremor leveled the entire city and afterward the surviving population pitched tents and scrambled for food and water, a description befitting January 2010. Thus ever and always: an unwitting partnership of earth and a tacit socioeconomic contract that elevates a natural disaster into unspeakable human tragedy.

In those distant years there were artists, writers, and musicians among the population of African and Afro-Creole slaves and free coloreds, some of them trained in Paris or Rome, and in service to or economically tied to French colonists. Nearly out of sight in the slave quarters and in the nearly impenetrable backcountry, the Blacks were creating graphic arts, an oraliture, and a music binding the homelands to the new lands. European observers would disdain these as barbaric expressions. Only under pressure of the US occupation of 1915–1934 and the rise of a new consciousness in Haiti and the wider Caribbean would these "barbaric" Creole expressions emerge into public acclaim. Illustrious dancers, musicians, and visual artists would come to Haiti in the 1940s and 1950s to study this Afro-Creole heritage. The Centre d'Art opened in 1944, and by 1948 the Kreyòl-speaking painters and sculptors would garner international praise. More importantly: artists and latent artists all over Haiti began bringing their works to the Centre, galleries opened, and the streets of Haitian port cities were festooned and muraled with thousands of

Figure 1. Art vendor unrolling paintings. Photograph by Tequila Minsky.
Reprinted with permission.

landscapes, depictions of Vodou *lwa* and ceremonies, market scenes, and beautiful women. The Pearl of the Antilles became its art center.

The day after the earthquake, journalists already there or converging upon a newsworthy horror began to report from Port-au-Prince, Léogâne, and Jacmel. One of those already present and familiar with the country for years related her astonishment as she went through the streets and into the emerging tent cities:

> I couldn't believe it! I tried to get some pictures as we drove by. When we were walking on the street between Comité Artisanal and another gallery we saw this guy sitting there on the sidewalk with all these paintings rolled up. As I eyed his stack he unrolled them and showed me some of what he had.

Tequila Minsky continued:

> And when we were driving by one of the tent cities a day or so later I noticed people had their paintings beside the doors. A couple of days after that, driving on that same major artery, there were paintings strung up on the fence that separated the tent city from the street. And there was

Figure 2. Partially fallen house with art for sale. Photograph by Tequila Minsky. Reprinted with permission.

a house with paintings for sale. It looked like they had already organized a "gallery" and were in business.

Frantz Zéphirin threw his distress and energy into ten paintings, one boiling into visibility after another. A work of his from the 2008 hurricanes was featured on the cover of the *New Yorker.* He depicted the rushing waters rising toward an open door. Every stone of the house is a staring, open-mouthed face. In the door are three skeletons clothed in nineteenth-century garments—the *Gede,* those powerful spirits who guide the living into the land of the ancestors. It was the artist's response to the four hurricanes of 2008, but it fit the new disaster all too well.

Trauma is intolerable. It hastens to sink down below the level of awareness so that one can keep going, keep living. It abides there, perhaps uttered in unrecognized ways as ordinary as snapping at a spouse or child, or as an ever-deepening depression. Sometimes it bides time like the tectonic plates underfoot, straining into a pressure that must be released. The television images of the quake disturbed a woman's dark memory. "I was in the San Francisco quake of 1989," she said, her voice catching in her throat. "I still have nightmares. It was almost twenty years ago." Old ceremonies, songs, and dances help in such circumstances. They can charge the familiar rituals, the singing and dancing, with the task of articulating the burden of inchoate fear. Artists, musicians, poets, dancers, players, and filmmakers offer double assistance, in that they have the ability to eject their own mute and invisible dread into a calculated and tolerable sound and fury and thus provide viewers and listeners with a vicarious release from the terror.

As dark fell on the first wretched night, Richard Morse stood on the porch of his Oloffson Hotel, the historic gingerbread confection miraculously intact while all above and below was in shambles. In the yard a few journalists already in Haiti slept on the ground like everyone else. From the ruins beyond the enclosure came singing. The profundities of trauma found place and voice to call on God's mercy against inexplicable chthonic forces. The members of Morse's musical group had all survived and were out there somewhere in the singing darkness doing whatever needed to be done.

While Haitians at the scene went into action immediately, those at some remove began to respond. A woman in London, just returned from Haiti before the quake, was troubled that she could feel nothing but a programmatic cliché of sympathy. As she crossed Embankment Bridge, for no apparent reason at all she began to sob and sob and sob. She kept walking slowly, shaking, glad that urban folk mostly ignore the faces of passersby. The British artists who had recently exulted in the success of the Ghetto Biennale held in Port-au-Prince were planning a gathering to celebrate. The celebration turned into a wake. They knew that one of the Atis Rezistans, Louko, of the Grand Rue, was dead under a collapsed roof. They knew that Reggie Jean François, managing artisan for the Brandaid group in the Cité Soleil district, had survived but had spent a wretchedly sorrowful day trying to remove the bodies of his apprentices from under lethal rubble. They heard news about Flo McGarrell from Vermont, a Biennale participant who was setting up an art center in Jacmel and mentoring students in the film program. Flo had been at the computers in a hotel when the building buckled and fell to earth. The British group collected funds to enable one artist to go back to the site of the Biennale. She would assess the damage, participate in the salvage and safekeeping of artworks, and provide food and medical

Figure 3. Artwork by a young girl of the Ti-moun Atis Rezistans art lakou
in Port-au-Prince, 2009. Photograph by the author.

assistance for the downtown community (or *lakou*) closely associated
with the artists. A radio talk show planned as a report on the Ghetto
Biennale became a fundraiser that then took on a formal status as
Foundry Fund/Haiti. They brought one of the artists to London to
spark a campaign to restore the Grand Rue community.

The Ghetto Biennale was conceived of by artists who consciously
utilized the detritus of "First World" consumer products dumped
in Haiti—old vehicles of every sort, old clothing and shoes ("Why
do they think Haitians can use winter boots?"), used oil drums,
salvaged lumber, and wire. One of them explained that they recycle

Figure 4. Child in temporary school. Photograph by Lois Wilcken. Reprinted
  with permission.

anything into something new. He pointed out that the only local
material is human skeletons. There will be many of these now. And
the reason for their incorporation into the sculptures and tableaus
of the Atis Rezistans of Grand Rue remains unchanged. The artists
honor the deceased with the ceremonial feeding that precedes use
in the artworks, and thus respect their presence as ancestors. To be
in the art is, as one artist explained, "to set them on another life
journey, and maybe this one will be better than the one they had."
It is a recycling in the sense of the great wheel of incarnation and
reincarnation. On January 12 the quake destroyed the studios and the
art class space for the youngsters of the *lakou*. It buried Louko, whose
portrait had been on the entrance to the festival of art. Already they
are rebuilding. The children are learning reading, writing, arithmetic,
and how to make art from the shards and pieces of disaster. The artist
who went to England is back at the site on Grand Rue, recycling
trauma into regenerated art and community.

In what may be one of the most active turnovers of art ever,
many paintings, sculptures, and craftworks have been on the auction
blocks to benefit Haiti. Auctions are happening in Canada, the United
Kingdom, France, Germany, the United States, Venezuela, Trinidad,
Cuba, Ireland, and other countries. The visual arts of Haiti are in the

public awareness as never before, even more so than in the 1950s, when there were exhibitions in Paris and New York. In those years viewers were largely an art market public. Today the work is in the eye of anyone who pays attention to the news or to his or her local church and civic association activities.

The music too has a broader audience now and a wider scope, in that Haitian music today ranges from classical concerts by survivors of the Sainte-Trinité school of music, Pentecostal gospel choirs in Brooklyn and Philadelphia, RAM roots music, Boukman Eksperyans, to music and dance groups such as Troupe Makandal from New York. The day before the quake, RAM musicians were recording the rehearsal for 2010 Karnaval. The name of the song was premonitory: "Earthquake." Now the recording is under debris. The new version is to debut at the first post-quake performance in April. The musicians all survived and on the evening after the quake set the music aside for the rescue effort. Other local groups did likewise. Lolo Beaubrun's Boukman Eksperyans wrote new songs, and played these along with some old ones in a memorial concert held in the garden of their home. Makandal members went to Haiti from New York as soon as possible to put a school back in operation and set up shelter tents for families.

While there the Troupe made music with a local group in some buildings that were still habitable. Such actions continue to be evident. In the meantime the songs everyone knew rose up in spontaneous chorus all over Port-au-Prince and Léogâne. These are actions where the diaspora, friends of Haiti, and quake survivors are working hand in hand now and for the foreseeable future, using long, long musical traditions to create new compositions for raising up a new Haiti.

Visual artists and collections in Port-au-Prince suffered incalculable losses. The Roman Catholic Cathedral of Notre Dame instantly looked like the ruins of Tintern Abbey, its priceless stained glass in shards. Stained-glass artist and photographer Kesler Pierre grew up in Port-au-Prince but now lives in the United States. He immediately went to Haiti to begin a restoration process. An article in the *New York Times* on January 15 headlines Pierre's work: "The Spirit of Port-au-Prince, Now Broken." This can only refer to the glass. Pierre's presence signifies unbroken spirit.

Figure 5. Troupe Makandal setting up tent. Photograph by Lois Wilcken. Reprinted with permission.

The renowned murals of the Episcopal Sainte-Trinité Cathedral suffered nearly total annihilation. Philomé Obin's *Crucifixion*, Castera Bazile's *Ascension*, Rigaud Benoit's *Nativity*, and Gabriel Lévêque's *Angels* in the apse around the main altar disintegrated into colored powders. Wilson Bigaud's *Marriage at Cana* returned to dust along with the murals of T. Auguste, Préfèt Duffaut, and Adam Leontus. Patrimony is held in high regard by most Haitians, so no one was surprised to learn that a group had made special efforts to prevent bulldozers from demolishing the remains before rescue and preservation efforts could begin.

The Centre d'Art where the Creole artworks began their journey into world attention collapsed almost completely. With the aftershocks still quivering, those who knew that some of the national art treasures might still be intact risked their lives to bring them out and pack them into the trucks and vans that would take them to safe storage. The Musée de l'Art Haïtien had withstood the earthquake better, and rescuers immediately went in to salvage treasures. Axell Liautaud held Wilson Bigaud's *Earthly Paradise*, while a *New York Times* photographer took a picture that would bring grateful tears to many. But close by, the Fondation Création collapsed completely with unknown losses. The collection of Issa ElSaieh, whose art gallery was the first to open after the initial success of the Centre d'Art, remained sturdy through the quake, as did the nearby Oloffson Hotel in all its gingerbread glory, with its collection of paintings and Vodou flags. But farther up the hill the priceless private collection of George Nader, whose gallery had opened almost as soon as Issa's, was a catastrophe. Nader's son John, photographed in the process of rescuing as much as possible, spoke of several thousand works, many of them now lost or damaged beyond repair. These were the classic works of the artists from the period Selden Rodman called "The Haitian Renaissance." Although privately held, most were on public view and part of public heritage. Many were relieved to see Marianne Lehmann on the Internet rejoicing that a miracle had happened. Buildings all around her had crumbled but the invaluable collection of Vodou religious art in the Fondation pour la Préservation, la Valorisation, et la Production d'Œuvres Culturelles Haïtiennes (FVPOCH) survived. Nearby, the Nader sales gallery also remained standing and the works unharmed. But several galleries, artists' studios, and homes sustained damage, ranging from serious cracks to total destruction. Each artist or gallerist was mourning a relative or co-worker who had perished, and grieving the work of human hands perished.

In Jacmel the Ciné Institut for young film and video hopefuls fell, but the students grabbed what equipment they had at hand or could rescue and took to the streets. They tirelessly documented the loss of buildings, of lives, and of the vivid Karnaval arts for which the city is famous. The mask shops were in ruins, some of the artists dead or severely wounded. Ciné Institut is in the process of reconstituting itself with the help of donors from the outside. With Karnaval—the event that is a major source of income for the city—canceled, the artists are now living in tents and have no income. Nevertheless, in place of the joyous event they held a spirited wake. Mask maker Onel Bazelais led the parade, holding aloft a caricature of the president. Behind him were all the traditional spoofs of politicians and the famous, power spirits like the horned Bossou, and cadaverous Gede, the death *lwa*. People fashioned costumes from whatever pieces they could cobble up. The drums and horns of rara paced their funereal march from the center of Jacmel to the cemetery. The record of it is there, because the students of Ciné Institut filmed it all.

There are so many stories. Many of them are the same tale: of being in a strange state of detachment then surprised with a tight throat and tears; grieving with the mind only and then with the whole body; singing and praying; picking up pieces; burying the dead, mourning irrevocable losses; helping an unending surge of the hungry, thirsty, and homeless; raising money with songs and paintings; creating new paintings and songs; and making sure the children would have school and be able to make art. They know how to do this, these Haitians. They have been rehearsing and performing this theatre since that first act of earthquake and revolution in 1751.

Yet. Yet. Stories of artists from the past indicate that the loss of a substantial part of a body of work has a serious and permanent impact. Arshile Gorky comes to mind. When a studio fire burned an important group of his works he spoke ruefully of "his beauties" deceased. He cleaned up the damaged studio and created *Charred Beloved* as one of the last works he would do. He went into a deep depression and eventually committed suicide. For Haitian artists and any Haitian who experienced the shaking of the foundations, the unfolding of the trauma lies now and in the future. For any Haitian caught up in the quake the memory of the event lies like seeds underground with a slow germination and a long row to hoe.

April 2010

Note

A version of this article was first published in *Haiti Rising: Haitian History, Culture, and the Earthquake of 2010*, ed. Martin Munro (Liverpool: Liverpool University Press, 2010). Reprinted with permission.

L'Espoir après le seisme

Danièle Mangonès

Cinq caciquats disparus et quasiment oubliés ! Le poisson représentant l'abondance accompagné de Danbala—esprit et maître de l'univers, protecteur du péristyle avec Ayida Wédo.

Ce tableau fut d'abord au vertical, mis à l'horizontal cinq mois plus tard, une partie de la mer disparaissait, montrant seulement un poisson qui y restait.

Trois jours avant le séisme, je peint au centre ce qui semble être des gens flottant dans un bain de sang.

Quelques heures après le séisme, je comprends la révélation du désastre et je sors courant chercher du matériel de construction et des pierres qui ont la propriété de transmettre des sentiments positifs et je retourne travailler. Dans mon âme et dans mon cœur, je rebâttis.

Kalfou ouvre les portes à tous les ayisyen.

Ogou est en guerre, fâché . . . Il représente aussi Grand Bois et tous les esprits positifs de Guinée. Seul l'amour nous permettra d'arriver à la reconstruction rationnelle d'Ayiti.

Le rouge c'est notre victoire de peuple noir, indépendant et brave. Les mornes décorés de maisons multicolores représentent le renouveau et l'espoir . . . Le firmament en feu d'artifice est la célébration du courage de notre peuple.

Le tableau représente aussi l'Espoir après le séisme. Les astres brillent pour cette nouvelle Ayiti. Le soleil, la lune se réjouissent du courage de notre people . . .

La présence de Grand Bois indique la connexion entre l'astral et le terrestre. Il porte en lui le grand cœur des Ezuli, l'amour inconditionnel qu'apporte Fréda et la protection pour la patrie et la

Figure 1. "L'Espoir après le seisme." Par Danièle Mangonès.

famille ayisyènn de Dantò . . . L'innocence est représentée par une
jeune fille insouciante qui sourit et demande à Kalfou de lui ouvrir
le chemin pour arriver à une Ayiti meilleure. Le rôle du Potomitan
est de protéger Ayida et Danbala Wedo.

Le soleil, la lune et les astres apportent leurs énergies aux esprits
protecteurs de notre peuple et de notre nation.

La Sirène qui est l'essence de l'amour inconditionnel et la Baleine
sont proches d'Agwe qui supporte le monde pour la zillième fois.

Ayiti ne saurait mourir . . . Ayiti ne pourrait cesser de se battre
pour que l'espoir renaisse pour cette première nation noire libre.

DIVINE DESCENT OF CHRIST

Gessy Aubry

Après le séisme en Haïti, j'ai ressentis un profond choc face à cette énorme tragédie. Ma quête a commencé immédiatement pour trouver une explication au phénomène des Croix du Christ encore debout devant tant d'églises dévastées. Ces Croix, restées intactes en face de ces bâtiments détruits par le tremblement de terre, relèvent du miracle et continuent de demeurer pour moi un mystère.

Ce phénomène m'avait beaucoup secouée et j'en ai cherché, intérieurement la signification. « Divine Descent of Christ » fut en quelque sorte la réponse à ma question avec en plus de son symbolisme, le message reçu que ce tableau était destiné à servir l'énergie feminine en Haïti. Le message s'articulait ainsi : Le Christ est là, ici, maintenant et tout comme il y a 2000 ans. Il reprend le chemin du retour avec les femmes !

J'ai eu le privilège de saisir le message que le Christ lancait à la population d'Haïti et que je traduis ainsi : « Même si les édifices disparaîssent, *Moi, je serai toujours présent. Je Suis le Support, Je Suis la Voie, Je Suis l'Espoir.* » Je pense que cette compréhension des événements m'a propulsée dans un univers nouveau où les *Cris* et les *Larmes* ont pu être transmutés en *Cris d'Espoir.*

L'ordre vient du chaos. Ce tableau intitulé: « Divine Descent of Christ » est né des cendres du 12 Janvier 2010. Il représente la Conscience Christique sous la forme d'une étoile à 13 branches avec le Christ en son centre et le tout entouré d'un cercle. Cette représentation révèle la communion des 12 Apôtres avec le Christ pour former ce pont qui existe entre chaque être humain et l'âme qui vit en chacun. L'Eternel Féminin a lancé son appel avec le Christ ! Formons un cercle pour ancrer l'Espoir dans nos vies.

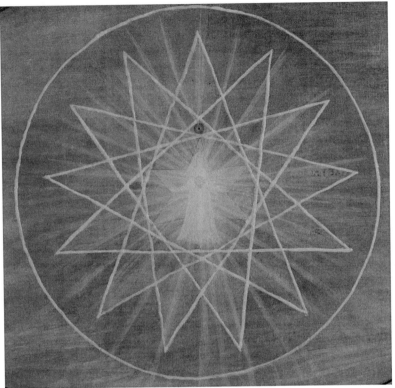

Figure 1. "Divine Descent of Christ" [détail]. Par Gessy Aubry, août 2012. Acrylique forme etoile a six branches 31" x 36".

BEFORE AND AFTER

Philippe Dodard

"Before and After" is a series of inks and paintings that speak for themselves about the experience of change in one's life after witnessing hundreds of thousands of souls disappearing within thirty seconds, spreading dust in the sky, leaving behind their light for us to remember how fragile we are and the responsibility to recreate Haiti and make it a better place to live. The solidarity of the whole world will transform our tears into healing seeds.

Figure 1. "12 janvier 2010." By Philippe Dodard. Acrylic on canvas, 30" x 36".

Her Saving Grace La Sirène

Edouard Duval Carrié

After more than a century of "La Sirène" providing solace to enslaved Africans ushered against their will to infernal sugar plantations in the New World, and after accompanying those tossed overboard back to their motherland, she is again ever attentive to their plight. Two centuries after independence, the country still needs the mighty La Sirène to come to her aid. There is a saying in Haiti that claims that our land is a slippery one. The severe and deadly earthquake which shook us to our core on January 12, 2010, adds new layers of meaning to that saying. In this painting, La Sirène comes to support what is left of the Cathedral and provide much-needed comfort to a people once again in distress.

Figure 1. "Her Saving Grace La Sirène." By Edouard Duval Carrié.

CONCLUSION

YO PRALE LAKAY:
A HOMECOMING

Claudine Michel

We are at times called to channel messages, to tap ancestral knowledge that we carry deep inside us, to access the collective consciousness of our people. If only we would listen . . .

In the summer of 2009, after attending the tenth KOSANBA conference in Mirebalais, in what was to be her last visit to her adopted country, Karen McCarthy Brown became too ill to write the new preface to her book. This would be the third edition of her 1991 magnum opus, *Mama Lola: A Vodou Priestess in Brooklyn*,[1] a book that had been so influential in the academy in the United States, yet remained sadly unknown for the most part to Haitians since the translation will not be available in Haiti until 2017.

That summer, Karen asked me if I would be willing to write the foreword and shared that Mama Lola was enthusiastic about it. Of course I accepted. It was a huge honor to craft the preface of such an acclaimed book, but it also seemed a relatively easy task at the time considering the richness of the material.[2] Moreover it was a way for me to pay respect to two elder sister-comrades—Karen herself as well as Alourdes Champagne, Mama Lola—whose lives and work had been so instrumental to my own development as a scholar of Haiti's national religion.

Though Karen was already weak and barely able to communicate she made another call to me on September 12, 2009. She was clear-minded that day (maybe herself channeling a message from that faraway place where we all come from and to which we shall return). Just before she hung up: "I have an insight," she blurted, "I now know what the book is about . . . it is about what Haiti *gives* to us." This luminous statement resonated like a calling. Mama Lola and

Karen Brown had created a captivating harmony of voices within Vodou, sharing its *konesans*[3] and exchanging their respective cultural wisdoms. Now they had extended an invitation to me to join their chorus. Heeding this call to service, I went to work.

A WRITING PROJECT TURNED EULOGY FOR THE EARTHQUAKE VICTIMS

On November 2, 2009, as I began drafting the foreword to *Mama Lola*, I thought what a propitious day it was: the Day of the Dead— *Fèt lè Mò*, a most venerated holiday in Haiti. Little did I know then what was in store for Haiti. The first words I penned were: "May all the Gede[4]—Bawon Samdi, Gede Nibo, Ti Malis, Ti Pise, Brav, Gede Simityè, Luciani Bawon Lakwa, Britis Jean Simon, Grann Brijit, and Gedelia, the female Gede that Karen summoned at the end of *Mama Lola*—guide my path and meet me at the crossroads as I humbly offer these reflections." I further implored the Gede—masters of life and death, Eros and Thanatos, the deity that personifies best the contemporary urban struggles of our people—to let the ancestors speak through me, as I would in essence be writing about the book's impact on us as Haitians, on the ramifications of this work for Haiti, and on the new place *Mama Lola* created for Vodou and its practices in both the scholarly world and the larger international community. Knowing that this celebrated text had been both widely used and positively reviewed by scholars throughout the world, I went deep inside my soul to unearth what others—particularly practitioners, elders with more *konesans*—would say about it. I asked if the book was in harmony with the spirits that had guided the work. I asked about balance that the text might offer.

Our national religion is grounded in a system of balance: balance within ourselves, in interpersonal relationships, in our rapport with the divine, in the way we understand and use power, in the task of negotiating life morally, in the harmony we seek with nature. I reflected that for too long our nation has been out of balance; the world has been out of balance. Could Vodou offer healing modalities for an ailing society? For a world no longer in equilibrium?

I felt the strong presence of the *Lwa*,[5] the Gede for sure, as I tried to organize my thoughts and find direction. Though writing down some ideas about a book, especially one so rich, might seem to be a simple task, at that moment it was a daunting challenge. For the task was not about crafting another academic commentary; I felt it was a summons to mull over Vodou's deepest meaning and the role that the ancestral religion can play in sustaining Haiti, its people, and its culture, and how it might address larger questions about the country's history and politics. The question became, "How could the spirit world and its figuration of the dead help reshape the decadent political and economic conditions in Haiti and stitch together its social fabric?" Could the *Lwa* help make sense of the current situation in Haiti? In an ultimate act of mirroring and inversion, might they turn chaos into order?

Karen Brown provided unique and perceptive views on Vodou rituals and practices as an alternate form of morality, a creolized worldview embracing "a moral vision that is not abstract but interpersonal, with a complexity that does not paralyze and a tolerance that is not abdication of responsibility."[6] I grappled with something even more unique about the book: Karen Brown's insights on the moral imperative to reclaim our humanity and our planet, and specifically the need for Western hegemonic powers to realize that they may indeed be able to learn something about being human from non-Western societies, so-called Third World agrarian societies where both the land and the people still matter. In her work she intentionally disrupted established standards of objectivity with the world-shattering view that the West must not believe itself to "have truth that rules out the truth of others."[7] Noting how Haiti has "become increasingly under the sway of US popular culture . . . and [how] all the learning tends to flow in one direction," she wrote that "the time may be right to test what can flow in the other direction"[8] and place the nexus of learning in Haiti.

In my preface I had to allow *Mama Lola* to stand as a powerful account of the contributions that Haiti can and does make to the larger conversations about religion, about life, and ultimately about being human.

I felt I had been entrusted with a precious gem but also a heavy responsibility. I pondered if it was perhaps my role to try to expound what Karen McCarthy Brown had meant when she exclaimed that she had finally figured it out: that the book was about "what Haiti gives to us!" Did I feel uneasy not because I had to write an introduction to a well-respected book but because I had to attempt to explicate Karen's truth-seeking insight about both the religion and the nation—what Haiti gives to us? Or because I sensed that, considering the illness she was battling, this might well be Karen McCarthy Brown's last gift to us? Or because I believed that this might be one of her most profound statements about her work of the past thirty-five years, about her complex understanding of the Vodou religion and the role it might play in rehumanizing a world turned egocentric, materialistic, and ecologically unsound?

Note that Karen did not say, "what Haiti *gave* to us." That phrase would have had a different meaning, referring to Haiti's unique place as the first independent black nation of the Western Hemisphere, inspiring revolutions in Venezuela and elsewhere in the Americas; referring to the role that Haiti's history had played in the Louisiana Purchase and the subsequent expansion of the United States; referring to the fact that in the black diaspora Haiti has been a beacon of hope, constantly leading struggles for social justice and creating extraordinary literary and artistic productions within the country and beyond. All these things would locate Haiti's contributions and gifts to the world in the past. Karen spoke in the present—what Haiti has to offer right now. Perhaps I had to leave academia and go into the realm of popular wisdom to seek an answer. Haiti's prized gift might then be its profound and proverbial *onè/respè*, honor and respect, and its ethos of sharing as *pataj*—concepts best conveyed in the simplicity of Toto Bissainthe's song "*Ti mòso manje fèt pou l separe*" (Every inch, every morsel of food must be shared), in the traditional proverb *Manje kwit pa gen mèt* (A cooked meal belongs to all), or even in Mama Lola's exclamation "When I eat alone, I have nothing."

I was clearly apprehensive about the prospect of trying to explicate Haiti's nonquantifiable riches, helping perhaps to dispel the media-constructed image of Haiti as eternal taker and recipient of world charities. Though Haiti is a very poor country materially speaking, it is also a giver, rich in all sorts of wisdom, knowledge, and hope as well as beauty, a country that captivates foreigners and impels them to return to its shores, a country that is after all for us, native sons and daughters, our *Haïti chérie,* our beloved Haiti.

A deeper revelation of Vodou's *konesans* was needed to dispel myths and misrepresentations and demonstrate that the Haitian imaginary differs from that of the West in profound and crucial ways that are nevertheless solid and worthy. This may well be the key to it all—that Haiti indeed has something to teach this world, especially in the area of religion and through the unique epistemologies that have been so disparaged and maligned by the Euro-American imaginary. My challenge was to reveal the riches in the practices and beliefs of Vodou and to demonstrate that this ancestral religion is ultimately about forces and values that transcend any particular nation-state or culture and, ultimately, how Vodou encompasses the ideals of spiritual democracy and service.

***

Late on November 2, the words didn't seem to want to come. I stopped. I traveled later that week to a Vodou ceremony at the home of *manbo*[9] Jacqueline Epingle in Montreal. I then went to the Haitian Studies Association meeting in Bloomington, Indiana, and then to Washington DC. Upon my return in December, I worked on the *Journal of Haitian Studies'* anniversary issue. I still could not write this text. The inspiration did not come.

On January 1, 2010, I awoke troubled from a strange dream. I told my husband about it; I told others. I resumed writing on January 3, 2010, still confronted by the extraordinary challenge of explicating the richness of Vodou, the richness of Haiti, and Karen Brown's unique ability to find beauty and truth in the daily lives of what some may call ordinary people—in their struggles and tribulations, their hope and despair, their love and lovelessness. I was anguished because I had to articulate what Haiti gives the world against the media's master narrative of Haiti as the poorest nation of the Western Hemisphere (how long will this painful descriptor be applied to us?) and against the never-ending stereotypes attached to Haitian religion.

And now I was also haunted by dreams in which I might have pre-sensed the apocalypse that was to come—troubling dreams that I had for twelve nights in a row before the quake. During what I now call the "ball of the dead of January 1," all the dead I had ever known visited me in dreams, their faces clear, even joyous, as if they were having a ball, a strange juxtaposition of family members buried in Haiti, close friends who had died in Santa Barbara, childhood friends who had made their transition thirty years ago, remote acquaintances, writers I might have met. There were more intimate dreams where dear departed ones, James Smith and Shirley Kennedy,[10] offered comforting words; there was an in-law who died in May 1973, Pierre was his name, who came to pack the belongings of his wife in a car and take her away, as "she needed to leave that house" (this same residence crumbled during the quake, and its sole inhabitant, this elderly lady, his wife, was saved). Dreams have such significance in Vodou, and I know they do for Karen and Mama Lola. These dreams have meaning, I thought, and I felt they were somehow connected to this foreword. Perhaps my invocation early on of the Gede, destabilizers par excellence, had something to do with it. What unearthly forces had I disturbed? I felt ill at ease, burdened, scared. I shared this with Phyllis B., a dear friend, the day before my birthday on January 10, what is now National Vodou Day in Benin. I asked her: Am I dying, or are others?

I was haunted in particular by the dream I had on January 11, in which I saw hundreds of thousands of people at Toussaint Louverture Airport in Port-au-Prince, running in all directions and screaming—chaos in Port-au-Prince and in the country at large. Something was out of balance.

I felt like a chosen mourner.

During those early days of January, despite my uneasiness and a troubled soul, I continued to write. On January 12, I was putting finishing touches to this text, perhaps crafting one of the last few paragraphs. The phone rang at 2:01 p.m. Pacific Time—5:01 Eastern Time, Haiti time. With a tremor that sounded like the tremble of the earth, the Haitian voice on the other end said, "Turn on the news. *Tranblemantè an Ayiti.* An earthquake has hit Haiti. Seven-point-three, they say, on the Richter scale. It hit Port-au-Prince. The National Palace is destroyed. *La Cathédrale* gone. The epicenter is in Carrefour." Did I hear right? Hit Port-au-Prince, the city where I was born. My Haiti. Carrefour, where my parents' home was located.

I stopped writing. I was numb, petrified. My people, my Haiti! No, it cannot be. (I am ashamed to admit it, but I almost felt relieved for a short minute. *This* was what I had been carrying.) Why Haiti? Why now? Why?

I felt as if I had been stabbed in the stomach. I had a vision of a razed Port-au-Prince reduced to nothingness. A heap of rubble and bodies everywhere.

I rushed to turn on the television set. My eyes shifted focus between two screens. On the one screen, the words I was writing. On the other, images of a wrecked city, collapsed buildings, rubble everywhere, bodies littering the street, corpses dumped in large mounds in the yard of the Hôpital Général. People covered in dust rushing, running, wailing. Children lost, shrieking. It was as if we had been bombed.

Prayers and blessings for the departed kap tounen lakay . . .

For those souls journeying to our ancestral home.

The foreword would now need to be a eulogy for the earthquake's victims. This outpouring of words could perhaps offer testimony and bear witness to our collective trauma, suggesting that our inner sanctuary could provide a space for healing and a chance to begin mourning and honoring our lost lives. Maybe these words would also move us toward higher levels of consciousness and a deeper appreciation of the immensity of a divine presence.

We needed all our *Lwa* and then some!

***

Details were not forthcoming at first. The hours seemed long; the moments were intense. Everyone was trying to obtain news of family and friends; phones did not work. I got word that my brother and his family were safe; I could not reach my parents until a week later.[11]

For the next few days, our attention was riveted to the TV screen.

We cried. We mourned.

The phone rang continuously. We feared for this one or that one we had not heard about; the list of names of those who had died grew longer. A list next to my computer was updated daily. What we saw on television was gruesome. *Goudougoudou*[12] had hit us hard.

Despite reports of airplanes loaded with supplies for the post-earthquake relief of Haiti, aid was not arriving fast enough. The image of Haiti begging for international aid contrasted so vividly with what I was writing about—Haiti, a plentiful Haiti.

Haitians everywhere contacted other Haitians. Haitians everywhere supported other Haitians, and other friends of Haiti called and tried to assist in what ways they could. The international community joined us in mourning; the earthquake catastrophe became a global phenomenon overnight. We witnessed moments of despair and hope, heroic rescues and loved ones reunited in the midst of this apocalypse. The outpouring of support was incredible but not enough to prevent seven thousand people from being dumped in a mass grave the first two days, and more after that.

Every society guards its rituals to bury the dead; we all need to lay our deceased to rest with dignity and respect. But many in Haiti did not have even the time or luxury to identify their loved ones before they were thrown into public trucks and then tossed like garbage. Proper burial might have brought some minimal comfort and a modicum of meaning to their losses. Yet even that was denied to the poor—being able to honor lives that mattered to them, grieve properly, and have the luxury to remember.

During the next two months, like most Haitians, and like those from the international community who wanted to assist, I worked relentlessly on the bit of relief efforts I could help organize with the support of Direct Relief International. I had a supportive talk with the editor at UC Press and a new deadline. We agreed that I would add "something about the earthquake." Of course, at the time I had no idea how much the text would be reshifted. I told myself that I would return to writing on March 12. These anniversaries have meanings for Haitians and now for the world. These are archived in our minds and our bodies, marking the date when our country was fractured, when the earth opened up and asked for a rebalancing. In the words of A-lan Holt, "Haiti was broken, then broke open the universe."[13]

This task weighed on me. It was time to finish. Clearly what I had first written no longer fit. This is where things stood for me: the text needed to be rethought. More than ever, the preface could no longer simply praise the value of the book, highlighting Mama Lola's many profound contributions or even discussing Karen's courageous self-reflexivity in her writings. I now had to delve even deeper into the question Karen posed about what Haiti gives to us. I knew that along with the work of other writer-artist first responders, I would need to provide counterbalance to this moment of indescribable physical destruction, utmost devastation, and sheer despondency among those who continued to mourn their dead.

Might I have intuited in my dreams the catastrophe that was to come? Might I have sensed that the Gede would need to be summoned to carry and soothe those three hundred thousand souls who perished in the earthquake on January 12, 2010? Were those whose faces I had seen in my dreams those who were preparing an embrace for the departed souls to be reunited with spirits of other realms?

May the ancestors continue to steer us home.

My words in the foreword emerged from an intimate place. With mystic instruction to listen intently to elders Mama Lola and Karen Brown, I learned to become receptive to the wisdom of the ancestors and the Vodou spirits who speak in our dreams and who, in time, carry us to ethereal dimensions.

In *Ginen*,[14] we find the ancestral realm of the unborn and the afterlife, where ancestors who have passed from this life reunite with those not yet born; where the conjoining of spirits—old and new—creates a seamless tapestry of past, present, and future that simultaneously shields and strengthens the living. May we always remember to remember, and continue to honor these ancestral names as we continue our paths forward, and home.

Notes

Adapted from Claudine Michel, "Foreword. Mama Lola's Triplets: Three Decades, Three Rituals, Marasa Twa," in Karen McCarthy Brown, *Mama Lola, A Vodou Priestess in Brooklyn*, 3rd ed. (Berkeley: University of California Press, 2010). Another version appeared in the *Journal of Haitian Studies* (vol. 18, no. 2 [2012]) and was also presented at the Conference on Vodou and Créolité, Franklin College, Lugano, Switzerland, April 6–9, 2011. I dedicated the presentation to my mother, writer and feminist Paulette Poujol-Oriol, who died less than a month before that conference. This essay is dedicated to Karen McCarthy Brown herself, who made her transition on March 4, 2015, and to Mama Lola, who has created such a meaningful legacy for our national religion.

1   *Mama Lola* is the first biography of a Vodou devotee, Alourdes Champagne, a priestess in this case. The text portrays the real lives, longings, and social and personal struggles of Alourdes and her family to maintain traditional Haitian religious values in Brooklyn where they live. This multidimensional narrative is at once a story of rootedness, departure, and new beginnings.

2   The book enriched indigenous religious studies, feminist studies, anthropology, and research methodologies, and offered a repositioning of notions of race, class, gender, and sexuality. Its in-depth exploration of themes such as Diaspora and transnationalism within Vodou created a paradigmatic shift that has paved the way for a greater acceptance of the cultural philosophy and religious experience of Haitians as a legitimate field of academic inquiry.

3   An important notion in Vodou metaphysics, *konesans* is knowledge accompanied by wisdom.

4   Gede is the spirit of death, life, and sexuality in Vodou. There are twenty-one different spirit manifestations in the Gede family; many are known to love children.

5   The *Lwa* (singular and plural in Kreyòl) are the spirits of the Haitian pantheon. There are 401 such deities.

6   Karen McCarthy Brown, "Plenty Confidence in Myself: The Initiation of a White Woman Scholar into Haitian Vodou," *Journal of Feminist Studies in Religion* 3, no. 1 (1987): 75.

7   Ibid.

8   Karen McCarthy Brown, "The Moral Force Field of Haitian Vodou," in *In Face of the Facts: Moral Inquiry in American Scholarship*, ed. Richard Wightman Fox and Robert B. Westbrook (Washington, DC: Woodrow Wilson Center Press, 2002), 200.

9   A *manbo* is a Vodou priestess. Manbo Jacqueline Epingle is a founding member of KOSANBA, A Scholarly Organization for the Study of Haitian Vodou, housed at UC Santa Barbara, Center for Black Studies Research. See http://www.research.ucsb.edu/cbs/projects/haiti/kosanba/index.HTML.

10 In the book's actual foreword, I did not reveal James Smith's and Shirley Kennedy's full names. *Yo fè chimen yo deja. Kouneya, mwen ka nonmen non yo.* Somehow I feel that these close friends have made their safe journey "home" and that they may now be named.

11 Mother miraculously escaped death during the Haiti earthquake as the old family home collapsed only a few feet from where she was; yet it is interesting that she died on the day of the Japan earthquake on March 11, 2011. She was a big presence and it is not surprising that she made her exit on that day. In Vodou, all dates have meanings.

12 *Goudougoudou* is the name that Haitians have given to the earthquake of January 12, 2010. Many Haitians explain that this onomatopoetic term is what the rumble felt like.

13 A-lan Holt, "A Poem for Haiti," unpublished poem, January 2010.

14 Before reaching Ginen, the soul, free from the cosmic force of the *Lwa*, will reside "one year and one day" in the water before returning to the land where it becomes a protective spirit for the living. The third edition of *Mama Lola* was released around the first anniversary of the January 2010 earthquake. May it be received as a eulogy for the earthquake victims and a celebration of their lives.

AUTHOR BIOGRAPHIES

Anne-christine d'Adesky is an Oakland-based writer with Haitian family roots. She is a journalist, activist, documentary filmmaker, and author of four books including *Beyond Shock: Charting the Landscape of Sexual Violence in Post-quake Haiti* (2013) and a forthcoming activist memoir, *The Pox Lover: Chronicle of the Hot 90s in New York and Paris*. She was the Global Coordinator for Haiti for the One Billion Rising (V-Day) campaign against sexual violence from 2013 to 2015.

Gysèle Th. Apollon was born in Cap-Haïtien and studied in Madrid and Paris. She then resided and worked in Geneva, Switzerland, until 1984. After twenty years abroad, she returned to Port-au-Prince to devote herself to writing. She has published two novels—*Lea* and *Croisière pour dame seule*—as well as a collection of short stories, *Les Seigneurs de guerre*. She also contributes to the opinion section of the Haitian newspaper *Le Nouvelliste* and also to the journals published by the Centre de Recherche et de Formation Économique et Social pour le Développement (CRESFED), including *Rencontre*.

Jacinthe Armand received a M.A. in international affairs from Columbia University. She worked as a program officer for the United Nations Development Programme in Vientiane, Laos. She then moved on to Wall Street as an international banker before returning to her native Haiti, where she managed a family travel business. She is now developing a self-sustaining farm in southern Haiti as a model of local community development.

Gessy Aubry is the owner and manager of Louve LLC, a manufacturer and wholesale retailer of handmade natural soaps in Weston, Florida. She is a self-taught artist who has exhibited solo and in collaboration with other artists in Haiti and elsewhere and was also featured in the film *Pluie d'Espoir* (Rain of hope). She has served as an independent consultant for organizations in Haiti, the United States, and Morocco, and provides French/Creole/English interpretation services.

Mathilde Baïsez studied pedagogy and theater at Université du Québec in Montréal (Uquam), where she later taught theater for twelve years. She was a professor of French at Université de Montréal and directed a theater group for seniors. She has also worked with grassroots organizations to develop popular theater programs.

Françoise Beaulieu-Thybulle holds an M.A. in library and information science and served as director of La Bibliothèque Nationale d'Haïti in Port-au-Prince for over thirty years. She is currently the president of the Association of Caribbean University, Research, and Institutional Libraries.

LeGrace Benson holds an interdisciplinary Ph.D. from Cornell University with an emphasis on an ecological approach to perception and the arts. She has taught at Cornell University, Wells College, and the State University of New York and has published numerous articles and book chapters. Her book *Arts and Religions of Haiti: How the Sun Illuminates under Cover of Darkness* was published in 2015. She is currently vice-president of KOSANBA, A Scholarly Association for the Studies of Haitian Vodou, and is the 2016 president of the Haitian Studies Association (HSA).

Edouard Duval Carrié is a visual artist working in mixed media. Though he no longer resides in his native country, Haiti remains a great source of inspiration for him. A painter, sculptor, and curator, he has exhibited in major galleries and museums around the world, including solo exhibits in Paris, Mexico, Holland, and the United States. He is the recipient of many awards, including the Southern Arts Federation Visual Art Fellowship and the South Florida Cultural Consortium Visual Art Fellowship.

Evelyn Ducheine Cartright received a B.A. in English and philosophy and an M.A. in English from Stony Brook University. Her doctorate in public administration is from Nova Southeastern University in Florida. She is an assistant professor and the director of the Africana Studies Program at Barry University in Miami, teaching Caribbean and African American literature. Her publications have appeared in the *Journal of Haitian Studies* and the *Encyclopedia of Racism*.

Manoucheka Celeste holds a Ph.D. in communication and a graduate certificate in feminist studies from the University of Washington. She is an assistant professor in the Center for Gender, Sexualities, and Women's Studies Research and the African American Studies Program at the University of Florida. Her book *Race, Gender, and Citizenship in the African Diaspora: Travelling Blackness* was recently published with Routledge. She has also published in *Feminist Media Studies* and the *Journal of Haitian Studies*.

Johanne Elima Chachoute was born in Haiti. Encouraged by her father, she became an avid reader in her youth, reading novels and magazines during summer breaks. Her love of reading nurtured a passion for writing that began at the age of thirteen. Her role models include Gary Victor, Margaret Papillon, and Évelyne Trouillot. She is a blogger for *Ayibopost*.

Nadège T. Clitandre received a B.A. from Hampton University, a M.A. from the University of Chicago, and a Ph.D. in African Diaspora studies with a designated emphasis in women, gender, and sexuality at the University of California, Berkeley. She is currently assistant professor of global studies at the University of California, Santa Barbara, where she specializes in issues of Diaspora, migration and displacement, and transnationalism. She is the founder of Haiti Soleil, a nonprofit organization that focuses on engaging youth and building community through the development of libraries in Haiti.

Carolyn Cooper is a professor of literary and cultural studies at the University of West Indies, Mona, Jamaica. She is the author of two influential books, *Noises in the Blood: Orality, Gender and the "Vulgar" Body of Jamaican Popular Culture* (1993) and *Sound Clash: Jamaican Dancehall Culture at Large* (2004). She is also the editor of the award-winning *Global Reggae* (2008) and writes a weekly column for the *Jamaica Gleaner*.

Edwidge Danticat is the author of several books, including *Breath, Eyes, Memory*, an Oprah Book Club selection; *Krik? Krak!*, a National Book Award finalist; *The Farming of Bones,* an American Book Award winner; and *The Dew Breaker*. Her memoir *Brother, I'm Dying* was a 2008 winner of the National Book Critics Circle Award. *Create Dangerously* and *Claire of the Sea Light* are her most recent publications. She is also the editor of *The Butterfly's Way: Voices from the Haitian Dyaspora in the United States* and *The Beacon Best of 2000: Great Writing by Men and Women of All Colors and Cultures.* Danticat is a 2009 recipient of the John D. and Catherine MacArthur Foundation Fellowship.

Olga Idriss Davis is currently a professor in the Hugh Downs School of Human Communication at Arizona State University and principal investigator of health literacy and community engagement with the Southwest Interdisciplinary Research Center (SIRC). Her work explores the sociocultural determinants of health on communities of the African Diaspora. She has published in interdisciplinary academic journals and is coeditor of *Centering Ourselves: African American Feminist and Womanist Studies of Discourse.* She is president and CEO of Davis Communication Group, LLC, a communication and multimedia consulting company located in Phoenix, Arizona.

Charlene Désir is associate professor at Nova Southeastern University's Abraham S. Fischler College of Education. Her academic interest include social, psychological, and spiritual adjustment of immigrant students to the United States; schools' social curriculum; and psychosocial trauma occurring among immigrant children and youth. Désir has developed cultural literacy projects in Haiti and for immigrant children in the United States. She also worked as a school psychologist, K–12 school counselor, and school administrator in Massachusetts district and charter schools. She has published in the *Harvard Educational Review* and the *Journal of Haitian Studies.*

Philippe Dodard is a graphic artist and painter. Born in Port-au-Prince, Dodard worked for many years as an advertising illustrator. He has headed numerous cultural and artistic missions and events nationally and internationally. His work has been exhibited throughout Europe and the Americas in solo and joint exhibits. A book on Dodard's artwork, *Philippe Dodard: The Idea of Modernity in Haitian Contemporary Art*, was published in 2014. Dodard is currently the director of the premier arts school in Haiti, the École Nationale des Arts (ENARTS).

Jan J. Dominique received a degree in arts and letters from Université de Montréal. Born in Port-au-Prince, she taught for many years in the school system and at the university level in Haiti. She was a journalist at Radio Haiti Inter, where she also served as director until she left the country in 2003. She has published a number of short stories and novels including *L'Écho de leurs voix*, released in 2016 by the Éditions du Remue-Ménage in Montréal, where she currently resides.

Dolores Dominique-Neptune. I am fifty-six years old, and the most extraordinary thing in my life is the fact that I created three beautiful human beings with my husband, Jean-Claude: Jakaranda, Anne Claude, and Jean Olivier. From this world and the other, they are my biggest teachers and I learn every day from them; they raised me more than I raised them. They are indeed wonderful. They inspire me and sometimes it even feels as if I have a dictaphone and am being ordered. Even my three grandkids seem to do the same.

Michèle Duvivier Pierre-Louis is a professor and economist who served as prime minister of Haiti from 2008 to 2009. She was born in Jérémie and attended secondary school in Port-au-Prince. After graduating from Queens College of the City University of New York, she pursued her M.A. in economics. She then returned to Haiti, where she worked in many different sectors involving national development, planning, literacy, and cultural activities. Her work has appeared in various academic publications, popular venues, and specialized magazines. Today she is president of the Fondation Connaissance et Liberté—FOKAL, an organization that works to support education, culture, and development in the capital and throughout the country.

Marie Andrée Manuel Étienne studied English at Hunter College and bilingual business administration at the Latin American Institute of New York. Upon her return to Haiti, she studied sociology at the university in Port-au-Prince. From 1970 to 1992, she taught French, English, Creole, and natural sciences in a number of different schools and venues. In 2001 she published the novel *Déchirures* with Vents d'Ailleurs. She was president of the Club des Femmes de Carrières Libérales et Commerciales in Port-au-Prince from 2002 to 2005 and again from 2008 to 2015.

Raymonde Maureen Eyi was born in Oyem in the Woleu-Ntem province in Gabon and attended the Val-Marie de Mouila and the Sœurs du St-Esprit et de l'Immaculée Conception of Libreville.

She then studied in London and Grenoble, where she obtained her diploma in political science in 1982. In 1984 she became involved in public service in Gabon, notably working with the Department of Culture, Housing, and Urbanism; the Economic and Social Council; and finally the Ministry of National Education until she retired in 2016. She considers herself *haïtienne de cœur* as she has always been interested in the history of that first black republic.

Michele-Jessica (M.J.) Fièvre obtained her M.F.A. from the creative writing program at Florida International University. Born in Port-au-Prince, she is the founding editor of *Sliver of Stone Magazine* and the author of *A Sky the Color of Chaos* (Beating Windward, 2015). She is also the editor of *So Spoke the Earth* (2012), a collection of essays on the 2010 earthquake. Her short stories and poems have appeared in numerous anthologies and magazines.

Lyvie François-Racine was born in Haiti and moved to the states at the age of thirteen. She resides in Scottsdale, Arizona, and works as a national account manager at Philips Lighting. She cofounded Phoenix Rising for Haiti, a nonprofit organization run by a medical and rehabilitation team, and has made three mission trips yearly to Haiti since the earthquake. She is currently working on the grand opening of the first PRH rehabilitation clinic in the Northwest of Haiti. Her dream is to have PRH rehab clinics all over rural Haiti.

Geneviève Gaillard-Vanté received the Prix d'Aptitudes Linguistiques from ONU 1983, a Choice Award in 1997, and the coveted Haitian literary prize Prix Deschamps in 2001 for her novel *Ombres du Temps*. She has also published another novel, *Parfum de Cèdre* (Editions Calliope, 2003), and is the author of many other texts that have appeared in various anthologies, notably in Spain and the United States. *Magie Bleue,* a poetry book, was published in 2009 by Multicultural Women's Presence Press, Inc., in Florida.

Danielle Legros Georges is a professor in the creative arts at Lesley University and a faculty member of the William Joiner Institute Summer Writers' Workshop, University of Massachusetts, Boston. She was named poet laureate of the city of Boston in 2015, and is the author of two books of poems, *The Dear Remote Nearness of You* (2016) and *Maroon* (2001). She also serves as a consulting poetry editor for *Solstice* and *Salamander* literary magazines, and has curated poetry activity for exhibitions, including the Institute of Contemporary Art/Boston's Black Mountain College Exhibition (2015–16).

Josiane Hudicourt-Barnes was born and raised in Haiti. She lived in the United States for thirty years before returning to Haiti. She has been a teacher of immigrant children and a researcher focusing on Haitian Creole, multilingual education, and cultural differences in the classroom. She has also worked on teacher training and school administration. After the earthquake of 2010, Hudicourt-Barnes spent six months working at Hôpital de la Communauté Haïtienne in Pétion-Ville to support victims of the quake in affected areas and to coordinate volunteers and donors.

Carolle Jean-Murat is a board-certified gynecologist and intuitive healer. In 2005 she built the Dr. Carolle's Wellness and Retreat Center of San Diego, where she currently resides. She also serves there as medical director for the True Healing and Wellness Institute. As a motivational speaker, she conveys her empowering message through her books, TV, podcasts, workshops, and in one-on-one consultations. She is the author of numerous books, including *Natural Pregnancy A–Z* and *Staying Healthy: 10 Easy Steps for Women.*

Grace L. Sanders Johnson is an assistant professor in the department of Africana studies at the University of Pennsylvania. She received her Ph.D. in history and women's studies at the University of Michigan. A historian of gender and the Caribbean, she researches women's intellectual thought, sexuality, migration, and oral history in twentieth-century Haiti.

Kathuska Jose was born in Port-au-Prince in 1986. She holds a B.A. in English and a specialization in creative writing from the University of Massachusetts, Amherst. Her poems have appeared in *A Lime Jewel: An Anthology of Poetry and Short Stories in Aid of Haiti* (2010); *Jabberwocky*; *Short Cuts*; *Mother Tongue*; and *Bang and Whimper.* She lives in Everett, Massachusetts.

Yanick Lahens was born in Haiti and educated at the Sorbonne in France. She taught literature at the École Normale Supérieure,

State University of Haiti, until 1995. In 1996–1997, she was a cabinet member in the Ministry of Culture under the leadership of Raoul Peck. She is a journalist, a radio talk-show host, and a social activist. Lahens is most recognized as an essayist, novelist, and short-story writer. She has published, among other books, *Dans la maison du père* (2000), *La Couleur de l'aube* (2008), *Failles* (2010), and *Guillaume et Nathalie* (2013). She has won several prizes, including the Prix Femina in 2014 for *Bain de Lune*. She is one of the founding members of l'Association des Écrivains Haïtiens and contributes regularly to critical journals on Haitian and Caribbean culture such as *Chemins critiques*, *Cultura*, and *Boutures*.

Edith Lataillade was born in Port-au-Prince. She earned a degree in economics and in applied communications at l'Institut des Hautes Études Commerciales et Economiques (IHECE). For twenty-five years she worked at the United Nations with various programs such as PNUD and the Fonds de Contrepartie Haiti/Canada (FNUAP), and also concentrated on projects on health and education with the Centre de Gestion des Fonds Canadien (Fonds Kore Famn). She has published numerous technical articles, short stories, and essays and was the recipient of the Prix Deschamp in 2001. Also a painter, she has participated in numerous art exhibits.

Danièle Mangonès has more than twenty years of experience in business, public relations, and international development. Combining her creative spirit and her business skills, she founded and managed an art gallery. She also contributed to the promotion of Haitian history and culture through radio shows, round-table discussions, and art shows in Berkeley, California. She currently resides in Florida and is preparing an exhibit of traditional Haitian Vodou vèvè paintings on canvas.

Michèle Voltaire Marcelin is a writer, poet, actor, and visual artist who has lived in Haiti, Chile, and the United States. She is the author of the novel *La Désenchantée*, translated to Spanish as *La Desencantada*, and two other books of poetry and prose: *Lost and Found* and *Amours et Bagatelles*, translated to Spanish as *Amores y cosas sin importancia*. Her work is also included in diverse anthologies published in France, Canada, and the United States.

Kettly Mars was born in Port-au-Prince, where she resides today. A prolific writer, she is the recipient of many literary awards including Le Prix Jacques Stephen Alexis for best novel; Le Prix Senghor for literary creation, Le Prix Prince Claus, and Le Prix Ivoire. In addition to many volumes of poetry and short stories, Mars has written six novels, including *Kasalé* (2003), *L'Heure hybride* (2005), *Saisons sauvages* (2010), and *Aux Frontières de la soif* (2013). A number of her books have been translated into Italian, German, English, Japanise, and Dutch. She explores and complicates the intimate spaces of the self to counter problematic discourses on the creativity of women.

Nadève Ménard is a professor of literature at the École Normale Supérieure of Université d'État d'Haïti. Her first book, *Écrits d'Haïti : Perspectives sur la littérature haïtienne contemporaine (1986–2006)* was published in 2011, and she is one of the coeditors of *The Haiti Reader*, forthcoming from Duke University Press. She is currently working on a book that focuses on the critical reception of Haitian literature.

Claudine Michel is currently assistant vice-chancellor of student affairs and professor of Black studies at the University of California, Santa Barbara. She has published widely in the areas of education, Black studies and religion. She is a founding member of KOSANBA, A Scholarly Association for the Study of Haitian Vodou, and *Kalfou: A Journal of Comparative and Relational Ethnic Studies*, both housed at the UCSB Center for Black Studies Research. She is a former president of the Haitian Studies Association and has served since 1997 as editor of the *Journal of Haitian Studies*. Her work has been recognized by the Haitian Studies Association and a 2013 Jean Price-Mars Médaille, Faculté d'Ethnologie, Université d'État d'Haïti.

Myriam Nader-Salomon is an art dealer and appraiser. She developed an appreciation and passion for art at an early age under the influence of her father, Georges S. Nader, founder of the internationally renowned Nader's Art Galleries and Musée d'Art Nader. From 1989 to 1999, Myriam assisted her father in managing art galleries in Port-au-Prince and in Croix Desprez. In 2003, Myriam opened Galerie d'Art Nader, LLC, in Coral Gables, Florida. Today, her art gallery is an online family trade business based in New York.

Viviane Nicolas is a trailblazer in anthropo-psychological studies who studied Vodouist populations in Haiti. She developed successful pedagogical approaches that assisted in the education of Haitian students in both Protestant and Catholic schools in Montreal. She is about to open in Jacmel a school for adult Vodouizan with a curriculum based on the local ethos and grounded in the experience, creativity, and artistry that characterize the Haitian people.

Christalie Parisot has been in the public eye since childhood. With over seventeen years of experience in the media, Christalie has hosted radio and TV shows in Haiti and in the United States. Christalie currently anchors the Haitian/Caribbean News on NBC6 Cozi in South Florida and Tropik TV in the Caribbean. She also manages Imaginart Media Productions, a marketing and production company specializing in the Haitian/Caribbean markets in the United States, Canada, and the Caribbean.

Lucie Carmel Paul-Austin, Ph.D., is a professor at the State University of Haiti (UEH). Her research interests are history, phenomenology, and the poetics of the francophone Caribbean. She is particularly interested in the historical roots of the political morass that Haiti currently finds itself in. She is a former education minister and a former member of the CEP (Provisory Electoral Council).

Claire Antone Payton is a Ph.D. candidate in history at Duke University and the creator of the Haiti Memory Project. She is the author of *Vodou and Protestantism, Faith and Survival.* Her article "The Contest over the Spiritual Meaning of the 2010 Earthquake in Haiti" was published in 2013 in the *Oral History Review.* She was awarded a Fulbright-Hays Fellowship for her project on the history of Port-au-Prince between 1957 and 1986.

Jerry Philogene is an associate professor and chair of the American studies and Africana studies departments at Dickinson College. Her research and teaching interests include interdisciplinary American cultural history, Caribbean cultural and visual arts, black cultural politics, and theories of the African diaspora. Her articles have appeared in *Small Axe: A Caribbean Journal of Criticism, Magazine, Radical History Review, MELUS,* and most recently *Journal of Haitian Studies.* She is currently working on a book manuscript titled *The*

Socially Dead and the "Improbable Citizen": Cultural Transformations of Haitian Citizenship.

Alexandra Philoctète was born in Jérémie, Haiti. She studied in New Hampshire and New York. She earned a degree in sociology and history at the Université Laval in Montréal and served as a member of the administrative councils of YWCA, the Point de Ralliement des Femmes d'Origine Haïtienne, and the Association of Francophone Writers of America. She was also active at the United Nations. Today, she holds the position of "Agente de Programme et de Développement de la Condition Féminine du Canada." She is the producer and host of the radio broadcast "Réalités diverses" in Montréal. She has received the Prix de la Condition Féminine and the Prix de la Jeune Chambre de Commerce Haïtienne in Montréal.

N. Frédéric Pierre is completing a Ph.D. in the department of history at New York University. Her dissertation examines the historical development of a Black state in a period characterized by racialized slavery and turbulent revolution. She is board chair of the Flanbwayan Haitian Literacy Project, an immigrant education advocacy group. She was born in Cap-Haïtien and looks forward to uncovering more of Haiti's past.

Toni Pressley-Sanon is assistant professor of African American studies at Eastern Michigan University. She is the author of *The Haitian Peasantry through Oral and Written Literature: Roumain, Alexis, Endore, Carpentier and Fountain* (2015) and *Zombifying a Nation: Race, Gender and the Haitian* Loas *on Screen* (2016). Her latest work, Istwa *across the Water: Haitian History, Memory, and the Cultural Imagination,* is forthcoming from the University Press of Florida.

Marlène Racine-Toussaint received a B.A. in journalism and an M.A. in modern languages from SUNY–Stony Brook and a Ph.D. in women's studies from the Union Institute/University of Ohio. She worked at SUNY–Old Westbury in the area of international education and taught French and Spanish for over ten years. A staunch feminist passionate for social justice, she joined the feminist branch of JEUNE HAITI, a resistance movement for the advancement of Haiti, in 1964. In the early 1970s she founded L'ÉTRIER Cercle Féminin and CHANDELLE and, in 1999, Multicultural Women's Presence

(MWP). She is the author of *Chants de femme, Ces femmes sont aussi nos soeurs: Témoignage de la domesticité féminine en Haïti et en diaspora*, and *Gerbe d'amour, poèmes*. She has edited or coedited *Le Temps qui passe... Anthologie de poemes d'amour et de souvenirs* and *Brassage: Anthologie poétique de 68 femmes haïtiennes*.

Kate Ramsey is associate professor in the department of history at the University of Miami. She is the author of *The Spirits and the Law: Vodou and Power in Haiti* (Chicago, 2011) and coeditor of *Transformative Visions: Works by Haitian Artists from the Permanent Collection* (Lowe Art Museum, 2015).

Florence Bellande Robertson holds a doctorate in francophone literature from the University of California, Los Angeles (UCLA), and taught language and literature at La Sierra University and the University of Redlands. In 1966, as a social activist, she joined the feminist branch of JEUNE HAITI, a resistance movement in the Diaspora. In 1995, she founded La Fondation Espoir (Haiti) with a branch in Florida, Foundation Hope for Haiti (2002), which she continues to direct. She is also a founding member of KOSANBA and of Multicultural Women's Presence (MWP) and was president of the Haitian Studies Association (HSA) in 2007. She has published several articles, books of poetry, and a volume of literary analysis (*The Marassa Concept in Lilas Desquiron's Reflexions of Loko Miwa* [1999]), and is coeditor of *Brassage: An Anthology of Poems by Haitian Women* (2005).

Odette Roy-Fombrun was born in Port-au-Prince and completed her studies at Haiti's École Normale d'Institutrices. After attending the Preschool Training School of Boston, she devoted her entire lifetime to public education and in 1946 founded the first kindergarten in Haiti. She has written numerous manuals on civic history and geography and many textbooks that have been a staple in Haitian schools since her first book was published in 1949.

Lynn Marie Selby received her Ph.D. in sociocultural anthropology in the African Diaspora program at the University of Texas at Austin in 2015. She is writing a monograph on Haitian women's community activism and participation in popular politics in Port-au-Prince based on ethnographic fieldwork from 2008 to 2010. She is currently a lecturing/research Core U.S. Fulbright Scholar with dual affiliation at the State University of Haiti in Port-au-Prince and the Public University of Nippes in Miragôane. She teaches qualitative research methods and methodology and conducts research on post-earthquake aid to public Haitian higher educational institutions.

Florence Etienne Sergile is an agronomist and conservationist with more than thirty-seven years of experience in the management of the environment. She is also a researcher at the University of Florida. She coordinates agricultural research, the screening of pathogenic emergences, and the application of novel ideas and visions in Haiti. She is the author of various documents on the nature of the islands and of the children's book *A la découverte des oiseaux d'Haïti*. She is one of the editors of *Biogeography of the West Indies: Patterns and Perspectives* and *Terrestrial Mammals of the West Indies*.

Évelyne Trouillot is a professor at l'Université d'État d'Haïti and l'Université Caraïbe in Haiti. She left Haiti at an early age to study in the United States, but returned in the early 1980s and has lived in Haiti ever since, dividing her time between teaching and writing fiction, poetry, and children's books. In 2004 Trouillot received the Prix de la Romancière Francophone du Club Soroptimist de Grenoble for her novel *Rosalie l'infâme*, which was translated into English as *The Infamous Rosalie* in 2013. Trouillot is also the author of *Sans parapluie de retour*, *La Chambre interdite*, *Parlez-moi d'amour*, *L'Oeil-totem*, *Absences sans frontières*, and *Le Rond-point*, which received the Prix Barbancourt in 2015. Along with her brother Lyonel Trouillot and her daughter Nadève Ménard, she is a founder of Pré-texte, an organization that sponsors reading and writing workshops.

Catherine Tutter currently serves as administrative coordinator for the David and Roberta Logie Department of Textile and Fashion Arts at the Museum of Fine Arts, Boston. She is trained in ancient Japanese fiber art processes. Her most recent work explores the social, textual, and performative dimensions of spinning and weaving. She is co-creator of *Spin a Yarn, Weave a Life*, an award-winning innovative project that transformed the life stories of five elders into fabric. The project has evolved to build community and strengthens bonds between veterans, trauma survivors, educators, students, clinicians, elders, and families.

Gina Athena Ulysse is a feminist artist-academic-activist and self-described Post-Zora Interventionist. She is the author of *Downtown Ladies: Informal Commercial Importers, a Haitian Anthropologist and Self-Making in Jamaica* (2008), *Why Haiti Needs New Narratives: A Post-Quake Chronicle* (2015), and *Because When God is too Busy: Haiti, me & THE WORLD* (2016). She edited "Pawol Fanm Sou Douz Janvye" in *Meridians* (2011), and "Caribbean Rasanblaj" in *e-misférica* (2015). A committed public intellectual and intermittent blogger, she is a professor of anthropology at Wesleyan University, Connecticut.

Joëlle Vitiello received her Ph.D. from Stanford University and is now professor of French and Francophone studies at Macalester College in Saint Paul, Minnesota. She coedited *Elles écrivent des Antilles (Haiti, Guadeloupe, Martinique)* with Susanne Rinne (1997) and *Women in French Studies: Women at the Threshold of the XXIst Century: Historical and Contemporary Perspectives* with Dana Strand (2003). She has published numerous articles and chapters on Haitian literature and culture in professional journals and anthologies of essays. She wrote the introduction to the anthology *Comment Ecrire/ Mou Pou 12 Janvier? How to Write an Earthquake?* (2011).

Laura Wagner received her B.A. from Yale University and her Ph.D. in anthropology from the University of North Carolina, Chapel Hill, where her research focused on the aftermath of the 2010 earthquake in Haiti. She is currently a project archivist at the Rubenstein Rare Book and Manuscript Library at Duke University, where she is processing the archive of Radio Haiti-Inter, Haiti's revolutionary independent radio station. She is also a fiction and nonfiction writer; her first novel, *Hold Tight, Don't Let Go*, was published in 2015.

Anna Wexler is an interdisciplinary artist and scholar/writer working with text, installation, and ritually configured performance to distill specific legacies of oppression and visionary resistance. Her doctoral dissertation at Harvard University, and subsequent publications on ritual art and healing, were based on an artistic apprenticeship with the late Clotaire Bazile, a Haitian Vodou priest and flag maker. She has worked in the Boston-area Haitian community in educational and social service settings and is a member of Mobius, an artist-run group that supports experimental work in all media.

Women's Presence

MULTICULTURAL WOMEN'S PRESENCE

Mission Statement

Multicultural Women's Presence is a small publishing house established in 1999. Our main purpose is to give precedence to the writings of women and to provide a new forum for women all over the globe. The women involved are from various cultural backgrounds.

We dedicate ourselves to helping women make their voices heard: to alleviating the pain and eliminating the difficulties that many women face in getting their work published. We encourage those who probably think that they have little or no chance of being published.

MWP seeks to empower women and promote their cultural, economic, social, and political development. Our activities also include literary events, book signings, public readings, social and cultural events, and writing workshops.

MWP publishes challenging books written by women and about women. Our publications range across many subjects and genres, including children's books, short stories, novels, anthologies of articles, feminist books, cookbooks, poetry, history, nonfiction, and literary criticism.

For further inquiry or to submit a manuscript, contact:

Marlène Racine-Toussaint

Multicultural Women's Presence

9441 NW 15th St.

Pembroke Pines, FL 33024

Phone: (954) 447-7277

Email: multiculturpress@aol.com